New York Café Society

New York Café Society

*The Elite Meet to See
and Be Seen, 1920s–1940s*

ANTHONY YOUNG

McFarland & Company, Inc., Publishers
Jefferson, North Carolina

LIBRARY OF CONGRESS CATALOGUING-IN-PUBLICATION DATA

Young, Anthony, 1950–
 New York Café Society : the elite meet to see and be seen, 1920s–1940s / Anthony Young.
  p. cm.
 Includes bibliographical references and index.

 ISBN 978-0-7864-7437-0 (softcover : acid free paper) ∞
 ISBN 978-1-4766-1906-4 (ebook)

 1. New York (N.Y.)—Social life and customs—20th century. 2. New York (N.Y.)—Intellectual life—20th century. 3. Nightclubs—New York (State)—New York—History—20th century. 4. Elite (Social sciences)—New York (State)—New York—History—20th century. 5. Intellectuals—New York (State)—New York—Biography. 6. Artists—New York (State)—New York—Biography. 7. Socialites—New York (State)—New York—Biography. 8. New York (N.Y.)—Biography. 9. Depressions—1929—New York (State)—New York. 10. New York (N.Y.)—History—1898–1951. I. Title.
 F128.5.Y68 2015
 974.7'043—dc23   2015013516

BRITISH LIBRARY CATALOGUING DATA ARE AVAILABLE

© 2015 Anthony Young. All rights reserved

No part of this book may be reproduced or transmitted in any form or by any means, electronic or mechanical, including photocopying or recording, or by any information storage and retrieval system, without permission in writing from the publisher.

On the cover: Café Society photographer Jerome Zerbe took this photo of Julian Gerard, Marian Tiffany Sapportas, Joseph J. O'Donohue IV, Howard Cagle, Robert Bruce, Anne Andrews and newspaper columnist Lucius Beebe (Jerome Zerbe: by permission)

Printed in the United States of America

McFarland & Company, Inc., Publishers
 Box 611, Jefferson, North Carolina 28640
  www.mcfarlandpub.com

Table of Contents

Acknowledgments	vi
Preface	1
Introduction	3
1. Ward McAllister, Caroline Astor and the 400	11
2. Prohibition, the Speakeasies and Nightclubs of the 1920s	24
3. The Cult of Personality	44
4. Café Society's Writers, Journalists, Editors and Playwrights	60
5. Boom and Bust: Music, Skyscrapers and Wall Street in the 1920s	89
6. Effect of the Great Depression on New York Society and Café Society	107
7. This New York: Maury Paul, Lucius Beebe and Walter Winchell	122
8. The Colony, the Plaza, the Rainbow Room and the Waldorf	149
9. Jack and Charlie's 21 Club	163
10. The Stork Club	176
11. El Morocco	185
12. Café Society Fades Away	198
Chapter Notes	205
Bibliography	208
Index	211

Acknowledgments

Marcie Rudell and Shermane Billingsley were helpful in correcting the chapter on the Stork Club and I am grateful for use of the photo of club owner Sherman Billingsley with that dapper man-about-town, Lucius Beebe.

I dedicate this book to my daughters Erin and Katie.

Preface

In 1978, three years after I graduated from Pratt Institute, I discovered the writings of Lucius Beebe. He was one of the 20th century's more interesting individuals. Beebe was a man out of time, who would have felt eminently comfortable during the Gilded Age in Caroline Astor's huge Fifth Avenue mansion salon, riding aboard J. Pierpont Morgan's yacht *Corsair*, or rubbing shoulders with the Vanderbilts in one of their Newport, Rhode Island, mansions. Beebe had been a journalist with the *New York Herald Tribune* from 1929 to 1950, and was a prolific author from the 1930s to the 1960s.

Beebe wrote a great deal about his years in Manhattan during the Great Depression and the charmed life he lived there. He was one of the central figures of New York Café Society. He looked, acted and dressed the part. I wanted to know more about him but in searching for a biography of him, I discovered no one had written one. I was not yet a published author, but I had written several articles for the *New York Times* and I was writing articles on automotive history for a number of magazines. I considered what might be required to write a biography on Beebe and got to work outlining the task.

Beebe had passed away in 1966, but a number of his associates, friends and acquaintances were still alive. Among them were photographer Jerome Zerbe, socialite Gloria Braggiotti Etting, and independently wealthy man-about-town, Joseph J. O'Donohue IV. I spoke on the phone to Eve Brown, who wrote *Champagne Cholly,* the biography of Maury Paul. I also spoke with socialite Marion Tiffany Sapportas. Knowing I would have to have sample chapters and a comprehensive outline to interest a literary agent, I began to make phone calls. Zerbe invited me to his Manhattan apartment and regaled me with stories of his career during the 1930s. He also loaned me the negatives of 50 of his best photos he had taken of Beebe with friends and business associates. He told me, "You can make prints from those and when you come back, I will identify the people in every photo. You can use the ones you like in your book about Lucius." I also interviewed Gloria Braggiotti Etting in Florida and flew to California to interview Joseph J. O'Donohue, who knew Beebe well.

I spent several months putting together the sample chapters and book outline. I also queried about a dozen agents in New York before I found one who was interested in representing me for my proposed biography of Beebe. The agent spent nearly half a year trying to interest various publishing houses, before she told me she did not think she could get me a signed contract since I did not have a single published book to my name. I shelved the idea and it remained dormant for over 25 years.

I chose to focus on automotive history and succeeded in publishing ten books on various makes, models and periods. In 2012 I discovered the envelope with Zerbe's 50 photographs and looked at each one. I made the realization that my original idea may have been too narrow. A book on New York Café Society would prove a much more interesting topic. There was also a lot more source material.

During the ensuing years between the time I abandoned the Beebe biography and chose to compile the history of Café Society, there had been a number of biographies published about some of its most notable members, as well as some of the clubs they frequented, but no comprehensive history of this fascinating period of New York. Café Society emerged in the late 1920s, flowered during the 1930s and began to fade in significance and public interest during the 1940s. There was a larger story I discovered about Café Society; it thrived predominantly against the economic backdrop of the Great Depression. The members of Café Society lived and enjoyed a lifestyle totally apart from those struggling to survive. Many New Yorkers in particular and millions of readers across America read such columns as "This New York," written by Lucius Beebe, and "Cholly Knickerbocker," written by Maury Paul, as entertainment and a diversion. Class envy never seemed to be an issue.

This book is about the "names that made news," in the words of Beebe, the places they frequented, the work they performed and the events that happened prior to, during and after the worst economic time in American history.

Introduction

There are many enduring, even iconic, images of life in New York City during the Great Depression of the 1930s. Men and women could be seen with their makeshift fruit stands selling apples for five cents each. The long lines of unemployed, bedraggled and despondent men were seen waiting for a bowl of hot soup outside the Salvation Army soup kitchen. Overcrowded homeless shelters in the Bowery often had an entire family occupying a single room—with the communal bathroom down the hall.

The established unemployment figure nationally and in Manhattan was 25 percent. That meant, of course, that the remaining 75 percent had kept their jobs, albeit often at reduced wages. The lives of the still-employed went on, still somewhat comfortable in their ability to pay rent, buy food and clothing, meet their other needs and even enjoy entertainment on occasion.

There was a very small segment that enjoyed a style of living that by every measure was lavish, stylish, entertaining and rewarding. Who were these men and women who managed to deftly skirt the economic calamity in New York City that affected so many others? These people were the creative, the talented, the humorous, the accomplished and sometimes the rich. They frequented the most glamorous nightclubs, restaurants and drinking establishments that existed at the time and were the object of numerous newspaper writers in the New York dailies, occasionally with photographs of these fortunate elite. Columnist Maury Paul—using the *nom de plume* "Cholly Knickerbocker"—was descriptive and accurate in labeling this group. He was the first to call it Café Society, and the phrase stuck. Lucius Beebe, reporter for the *New York Herald Tribune*, and one who himself cut a handsome figure in his dinner tuxedo, coined a phrase to describe these people and the glittering lifestyle and environment they swirled around in as the Chromium Mist.

Café Society, which flourished in the 1930s, had its basis in the people, their professions and events of the 1920s, and it was uniquely confined to New York City. It was not a societal phenomenon that spread to Chicago or even Hollywood. That is because Café Society was a product of Manhattan itself; it was a confluence of political events surrounding prohibition and its eventual repeal, literary trends and the power of the printed dailies, the bull market of the 1920s followed by the stock market crash and the impact of the Great Depression on countless businesses and individual lives, the rise of jazz music and its immense popularity, and the transformation of a few speakeasies into elite and posh nightclubs that were homes to the names that made news.

It was during the ever-worsening Depression that Café Society proved an object of fascination to tens of thousands of newspaper readers every day. The economic devastation was felt acutely in New York City, with the collapse of personal fortunes, closure of countless businesses, and an estimated one-fourth of the adult population unemployed. The Forgotten Man became a symbol for the condition of the entire economy, but this was a fallacy. There were indeed soup lines in the Bowery, men hawking apples and pencils, and shelters housing the homeless. Nevertheless, much of the city still hummed with the activity of commerce.

Central to the mystique of Café Society were the clubs and restaurants that served as the backdrop for it. Speakeasies had been the meeting place to socialize and drink, eat and often be entertained. Prohibition was an unsustainable law, but it took more than a decade to reveal the lofty goals its proponents promised were not achievable. It spawned an entire criminal cartel that spread its tentacles into other businesses throughout the city. The speakeasies were battling both the mob and the local and national government agents' intent on shutting them down. In many cases those agents succeeded. In those cases that they didn't, they were in the pocket of the speakeasy owner.

With the Depression bearing down on establishments even after repeal of Prohibition, many of the small places went out of business. Owners of larger, better-established places sought clever ways to bring in needed clientele. One enterprising photographer by the name of Jerome Zerbe convinced the manager of the Rainbow Room he could pack the dining room of the dazzling Art Deco-styled supper club and have his photographs published in the New York dailies that would act as a magnet to well-heeled customers, and even have them standing in line to get a table. Zerbe did just that. When Zerbe boasted to John Perona, proprietor of the elite El Morocco nightclub, of his new job, Perona implored Zerbe to do the same for his place. Zerbe did so with equally dazzling success at El Morocco from 1935 to 1939.

Zerbe's photography alone did not cause the daily papers to sell out, but the witty and revealing writing that always accompanied the photos in several daily columns often did. This was not tabloid journalism, although the papers also carried that. No, these daily columns, and the articles that appeared in *Vanity Fair*, *Town & Country* and *Vogue*, were something different altogether. These writings were a journalistic profile of notable people, not just the beautiful and handsome, but the accomplished who had something to their credit. And in 1930s Manhattan, there was always something to write about. It was not simply what was written, but the style in which it was written that made it so ingratiating, and did so in the pages of the *New York Herald Tribune*, *New York Daily Mirror* and other newspapers.

A handful of staff journalists wrote columns for these papers and they were avidly read by New Yorkers every day. Maury Paul was among the first to break into the New York 400 with a writing style that was decidedly caustic at times, and that was part of his appeal. He often had disparaging things to say about those he wrote about, and the objects of his barbs rarely complained about it. Paul's readers enjoyed stories about how the stuffed shirts were brought down to size, even if those stuffed shirts happened to be themselves. Paul also had his web of informants, and he often dished the dirt along with the truth so well it was often difficult to distinguish between the two, which was probably Paul's secret of success and longevity.

Walter Winchell wrote about the frenetic life on Broadway, first for the *Evening Graphic* in the mid–1920s before he moved on to the *Evening Journal* in 1929. Winchell wrote about not only the new and notable events in the New York theater, but through a small network of tipsters was able to get the scoop who was being considered for the next big Broadway production—and who was quite possibly going to get the ax. He also laced his columns with who was indiscreetly on the arm of whom and what nasty habits—or addictions—a certain individual might be coping with. It was an intoxicating mixture for many readers of his column and it became so successful, Winchell was syndicated in hundreds of newspapers across the United States. He became one of the most powerful and successful journalists in print.

Without question, the classiest journalist to chronicle the glittering life of Café Society with unmatched literary panache was Lucius Beebe. With a master's degree in journalism from Harvard under his arm, he reported to Stanley Walker, city editor of the *New York Herald Tribune* in 1929, practically on the eve of the momentous stock market crash. For several years, Beebe simply wrote all manner of copy for the paper, from obituaries to theater production openings and performances at the Metropolitan Opera. Beebe finally convinced Walker that he would be eminently qualified to write a daily column on the New York high life, and Walker granted Beebe his request. "This New York" began appearing in 1934 during the depth of the greatest economic depression in American history. Beebe took the high road in writing about the people, places, food and drink, happenings and conversation he shared each evening, dressed in full dinner tuxedo, as indeed all the men were every night. Beebe discreetly avoided even a hint of scandal, but did manage to tastefully record who was with whom, and if they were married to each other, all the better. His reviews of culinary fare were particularly coveted by eating establishments, and Beebe often ate morning, noon and night without so much as removing his wallet to pay the bill. His trademark florid prose was distinctively his own, and his column, which was also syndicated, had an avid following.

The emergence of jazz music in the 1920s was a cultural marker that delineated the decade. Small ensemble jazz often served as the musical backdrop in many speakeasies during the 1920s, and not just in Harlem. Along with this came the evolution of symphonic jazz. Paul Whiteman emerged with his jazz band in 1918 in California, but two years later moved his band to New York City and almost immediately signed with Victor Records. Whiteman was a composer as well as a band leader; he recorded many of his compositions, and these records received air play. Whiteman knew many of the emerging jazz musicians and composers of the day. In 1924, he commissioned George Gershwin to compose a unique work that his orchestra would play with several other new compositions; Gershwin wrote "Rhapsody in Blue" and performed on the piano accompanied by Whiteman's Palais Royal Orchestra at the Aeolian Hall in February 1924. Whiteman billed the concert as "An Experiment in Modern Music." The evening proved to be a milestone in the history of jazz and further advanced the careers of Gershwin and Whiteman. Irving Berlin's 1924 composition "What'll I Do?" became a No. 1 hit for Whiteman. Whiteman became identified by many as the King of Jazz. He would prove a musical institution during the 1920s and 1930s, and Whiteman's orchestra was an immense draw in the finest Manhattan nightclubs, and toured the United States as well.

While Whiteman was the figurehead of that music style, he shared the stage with some of the most popular and successful songwriters and lyricists of the 20th century. The instrumental music and songs of the 1920s and 1930s were not only a staple of performers before the appreciative members of Café Society as they hobnobbed with one another; they also received airplay that were enjoyed by many who would never pass through the door of El Morocco or the Stork Club, or could even imagine doing so.

Introduction

The late 1920s signaled a new era of sophisticated compositions with decidedly romantic lyrics. "Jalousie" was composed in 1925 by Jacob Gade with lyrics by partner Vera Bloom; this couple wrote many endearing songs during the 1920s and 1930s. Hoagy Carmichael's "Stardust" was composed in 1927, but it was Mitchell Parish's 1931 lyrics that propelled it to become one of the most often played songs on the radio and in nightclubs. George and Ira Gershwin collaborated on many songs that are popularly played in concerts even today. The quintessential Depression song, "Brother, Can You Spare a Dime?" appeared in 1932 and echoed the mood of many of the unemployed. That year Cole Porter introduced "Night and Day," and soon people singing the hauntingly beautiful song practically everywhere. "Stormy Weather," composed by Harold Arlen in 1933, has been a staple of jazz singers for 80 years. Irving Berlin penned "Top Hat, White Tie and Tails" as an ode to Café Society that was performed by Fred Astaire in the film *Top Hat* in 1935. Also that year "Autumn in New York" was a most popular tune heard on record players and from radios and bandstands. Duke Ellington's "Blue Reverie" from 1936 was heard not only in Harlem but in the swank mid-Manhattan nightclubs. These are but a few of the classic, enduring jazz and popular compositions that arose during these momentous decades, and there were hundreds more.

Manhattan in the 1920s was home to hundreds of nondescript office and apartment buildings, with a few notable exceptions like the Woolworth Building and New York Life Building. All that changed with an unprecedented skyscraper building boom that started about the time of the stock market crash. In mid-Manhattan there began an epic building competition between the Chrysler Building on Lexington Avenue, which broke ground first, and the Empire State Building on Fifth Avenue. The Art Deco–styled Chrysler Building was the tallest in New York, standing 1050 feet, when completed in 1930. However, the Empire State Building surpassed it in 1931 and became the tallest building in the world at 1,250 feet and 102 floors. New Yorkers were astounded to watch the building rise floor by floor almost before their eyes. These buildings became a metaphor for the wealth and endurance of New York City in the face of the Great Depression and in real terms provided employment for thousands of construction workers and related trades. These workers moved on to other skyscraper projects: 500 Fifth Avenue also completed in 1931, the American International Building in 1932, and Rockefeller Center in the latter 1930s. At the top of Rockefeller Center was the Rainbow Room, which became the tallest meeting place of Café Society as it dined and danced on the 65th floor overlooking Manhattan.

The epicenter of Café Society revolved around select restaurants and nightclubs they frequented. Whereas the old Society 400 met in the Fifth Avenue mansions of their owners, New York's new elite moved into these new places to socialize, to enjoy one another's company, to see and be seen, and hopefully to be photographed by Café Society's photographer, Jerome Zerbe. A number of these clubs had their basis in 1920s Prohibition. In Manhattan, there were thousands of speakeasies, from full-fledged establishments to private apartments that doubled as secret drinking places, running all the way from Harlem down to Canal Street in lower Manhattan. Among the established formal places was Jack and Charlie Kriendler's 21. This place became a dining and drinking institution in Manhattan during the 1920s, weathered Prohibition and matured into a superb gathering place during the 1930s. John Perona had operated several different speakeasies during the 1920s before opening El Morocco in 1931. Nothing changed with the repeal of the 18th Amendment except the appearance of the now-required liquor license. Perona's mix of elegant if tightly packed seating, finest drinks, fine music and very selective approval of guests made El Morocco the most desirable place go in Manhattan at night. Just as lavish and definitely more spacious was Sherman Billingsley's Stork Club, which operated at several locations in mid-Manhattan before settling on East 53rd Street in 1934. The Stork Club became famous for its very fine cuisine, superb wine list and liquors from all over the world. Billingsley himself was present every night, greeting his famous guests at their tables and ensuring their time there was the very best. Those who aspired to the upper echelon of Café Society but were denied entrance at these exclusive places had other fine establishments to choose from. These included the Rainbow Room at Rockefeller Center, the Iridium Room in the St. Regis Hotel, and the Persian Room at the Plaza Hotel.

As new names came to the fore in the field of writing, playwriting, song composition, acting, or other notable professions, they would invariably make their way to one or all of these hallowed grounds of Café Society. Perona, Billingsley and the Kriendlers were always looking for new faces to create a buzz and draw attention to the establishment. And invariably, Maury Paul or Lucius Beebe would have something to say about that new name that was making news. Nowhere was the cult of personality more prevalent than within Café Society. New blood and new talent were needed to stave off the specter of monotony that could otherwise befall these establishments.

As the national economy laboriously recovered from the ravages of the stock market crash and the repercussions felt within the economy, business at these clubs also started to pick up. There were also fewer men and women hawking their wares on sidewalks and street corners. Formerly closed businesses opened once again, or new businesses were established in their places. For members of Café Society, the change was hardly noticeable at El Morocco, the Stork Club, 21 and the other haunts. Life for these fortunate had changed almost not at all during the economic depression. The drums of war emanating from Europe when Hitler's army invaded Poland were heard only faintly by members of the nightclub elite, although it was a topic of table conversation. However, the prospect of United States involvement was as far removed from their discussions as the prospect itself. It was certainly not a point worth mentioning in Beebe's "This New York" or Paul's "Cholly Knickerbocker" column, unless the person who was the subject of the column had family in Poland, Austria, France or the Netherlands.

Café Society's myopic view of the world changed with the bombing of Pearl Harbor in December 1941. President Franklin D. Roosevelt's chilling radio broadcast finally brought the war home to all Americans. Suddenly the war *was* a topic of conversation among the tables at El Morocco and the Stork Club. Maury Paul died in 1942, but Beebe continued to chronicle the comings and goings of those around him. Walter Winchell took up the mantle of the radio war correspondent, if only stateside. Jerome Zerbe was moved to serve in the Navy, so he enlisted as a chief photographer's mate. Zerbe served on the aircraft carriers *Essex* and *Hancock*, but any ship he might serve on could be the target of a German torpedo. He photographed using his trusty Speedgraphic practically every day. He rose to become Admiral Nimitz's personal photographer and often went ashore to photograph the fighting on the Pacific islands.

Many of the actors and actresses of stage and screen who had frequented El Morocco, the Stork Club and 21 joined the USO to entertain the troops in the United States, Europe and the Pacific theater. Rationing had its impact on the restaurateurs, and lavish entertaining for a period of several years was not considered in the best of taste in view of the privations of fighting men and women overseas and rationing in America. Many women were called to factories to help build the arsenal of democracy lauded in the film reels. The music also changed during the war, with band leaders and musicians like Artie Shaw, Tommy Dorsey, and Benny Goodman churning out a stream of new musical hits.

In many ways, life went on in Manhattan, and no better evidence existed than Broadway. *Oklahoma* opened at the St. James Theater in 1943 and it marked a dramatic shift in the musical genre on Broadway. *On the Town* by Betty Comden and Adolf Green followed in 1944. With the cessation of hostilities, New York City welcomed home many of the returning troops, and grieved when loved ones did not come home. Zerbe was one of those who did. Gradually the former pace of activity picked up at the glittering night spots that had become so famous in the 1930s. Paul Whiteman adapted to and embraced the new swing and big band sound. Whiteman and his band were as popular as ever. America in general and Manhattan in particular were in a celebratory mood.

No longer were Forgotten Men lingering on the sidewalks desperate for work. As the national economy began its postwar boom, prosperity returned and the popularity of El Morocco, the Stork Club, 21 and the other famous meeting places of Café Society were operating at their capacity, but the mood was indescribably different. By the late 1940s, even the phrase Café Society seemed overdone, as if a different phrase needed to be coined to describe the people, places and their activities. Even Lucius Beebe sensed the change, although he knew change was the only constant of Manhattan. Thinking it wise, Beebe wrote his profile of the Café Society years in *Snoot If You Must,* published in 1947. He had been a newspaperman for two decades and he looked for something new and different to do. Beebe had been a longtime railroad and train travel enthusiast and made plans to move west. With his partner Chuck Clegg, he moved to Nevada, where Beebe began publishing his own regional newspaper. He purchased a lavish, restored Pullman car and converted it into living quarters, occasionally hitching a ride on a train as it crisscrossed the West. Taking tips from Zerbe, Beebe and Clegg took up train photography and wrote numerous books on the subject.

The types of columns written by Winchell, Paul and Beebe lost the interest of their readership, and the activities of Café Society slowly became a memory. The original meeting places still welcomed the same clientele, but the Chromium Mist had started to fade away, just as the 400 had at the turn of the century. Nothing really replaced it. Gone were the evening tuxedos and top hats on the men and dazzling evening gowns on the women. Clothing was far less formal and standards were relaxed. Just about anyone could enter El Morocco or the Stork Club now and the exclusivity was gone. Café Society had been a moment in time, and its time had finally passed.

CHAPTER 1

Ward McAllister, Caroline Astor and the 400

When establishing a timeline for the rise of Society in New York City, much depends on how far back one wants to go and if there was a pivotal event that could signal its establishment. One could argue the roots of Society came with the Dutch immigrants who prospered in what was then New Amsterdam. Or perhaps it originated with members of the Founding Fathers who chose to make Manhattan Island their home. Some research, however, reveals that the great names that would resonate most loudly during what would become known as the Gilded Age were the promotion of one man. His name was Ward McAllister. He would become the focus of establishing the names of select wealthy families in New York City in the late 1800s, although wealth alone was not a guarantor of entry. These families were of interest to many New Yorkers and they rose to that level of interest through the city's newspapers and certain magazines.

McAllister was born in Savannah, Georgia, in 1827. His father had been a graduate of Princeton with a degree in law, who married a prominent young woman from New York. Raised and educated in Savannah, he had visions to moving to Manhattan and making his mark any way he could. At the age of 20 he did so. Using family connections on his mother's side, he managed to get invited to a number of lavish parties and balls, and found he liked this life very much. He was in a quandary as to how he might make a living or at least an avocation out of his desire to break into New York Society. Not much is known about what work, if any, he performed there. We do know the money he did have soon ran out and he had to return to Savannah. Both his father and brother were attorneys, and dispensing with a full college curriculum, he applied himself to studying the premier reference works on law written by

William Blackstone, and other law books, in order to pass the Georgia bar exam. He succeeded on the first attempt. He made his father proud in doing so.

The senior McAllister felt it would be more remunerative to practice law in California, so the father and his two sons traveled west. However, all three found it difficult to establish a client base. It may have been Ward who suggested having dinners in their home by inviting prominent individuals as prospective clients. He took to this task with great organizational skills and personal attention to every detail. The dinners were a supreme success and business boomed at McAllister & Sons. Young Ward worked in the law offices during the day and formulated dinner parties at discreet times during each month. He shared in the profits of the firm and soon amassed $100,000. He really had no love for the law profession, but did love to host dinners and he felt this might be his means of breaking into the wealthy circles of New York City if done just the right way. He did not want to be a restaurateur, although he probably would have succeeded had he done so. Instead, McAllister exercised his lavish dining presentation skills with an ulterior motive. He believed he could advise select people in New York Society on how to hold these all-important social functions, and he would be the one in New York they would come to for guidance.

He spent several years in Washington, D.C., and even helped to organize a presidential inaugural ball. He met and married Sarah Gibbons and they had one child. McAllister felt he was ready to move back to New York and in 1858 he was back in Gotham. He first worked to build his associations with prominent older men. A dinner he held at the New York Hotel in 1859 displayed the ambitious McAllister touch, having eleven courses. His wife's family had a mansion in Madison, New Jersey, but it had been effectively shuttered and placed under the watch of a single groundskeeper. McAllister dispatched a small army of servants, maids, gardeners, stable keepers and cooks to the estate to prepare the home for an extravagant hosting event that taxed even McAllister's abilities. All was ready for the arrival of his elite guests from New York City. The mansion with many guest rooms provided all the accommodations necessary. The several days they spent there were an immense success, and when they returned to New York, the reputation of McAllister spread among the upper crust of the city.

The war between the Northern and Southern states that raged from 1861 to 1865 made such lavish displays improper. The dinners McAllister did hold were more subdued, reflecting the trying times. However, those years bear hardly a mention in his memoirs. There is no record of his returning to Savannah to check on the fate of the city during the war in the South. After the suppression of the bloody Draft Riots of 1863, the bloody battlefields in Pennsylvania, Maryland and Virginia once again seemed far-removed from Park and Fifth Avenue. With Reconstruction, McAllister could resume his plans to get the favor and respect of New York City's finest citizens.

With a small circle of established wealthy contacts, McAllister planned another dinner gathering, but of men only. He believed Society could, indeed, be organized in an informal way and wanted the advice of the men he had surrounded himself with on how best this could be accomplished. Although McAllister was prosperous and had the additional wealth of his wife behind him, he was no captain of industry. During this momentous dinner meeting, McAllister laid out his vision of New York Society, how it might be organized, the qualifications for being included in the select circle, and even the entertainments that could be held as social activity. He then asked the men for their advice and consent. The concept was well received, and McAllister later wrote, "We resolved to band together the respectable element of the city, and by this union make such strength that no individual could withstand us ... that the good and wise men of this community could always control Society."[1]

McAllister broached some of the names of men he felt should be what he called Patriarchs of the city. The small group of men helped him to compile a list of 25 names who would make up this group of Patriarchs. Among them were John Jacob Astor, William Astor, Eugene Livingston, Benjamin Welles, Royal Phelps, A. Gracie King, William C. Schermerhorn, and other very prominent and wealthy men whose family trees could be traced back four generations. McAllister, of course, made sure he was on the list of 25. Each Patriarch could give a Society ball during the year, inviting only those with impeccable credentials and manners. The first such ball was held in 1872 in a home of one of the Patriarchs. McAllister worked behind the scenes to ensure it was a great success. The young ladies and gentlemen invited all had a wonderful time, and the self-appointed organizer of Society was quite pleased with himself. The gatherings evolved into formal dances, and when one of them was held in Mrs. William Astor's Fifth Avenue mansion, McAllister knew his vision was becoming a reality. Some of these dance balls were held at Delmonico's, known for its very fine food and luxurious furnishings. The time for the lavish event to be held was fashionably late, typically starting at 11:00 p.m. the formal dinners had been held earlier.

These dance balls also served as the primary means of introducing young women to Society and were probably the first debutante balls held in New York. These proved to be of utmost social importance for the Astors, Whitneys,

Goelets, and many other families McAllister considered not only socially prominent but also socially acceptable. It was during these debutante balls that the power and visibility of the mothers became increasingly apparent. Naturally, the New York daily papers soon began devoting column space to these elegant affairs, and announcement of the coming out as well as the event itself was coveted by these prominent mothers. These wealthy wives, who had once been relatively obscure, were now being written of in the papers, and they found it very gratifying. This would become a critical element in the formation and recognition of Society in New York City.[2]

While it was the men who organized these lavish events, soon the women came to the fore as being the rightful leaders. McAllister had wisely included William Schermerhorn in his small and powerful circle. Schermerhorn's daughter Caroline had married William B. Astor Jr., in 1853 when she was 23 years old. The Astors certainly qualified to be counted among McAllister's elite. In 1784, John Jacob Astor arrived in America from Germany just eight years after the nation declared its independence from England. He became a trader of gunpowder, firearms, and other necessities for Native American tribes in New England and in Canada. In exchange Astor received furs both common and rare that he then sold for large sums of money. He established the American Fur Company and became wealthy with its success. He expanded his trade to export and import a broad range of desirable goods that had a willing market.

In 1802, Astor purchased his first large tract of land leases in New York City. He knew the city would expand over the next several decades and pursued a methodical real estate acquisition plan to the point where he owned more land there than anyone else. This included prime land locations in the center of the island that would mark Fifth Avenue and Madison Avenue. He sub-leased the land on long terms instead of selling it. He married Sarah Todd and the couple had several children. At the time of his death in 1848, Astor's worth was estimated to be $20 million, which was inherited by Astor's second son, William Backhouse. Astor's confidence in his second son was well-placed. William B. Astor also had a shrewd business mind and he succeeded in expanding the Astor wealth through further real estate dealings. The second-generation Astor married Margaret Armstrong, whose family was wealthy and prominent in the Hudson River Valley. The couple had two sons: John Jacob Astor III and William Backhouse II.

Upon his death in 1875, William Backhouse had succeeded in quintupling his inheritance. The estate of $100 million was equally divided between the two sons, who lived very different lives. John Jacob III along with his wife

Charlotte cultivated New York Society and gave parties in keeping with their wealth and station. William Backhouse, Jr., held little interest in cultivating relationships with the same elite crowd. He had far more interest in breeding his horses at their Hudson River estate, sailing on his mammoth yacht the *Ambassadress*, and consorting with women who were willing to share his bed. His wife Caroline was left to her own devices, and she chose to make the very best of it.[3]

Caroline Astor had held numerous gatherings in her unpretentious home on Fifth Avenue and 34th Street, and McAllister was very impressed with Mrs. Astor's bearing and decision-making ability. There was something in the way she spoke and carried herself that attracted him to Mrs. Astor. Over time, they would become good friends, and at one point he adopted a term of endearment he used to describe her: Mystic Rose. Despite the fact the William Astor preferred the comfort of his yacht to his home, hearth and wife, the couple did manage to have five children. Their current multi-story home could not truthfully be called a mansion, judging from its bland exterior, which paled in comparison to the European-inspired architecture of the mansion belonging to department store magnate A.T. Stewart directly across 34th Street. Nevertheless, the interior of Mrs. Astor's home showed her complete interior design tastes. Her ballroom was large enough to comfortably hold 400 people, and that is the number McAllister would use as the upper limit of the socially acceptable.

However, Mrs. Astor's position as social arbiter of New York did not go unchallenged. There was another family arguably as wealthy as the Astors also having social aspirations, if not the necessary lineage: the Vanderbilts. Cornelius Vanderbilt, born in 1794 of Dutch ancestry, would be the founder of the family fortune. At the age of 16, he started a fledgling passenger ship line along the Hudson River. Over the next three decades he alternated between being a sole owner or partner with others in the shipping of passengers and freight. His methods became nearly ruthless and he sought monopolistic control of shipping. He established a passenger line to California to capitalize on the gold rush taking place there. The long voyage impressed on Vanderbilt the preference of railroads for passenger transportation and he began the acquisition of rail lines. He acquired the New York & Harlem Railroad, the Hudson River Railroad, and in 1867, the New York Central Railroad.

The vast fortune established by Cornelius Vanderbilt was inherited by his sons and passed to the third generation. The Vanderbilts became the premier mansion builders in the United States during America's Gilded Age. The mansions they built in New York City and in Newport, Rhode Island, were a conspicuous means of entering into Society—something the founder of the family fortune had no interest in. The second-generation Vanderbilts felt differently. They hired the finest architectural firms to design their Fifth Avenue residences and Newport summer cottages.

At the height of his powers within Society, McAllister made the first of several missteps. He had acquired a false sense of security enjoying the company and respect of Mrs. Astor, and he failed to believe he was fallible. In 1890, McAllister published his observations of New York's wealthy and notable in *Society as I Have Found It*. The book was written in McAllister's pompous style, and it offended those mentioned in its pages. Mrs. Astor's response to publication of the book was decidedly cold. McAllister tried to laugh off the criticisms, and he did not heed the warnings he should have been hearing. The very people he was so proud to associate with began to drop him from their list of invitees. Among them were Mrs. William K. Vanderbilt, Mrs. Odgen Mills, Mrs. Stewart Webb and Mrs. Hamilton McKown Twombly.

Just when it appeared he would do himself in completely, he managed to land a newspaper column with the *New York World*. The column was "Ward McAllister's Letters," which first appeared in 1891. He finally had a public forum for his observations and took great delight in pontificating his views on all matters pertaining to New York Society and the people in it. The pay was hardly substantial—only $50 per week, but it was worth far more in notoriety to McAllister than the paycheck. Having painfully learned from his gaffe in publishing his book, he strove in his column to be entertaining and inoffensive.

In 1892, Caroline Astor's husband William died. The estate was settled quickly and the widow Astor came into a personal fortune in the tens of millions. With no constraints on her ambitions, she realized her dream of having her own Fifth Avenue mansion in keeping with her status as the queen of New York Society and a home far more beautiful that the one she had occupied for years. She made an appointment with renowned architect Richard Morris Hunt. She outlined to him the style she wanted her mansion, the number of rooms, and where on Fifth Avenue she wanted it. After Caroline Astor reviewed and approved Hunt's architectural drawings, construction began in 1893 on the corner of Fifth Avenue and East 65th Street. The home was patterned after a French Renaissance revival design. The interior rooms rivaled the splendor of Versailles, from which Hunt took his inspiration, and were furnished with 17th and 18th century French furniture acquired from New

York's finest antique dealers. The picture gallery was three times the size of that in her previous home and could comfortably hold 1200 guests. Very prominent was a larger-than-life portrait of Caroline Astor by Charles Emile Auguste Carolus-Duran, painted in 1890. From the entry hall, there were reception rooms to the right and left. There were two dining rooms with adjoining salons, on the north and south side of the mansion, with a large kitchen and pantry to serve each. There was a large carriage garage and stable off 65th Street. On the second floor were several chamber rooms, one of which was Caroline's private bedroom, several maid's rooms, two nursery rooms and two guest bedrooms. The third floor was devoted almost entirely to guest rooms, but also had a large schoolroom and a sewing room.

The construction of the new Astor mansion took place at the onset of the financial panic of 1893 and the subsequent depression. Aggressive railroad expansion in the 1880s had led to widespread speculation in railroad stocks and other investment instruments. Large, existing railroads took on more debt by acquiring other rail lines. In March 1893, the Philadelphia and Reading Railroad filed for bankruptcy. This sent shock waves through the financial community, but this would be only the first of many failures of railroads. Tied with this was the failure of hundreds of banks, followed by the failure of the Northern Pacific Railway, the Union Pacific Railroad, and the Atchison, Topeka and Santa Fe Railroad. The panic became a financial contagion that precipitated bank runs and further bank failures and business closings across the United States. Unemployment had been only three percent in 1892 but more than tripled in 1893. Further closure of thousands of businesses and massive layoffs pushed unemployment in 1894 to between 15 and 19 percent, but a definitive number cannot be determined, as this was before government employment statistics were kept. Business and residential construction virtually stopped.[4] Mrs. Astor's mansion was one of most conspicuous exceptions to the contraction of building construction in New York City, and it kept several hundred masons, marble cutters, woodworkers, metalworkers, plasterers, glass cutters, cabinetmakers and other artisans busy and employed for two years as they worked to complete the magnificent home.

Managing the progress on her mansion also served as a conduit for channeling her grief upon losing her second daughter, Helen, in 1893. She had married James Roosevelt, older half-brother of Franklin Delano Roosevelt, in 1878. Caroline Astor lost her first daughter, Emily, who died in 1882 while giving birth to her third child from her marriage to James J. Van Allen. During the time of Helen's death and construction of the mansion, Mrs. Astor's third daughter Charlotte went through a well-known affair with a man by the name of Hallet Barrowe. This open scandal was a constant source of gossip in even the respectable New York papers. William Backhouse Astor, Jr., actually traveled to Paris in April 1892 in an attempt to talk sense to his daughter Charlotte to break off the affair. This was ironic, considering his known marital indiscretions. He died there in Paris from lung congestion and heart failure, and Charlotte accompanied the body back to New York. Charlotte was finally divorced in 1894 from James Drayton, who was the vice-president of the Equitable Life Assurance Society. Charlotte was the only daughter Caroline Astor had left; she was determined to reintroduce her to the elite circle she still controlled, and it would be done in the magnificent new mansion completed in 1894. This proved awkward, considering the scope of the scandal that was known to all. In 1896, Charlotte married George Ogilvy Haig and moved to London. This relieved Caroline Astor of an undeniable degree of embarrassment. Now, however, the queen of society was totally alone. Caroline Astor chose not to remarry.

The Mrs. Astor was a late participant to the mansion building boom of the late 1800s in New York City. When it came to conspicuous architectural consumption, the master builders were the Vanderbilts. Around 1878 William Henry Vanderbilt, the oldest son of Commodore Vanderbilt, ordered the construction of two similarly proportioned but differently designed mansions to be built on Fifth Avenue between 51st and 52nd Streets. On the next block going up Fifth Avenue, William K. Vanderbilt built his mansion, designed by Richard Morris Hunt. Between 57th and 58th Streets, Cornelius Vanderbilt—eldest son of William Henry—built one of the largest and most ornate mansions the city had ever seen. Cornelius also built the spectacular Breakers in Newport, Rhode Island, which may have been rivaled for grandeur by William's Marble House nearby. The obscure George Washington Vanderbilt II hired Richard Morris Hunt to design the largest mansion in the United State; Biltmore was built in Asheville, North Carolina, between 1889 and 1895. Nevertheless, Caroline Astor was quite pleased with her new mansion, and she intended to enjoy all it had to offer both for herself and for the Society she held sway over.

It was roughly around this time that Ward McAllister made several more societal missteps. To a reporter of the *New York Tribune*, he revealed that New York Society was made up, really, of no more than 400 individuals. When asked how he arrived at this figure, he casually mentioned that was the capacity of Mrs. Astor's original ballroom, as if to say the only ones who really mattered were those invited to Mrs. Astor's ball. Beyond that, McAllister wrote that there was an Inner Circle comprising 150 people, and the rest were broken down in four other descending scales. McAllister's means of selection was totally arbitrary and subjective. Who were these people? McAllister was queried. So then, in 1892 he methodically released the list of names, causing great consternation among the named, and particularly among those who were not included within the Inner Circle. He chose to release the list of Inner Circle members and did so alphabetically. This was a breach of protocol because they should have been ranked starting with Mrs. Astor. While releasing the list of names did not produce enemies, it did not result in winning any friends. He became further ostracized within Society, and Mrs. Astor stopped sending for him. He made polite inquiries and he received no response.

McAllister also managed to alienate Elbridge T. Gerry, the chairman of the Centennial Ball Executive Committee. The two men came to loggerheads over the protocol of the ball, with McAllister refusing to perform a simple request. McAllister resigned from the committee in a huff, and Gerry saw this as good riddance to the recalcitrant McAllister. The tabloid magazine *Town Topics* wrote scathing parodies of McAllister with appropriate cartoon illustrations.

Almost to the very end of his life, McAllister fought to defend his own standing among the New York elite, and while having lost the favor of Caroline Astor, he managed to secure the recognition of the Vanderbilts and others who counted him among their friends. His health began declining in 1894 and he slowly withdrew from the glittering social life of New York. He died in January 1895. The man who had counted himself among the 400 of New York Society had only five of the Patriarchs and 20 names among the 400 attend his funeral, and Mrs. Astor was conspicuously absent. Maime Fish took smug pleasure that the man who had humiliated her husband Stuyvesant Fish and denigrated her parties for their admittedly bizarre themes was now dead.

Caroline Astor was now 65 but she still wielded immense power over the social life of New York's wealthiest and most prominent citizens. Yet for all her influence and ability to organize balls and other highly desired social events, she still felt a need to have someone who could guide her or at least provide confirmation. At her age she may have also needed amusement. Perhaps for all these reasons she cast aside her own stringent restrictions and accepted a young man with no wealth and no genealogy that would qualify him to join the ranks of the 400. That man was Harry Lehr. While he lacked practically all the essential traits to be considered, Harry Lehr did have intelligence, wit, a way with words and a certain air that women found irresistible.

One of those women was Evelyn Townsend Burden. Lehr knew that the wealthy and connected summered in Newport, Rhode Island, and he made sure he was there for the summer social season during the late 1890s. When Evelyn Burden met Lehr for the first time, she was fascinated and asked him to join her and her husband for the summer at her Newport cottage Fairlawn.

It was just the sort of invitation Lehr had been seeking in his attempt to break into the upper crust of Newport, and ultimately New York. Through this venue Lehr met others who were equally fascinated with the socially adept though all but penniless man. His every expense was covered and his days and nights were filled with the presence of those whose company he coveted. It was at one of these gatherings he met Caroline Astor. She was bedecked in a magnificent dress and draped with diamonds that were so dazzling, Lehr remarked, smiling, she looked like a lighted chandelier. Caroline Astor laughed and was immediate taken by the brash and amusing young man.

Lehr immediately sensed Caroline Astor was needy, and he cleverly worked to fill the void left by McAllister while building the self-esteem of the woman who still held an impressive grip on society in New York and Newport. She asked Lehr to help her with her planned functions at her Newport cottage Beechwood, and Lehr gladly complied. He told her he would be glad to perform the same duties once back in New York at her magnificent mansion on Fifth Avenue. He also did something else, something Caroline Astor had never done as the head of New York Society. Lehr convinced her to dine publicly. When she entered Delmonico's Restaurant with Harry Lehr by her side, every head in the dining hall swiveled and jaws dropped. The event made the pages of every newspaper in New York.

Lehr was now everywhere in Manhattan. The invitations to him were more than he could fulfill. Other leading society ladies asked Lehr for his expertise in planning and arranging events. Mrs. Stuyvesant "Maime" Fish also called on Lehr to help her with her quirky balls and parties. Maime Fish and Harry Lehr were really two of the same kind and they got along as well as he did with Caroline Astor. No ball or party was complete without his presence. As the century turned from the 19th to the 20th, Lehr had overshadowed the memory of Ward McAllister. He was consulted in matters other than parties and fancy dress balls. He was called on regarding not only weddings but proper debutante balls and other social functions.

Lehr became one of the most famous shills of New York. Department store heir Tom Wanamaker secured a suite at Sherry's Hotel for Lehr to use at no expense, and his meals were covered as well. New York's finest tailors offered custom-fitted suits gratis for his mere endorsement and mention at parties. The same went for shoes, ties, jewelry, watches and other accessories. Lehr had to pay for virtually nothing.

Lehr had no wife as yet, because he really had no romantic interest in women. Nevertheless, for appearances and financial sake, he met a certain Elizabeth Drexel Dahlgren, daughter of the Wall Street financier. She, too, was taken by Harry Lehr, but he saw her only as a means to his ends. Dahlgren, a widow, was more or less pressured into the relationship by several of the matrons of the 400. The couple was married in 1901 but Elizabeth learned to her shock and her sorrow on her first honeymoon night that Harry Lehr had no romantic or sexual interest in her, he informed her coldly, and their marriage was never consummated. Theirs was a marriage of appearances only. Now that he had a wealthy wife, he feared all his free offerings to which he was so accustomed would soon dry up. He demanded from his wife an annual stipend of $25,000 and all expenses. To avoid any public embarrassment, Elizabeth acquiesced, and Harry continued to live in the style to which he had become accustomed. His unloved wife commiserated with her wealthy friends. Divorce was considered scandalous in the day, so she endured her empty married life for as long as her husband lived. Harry preferred the company of Tom Wanamaker, his chosen companion.

The Passing of an Era

In January 1905, Caroline Astor gave one of her last balls at her Fifth Avenue mansion. She was now 75 years old but she still put on a lavish display and the 600 invitees still came to pay her homage and bask in her legendary aura. From her diamond tiara down to her sequined shoes, she remained a commanding figure, but even she knew this would be her last such display. She no longer had the strength to carry the entire evening, and before the 1:00 a.m. multi-course dinner, she retired to her own bedroom.

Several years later, she did the unprecedented and granted an interview to an editor of a noted magazine of the day, *The Delineator*. She had pointed things to say about the vulgar and demeaning nonsense balls, often the brainchild of Harry Lehr, that were so popular with Maime Fish and Alva Vanderbilt Belmont. She was so candid and honest in her assessment of society as she knew it and as it was now, that the *New York Times* reprinted the key quotes in an article published in September 1908.

"Many people seem to think I could have done a great deal in making New York Society as democratic as it is in London and open to anyone of intellectual attainments, as it is in London," she said. "But one can only do one's best under the conditions.... We have to be more exclusive in New York because in America there is no authority in society."[5]

In her closing remarks, she frankly admitted New York would manage to get along without her and that there were women who would come forward to take her place as head of the city's society. She made a prophetic statement regarding the new generation growing up, saying their outlook on life was different from her conservative views, but she acknowledged they were "full of health and abundant spirits."

One day shortly after giving this interview, she lost her footing on the marble steps from the second floor of her mansion and fell headlong, striking her head on the steps and rolling to the bottom. She was bleeding from a scalp wound when servants discovered her. She refused to be taken to a hospital, and her physician Dr. Austin Flint was called to examine her. She insisted the doctor stitch her gash at home and she convalesced in her bed. Her mental health had been declining for some time and her servants witnessed her growing dementia and senility. Even her granddaughters saw her sadly slip into a fantasy world of greeting guests who were not there or imagining she was somehow pregnant. Her butler would listen politely to her plans for a new ball and those she wanted to invite, but the invitations never went out and the orders for flowers were never sent. She would still take her carriage rides through Central Park, which gave her a welcomed respite from the silent rooms of her mansion. The *New York Times* had also reported she had suffered mild heart attacks. She died in her Fifth Avenue mansion in October 1908. Her funeral was conducted on November 2 and her body was interred at Trinity Church Cemetery, next to her husband.

Even before Caroline Astor's passing, other women had continued to vie for the crown of the leader of New York society. Mrs. Stuyvesant Fish, Alva Vanderbilt Belmont and others carried on much as they had, both in New York and in Newport, Rhode Island. Nevertheless, life was changing among New York's wealthy. The financial panic of 1907 affected the financial holdings of many of New York's richest families. Nevertheless, the Vanderbilts, for example, still had millions of dollars at their disposal and they continued to enjoy their wealth and the most conspicuous and tangible display of their wealth, their many mansions. Harry Lehr continued to court the favors of many of New York's wealthy patrons to offer his services in making all arrangements for social events of all kinds.

The wreck of the R.M.S. *Titanic* in 1912 was a maritime disaster of unparalleled scope, with over 1200 men, women and children perishing in the icy North Atlantic waters. John Jacob Astor IV, 47 years old, known as Jack, was among the many who died, but his much younger, pregnant wife Madeleine survived and a son was born some months later. Together, they had both traveled aboard the White Star Line's sister ship, *Olympic*, just two and a half months before. Another first class passenger, Edith Rosenbaum, felt immediately ill at ease when she stepped into the reception room, and seriously considered leaving the ship. She ignored the premonition and chose to accompany her many steamer trunks filled with expensive gowns. Financier J.P. Morgan had purchased the White Star Line in June 1902 and placed J. Bruce Ismay as its director. Morgan booked a first class suite aboard the doomed liner, but canceled at the last minute and did not board the ship. Instead, he would die in his sleep in March of the following year. George D. Widener, president of the Philadelphia Traction Company and resident of the magnificent Lynnewood Hall, was on board with his wife and son Harry, but only his wife survived among the women who were able to get into a lifeboat. Benjamin Guggenheim, one of the heirs of the family fortune, was also on board the liner. There were many other first class passengers with comparable wealth, but not the recognition, on board the *Titanic* on its maiden voyage. Many of them wanted bragging rights of having experienced the epic ship's first voyage. Tragically, those voices would be silenced.

The sinking of the *Titanic* and the loss of life across all classes was the result of hubris and a conspiracy of events well recorded in many books and articles in the years that followed. In a sermon shortly after the sinking of the ship, the Bishop of Winchester was quoted as saying, "*Titanic*, name and thing, will stand as a monument and warning to human presumption." This maritime disaster also served as a metaphor to some, on the passing of the rich upper classes and their lifestyle. However, those surviving upper classes would continue to prosper, many of them, and continue to build their neoclassical mansions on Fifth Avenue, in Newport, Rhode Island, and in other wealthy enclaves around the United States. Nevertheless, the 400 would one day be supplanted by an equally famous but somewhat less wealthy class to become known as Café Society.

CHAPTER 2

Prohibition, the Speakeasies and Nightclubs of the 1920s

Instrumental to the formation of Café Society in New York City during the 1930s was the imposition of Prohibition nationwide and the emergence of establishments that became known as speakeasies, along with entertainment nightclubs, during the 1920s. The rise of the prohibition movement and its success in amending the Constitution of the United States to abolish alcoholic beverages in the country after more than 250 years of its consumption in America is one of the most curious events in the nation's history. Like any legislation that forbids certain behaviors or perceived rights by the individual to do what he or she wishes, those individuals will find the means to circumvent said legislation, and no legislation was more widely ignored than the Volstead Act that was crafted to enforce the ratification of the 18th Amendment to the Constitution.

To better understand the prohibition movement one must review the history and popularity of the various forms of alcoholic beverages from the earliest days of the American colonies. In 1630, a ship laden with 10,000 gallons of wine and countless gallons of beer arrived at the Massachusetts Bay Colony as essential staples of the residents there to be used for consumption as well as trading. The puritanism of the Puritans did not extend, apparently, to what was enjoyed at the table. Commercial distilleries sprang up in the Northeast and by 1763 there were more than 150 enterprises producing rum alone. No less than America's premier general in the War of Independence and its first president, George Washington, was quoted as saying, "[T]he benefits arising from moderate use of strong Liquor have been experienced in all Armies, and are not to be disputed." Liquor in various forms from over 14,000 distilleries became so common in the early 1800s that it was often less expensive than tea.[1]

2. Prohibition, the Speakeasies and Nightclubs of the 1920s

A century after Washington's endorsement of liquor for combat troops, Gen. Lewis Cass, as secretary of war under Andrew Jackson, eliminated soldiers' rations of whiskey and issued an edict forbidding consumption of liquor in all forms in forts and on bases. While such liquor consumption may have declined, it certainly was not eliminated. Soldiers found clever means to keep the spirits flowing. The argument was that water purity was often questionable at these forts and military bases.

Around the middle of the 19th century there began a temperance movement against liquor consumption which was small at first but like a planted acorn eventually grew to amazing size and strength. Such men as John Bartholomew Gough and Neal Dow backed this cause and worked tirelessly to convince many thousands of others that liquor in all its forms was evil, a menace to society, so laws were needed to curtail or even eliminate it. The first such law was enacted in Maine in 1851 with fines and imprisonment for those prosecuted for the manufacture or sale of liquor. This legislation emboldened others to pass similar legislation in other states. However, there was a backlash and pressure put on legislators in those states that enacted dry laws. By the end of the 1850s, all such state laws had been repealed, including the one in Maine.

There was a resurgence in the temperance movement starting in the early 1870s. It began in Ohio and the many of the believers in the movement were naturally drawn from the churches, with women often leading the way. The temperance movement coincided with the suffrage movement and the women involved were often supportive of both women's rights and prohibition. Susan B. Anthony became prominent in both movements but ironically found the male control of the dry efforts oppressive and threw her support totally behind suffrage. Women had virtually no rights whatsoever in the late 1800s and laws had to be changed to protect them within marriage and divorce, from abusive husbands ruled by liquor, and for the protection of children. Women could only improve their condition legislatively and this was the impetus behind women's suffrage.

The Women's Christian Temperance Union (WCTU) was founded in 1874 by Frances Willard, and over the next two decades the organization grew to a membership of 250,000. The WCTU became, essentially, the first political action committee and was immensely powerful. In 1876, before a large WCTU members' meeting, Willard stated women should have the right to vote in issues regarding liquor—decades before the right of women to vote was granted. By its very charter, the women in this organization fervently prayed for abolition of liquor manufacture and for the right to vote for legislation that could bring this about, as well as the many drunken sinners they encountered in their confrontations with saloon owners and patrons.²

Willard had some visionary and driven women within the WCTU who not only grew the organization but broadened its interest to men and women outside the group by appealing to the welfare of children. Mary Hunt was one of these women, and she had a plan to teach children to despise alcohol in all its forms. She wanted temperance instruction introduced in schools across the United States. By 1882, the first state to pass compulsory temperance education was Vermont, later followed by New York and Pennsylvania. Four years later, she went before the U.S. Congress and succeeded in getting legislation passed mandating Scientific Temperance Instruction in public schools and military academies. By 1901, every state had such laws on the books and the course was taught to every child attending school. This was a pivotal event in the push toward the eventual passage of the Eighteenth Amendment. It was that year that Carrie Nation adopted her weapon of choice—the hatchet—to destroy as much of a saloon's equipment and supply of booze as she could before she was arrested and taken to jail with her clothing soaked with beer, whiskey and other forms of liquor. The attention she drew to the temperance cause was out of all proportion to her practical impact on liquor consumption.

The distillers, brewers and wine makers marshaled their efforts to combat the attack on their ability to produce and distribute alcoholic beverages. With the dramatic growth in European immigration came with them the desire for drink, and America's consumption skyrocketed. By 1890, beer consumption was in excess of 850,000 gallons a year.³ Brewers like Adolphus Busch and the many other lesser companies and their distributors became fabulously wealthy meeting the market demand for brew, and they saw the leaders of the temperance movement as their enemies. However, the temperance movement had several decades of momentum behind it, and the liquor lobby was slow and anemic in its defense of its product.

The brewers, distillers and wine makers felt the most effective efforts should be spent on persuading legislators to block laws that affected their industry. The Distilling Company of America and its subsidiaries controlled over 90 percent of liquor production in the United States. Along with the country's brewers, revenues totaled three billion dollars annually by the first decade of the 20th century. The United States Brewers Association, the National Wholesale Liquor Dealers Association and the National Liquor League together formed their own powerful lobby to take on the prohibition juggernaut. Individually, many of the liquor and beer companies would actually advertise the benefits of their various alcoholic beverages. One Detroit brewer, George E. Gies, ran a series of advertisements against prohibition. The ads showed toddlers in a high chair or a mother holding her child, with ad copy that read: "Lager's amber Fluid mild, Gives health and strength to wife and child." Another ad read: "The youngster, ruddy with good cheer, Serenely sips his Lager Beer."[4]

The foot soldiers of the temperance movement, including the equally powerful Anti-Saloon League, methodically pushed for an amendment to the Constitution to effectively ban the manufacture, distribution and sale of virtually all alcoholic beverages. The strongest push for this took place in New York, and New York City may have been the wettest area of the country. The Anti-Saloon League targeted specifically Tammany Hall because the city government viewed the saloon as a focal point of deal-making both legitimate and illegitimate, and it was long-known for its rampant corruption. The ASL adopted a strategy of getting local districts to go dry one by one in upstate New York, working toward Manhattan, and then getting individual neighborhoods in the city to go dry. It intended to do this legislatively using what was called "local option," which had successfully closed over 1000 saloons in Baltimore alone. The ASL's William Anderson was brought in to do the job in New York state and the city. Anderson's efforts there were viewed as critical to getting a prohibition amendment approved by Congress and the states. By the ASL's estimates, New Yorkers spent $365 million a year on alcohol in all its forms and per capita liquor and beer consumption was three and a half times the national average.[5]

Anderson arrived in New York City the first week of January 1914 with a methodical plan proven over a period of 20 years nationwide. He even held a press conference in his hotel room and reporters recorded his brash proclamations that he would succeed in getting alcohol abolished in both the city and the state. While many who read his comments in the following day's papers laughed the comments to scorn, the ASL had a formidable success record, and others took Anderson more seriously. It would take him five years, but ultimately he and the ASL succeeded in the bold plan. The ASL became a powerful force in New York state politics over the next two years. One by one the state legislators threw their support behind prohibition. By May 1917, Anderson noted with satisfaction the local option legislation passed statewide. In particular, the legislation permitted New York City to hold a referendum on the matter. Those stunned by the success of these legislative efforts failed to recognize the mood of the Progressive era for reform and the fervent desire to reign in the Tammany Hall machine.

Finally, the Eighteenth Amendment came to a vote in the House of Representatives in December 1917. The final vote was 272 voting yes and 128 voting no. It then had to go through the state ratification process. State ratification moved with astounding speed, with many states ratifying the amendment on the same day. Two weeks after Nebraska ratified the Eighteenth Amendment, New York did as well, but by a narrow margin. However, by that point, New York's ratification was a moot point since more than three-quarters of the states had already done so. Ironically, though New York's ratification was unnecessary, symbolically it was very important. Ratification was completed in January 1919 and would go into effect one year later. The zealous advocates of prohibition rejoiced, naively believing that America was on the road to sobriety. Instead, the country was on the road to organized crime, an overwhelmed judicial system, millions of scofflaws, untold political and law enforcement corruption, and ultimately a completely discredited Prohibition movement.

The Volstead Act, as it was legislatively known, was drawn up to put teeth into the Eighteenth Amendment. The legislation got its name from Rep. Andrew John Volstead, who was the chief sponsor of the bill. He had been a prosecuting attorney until he entered Congress in 1903. He became chairman of the House Judiciary Committee in 1919, the year efforts began in Congress to draft the legislation with provisions to enforce Prohibition. Naturally, it was a contentious process, and by the time the bill was more or less suitable for a vote, it had more than 65 provisions written into it, right down to specific definitions of what was "intoxicating," what was or was not "beer" and what was "medicinal whiskey," defined "industrial alcohol," and "non-intoxicating cider and fruit juice," of which 200 gallons could be legally produced at home annually, among many others. It was a patchwork quilt of restrictions and permissions having numerous convenient loopholes. One of the most glaring was the provision that is was not illegal to *possess* liquor or any alcoholic beverage, and this just codified the hoarding of it by millions of Americans even before it was voted on by Congress. The weak link of the Volstead Act was the totally inadequate funding the bill provided for enforcement: $4.75 million.[6] This underfunding, which left the onus of enforcement on many state and local governments, was thus a serious impediment to the law's effectiveness. Nevertheless, when the legislation was voted on by Congress in October 1919, it was viewed by President Woodrow Wilson as draconian and he vetoed the bill. Congress overrode the president's veto several days later and the National Prohibition Act became the law of the land in January 1920.

Prohibition and the New Supply Chain

A great many national distillers, brewers and grape growers and wine makers were going to go out of business when the Volstead Act became law (with some exceptions), but other ways would be found to replace much of the lost alcoholic production capacity. Liquor would come from America's northern neighbor, Canada. In the first seven months of 1920, 900,000 cases of liquor were shipped from Canadian distillers to the port of Windsor, Ontario, alone.[7] From there it was a short transit by cargo ship of just one mile to the port of Detroit, Michigan. While this was a major hub for Canadian liquor, the entire border between Canada and the United States offered little barrier to liquor smugglers eager to get their premium alcohol into the United States via Washington, Montana, North Dakota, Minnesota and the northeastern states east of the Great Lakes. By the same token, Mexican distillers and brewers were eager to ply their product into California, New Mexico, Arizona and Texas.

However, it was the entire eastern seaboard of the country that became a giant port of imported liquor so vast it was nearly impossible for the Prohibition Bureau agents to stanch the flow. While much of the alcohol went into protective hiding, untold quantities were loaded onto cargo ships and sent to islands beyond the three-mile limit established by the Prohibition Act, and to Cuba, the Bahamas, Jamaica, Haiti, the Dominican Republic, Puerto Rico and the Virgin Islands. These Caribbean islands also became even larger importers of newly produced liquors, beer and wines. Grand Bahama was the closest island to the Florida coastline, and the sea lane between Florida and the island was thick with ships of all sizes moving booze to the Florida peninsula.

The 1920s truly became the age of the bootlegger. They were a vital link in the supply chain of getting needed liquor to distributors and to a now more powerful criminal element in New York City in particular. One of the most successful during this period was Bill McCoy, who ran several schooners out of Nassau. Legends grew up around him because he was, among other things, over six feet tall and handsome, a fine captain who literally ran a tight ship, he moved massive quantities of cases to the eastern shore with near invisibility, and he rarely touched the stuff himself. He would not sail his Nassau-registered ships into New York harbor but would drop anchor in places with less bureaucratic red tape such as Nantucket, Montauk, Long Island and Block Island. There he would offload his cargo, money would change hands, and he would sail out to sea again. McCoy had many imitators and most of them were successful—that is, they were not run out of business by the overworked agents of the Prohibition Bureau and state prohibition officers hired to run interference against the liquor flotilla that seemed to come in endless waves. These agents were supplemented by an increased Coast Guard during the mid-twenties.

The Prohibition Act demarcated the keep-out zone along the United States coast by establishing a three-mile limit where these ships of all sizes were permitted to move with their liquid cargo. Basically the supply of liquor moved offshore by 3.1 miles. Rum runners, in fact runners for all forms of liquor, would motor out to the anchored ships of the bootleggers to pick up the needed cases and return to shore. Many of these larger ships were permanently anchored and were supplied by other boats that came with supplies of liquor in their holds; the cargo would be transferred, and the supply ships would return to their respective ports in the Caribbean. Many times, individual retail customers with their boats or one hired for the occasion would also do business to buy for their private use. In these situations, the bootleggers preferred to have established customers who were repeat buyers. As a courtesy, many of these small customers would offer to take the ship's mail back to shore and deliver it to the Post Office and even take parcels to deliver personally. These same preferred customers would often bring needed supplies to the ship's crew. Other ships acted as floating restaurants and hotels where customers could come aboard, enjoy a fine meal with drinks, gamble, and perhaps sleep for the night and return to shore the following morning.

This vital network was also well established to supply the immense New York market, and Prohibition agents clearly knew this. The agents relied on the randomness of the ship boardings and inspections to act as deterrence, but tossing cases of liquid cargo overboard was often simply the cost of doing business. The supply ships offshore of New York were just part of an indistinct maritime warehouse line that ran the entire eastern seaboard. Appropriately dubbed Rum Row, it stretched as far north as Saint Pierre Island off the coast of Newfoundland. It is doubtful the advocates of Prohibition in the WCTU and the Anti-Saloon League ever imagined the extremes to which men would go provide alternate means of supply for liquor, beer and wine wiped out by the Prohibition Act, nor could they imagine the millions of otherwise law-abiding men and women who would become scofflaws in their simple desire to enjoy the alcoholic beverages of their choice.

On April 5, 1921, New York Governor Nathan Miller signed the Mullan-Gage Enforcement Law, which was written with even more stringent penalties than those called for in the Vollstead Act. Some of the New York press drew

This was a familiar scene in New York City during Prohibition. Two men pour illicit brew into the city sewer system as Deputy Police Commissioner John A. Leach looks on. Nevertheless, members of Café Society rarely went without their desired liquor or beer (Library of Congress).

the analogy that carrying a hip flask was now equivalent to carrying an unlicensed firearm. The NYPD rightfully feared this would overwhelm their police force with new enforcement duties, and district attorneys feared the courts would be clogged with cases of otherwise law-abiding citizens being prosecuted under the new law. Their worst fears were realized. Nothing symbolized the real consequences of the law like the case of seventy-seven-year-old Nora Kelly. Just one month after enactment of the new law, the elderly woman stood before a New York City magistrate, charged with possession of a small flask of whiskey. The judge rejected her explanation and she was sentenced to five days in jail, where the woman had probably never before spent one minute of her life.[8]

With the enactment of Mullan-Gage, the majority of cases coming before judges involved prohibition, not violent crime. Judges saw case after case of men and women who had never been charged with any crime whatsoever who learned the meaning of misdemeanor, and the length of their jail time was proportionate to the amount of liquor they had in their possession. The backlog of court cases became so overwhelming to the detriment of legitimate violent crime cases that pressure was brought to bear on the New York legislature. Gov. Miller lost his re-election bid to former governor Alfred Smith, who made repeal of the law a priority. On June 1, 1923, Smith signed the legislation repealing Mullan-Gage.[9] While the Anti-Saloon League and the WCTU decried this reversal, civil libertarians hailed it as a restoration of individual liberty and common-sense law.

Manhattan Nightclubs and the Emergence of Speakeasies

Examples of how existing liquor supplies already on hand were preserved are numerous. Before the first day the Prohibition Act became law, fully 80 percent of the alcoholic beverages held in reserve at the Union Club in Manhattan had been transferred into members' homes; some of these homes would become speakeasies. Similar efforts, multiplied hundreds of times, had been taking place up and down the length of the island for weeks. Liquor store owners were clearing their shelves of product in a panicked effort to prevent steep losses. Restaurants and hotels sold off their stocks and unsold liquor and beer also went into private homes. Forward-thinking individuals methodically stocked up on the liquor they wished to have that would form the basis of their new business as a speakeasy either in apartments or in hopefully obscure business locations throughout Manhattan. Nevertheless, many bars and virtually all liquor stores closed their doors forever. Legendary restaurants such as Rector's, Shanley's and Murry's could not operate profitably without serving liquor, wine and beer, and they all closed. However, much of the liquor simply moved to other locations where it continued to be served. Even President Warren G. Harding transferred his stash of liquor from his personal residence on Wyoming Avenue to his White House living quarters. He fully intended to continue serving booze to guests at 1600 Pennsylvania Avenue.[10]

Prohibition was directly responsible for the invention and vast expansion of furtive liquor serving establishments that became known as speakeasies. The word was coined from the quiet conversations between the customers and proprietors at the front door of the establishment, and the talk that went on once inside. Many of these establishments had small sliding panels so the doorman could view the person or persons outside, and often passwords were employed by customers sent from a referral. In New York City, there were literally thousands of speakeasies run out of apartments, and the furnishings indicated nothing less. There were also speakeasies operating in countless offices throughout Manhattan that had once housed other kinds of business, but whose owners discovered serving liquor was more profitable and cash left no paper trail.

At the upper end of businesses serving liquor were the nightclubs that had been in business before the advent of Prohibition, and new nightclubs that were the product of Prohibition. Those businesses which wanted to continue to operate under Prohibition in Manhattan had to pay exorbitant fees to Prohibition Bureau agents and New York City police officers. Those speakeasies and nightclubs owned by mobsters paid these bribes and hush money themselves. The businesses that refused to pay the money demanded, or which denied they were serving any liquor, or which dealt with law officers and agents who refused to take the bribes, were formally raided and the owners and often customers were hauled away for prosecution. Enforcement corruption became so widespread that even the *New York Times* reported that over 100 agents had been dropped from the Prohibition Bureau payroll for corruption by the end of 1920. Corruption was so prevalent that the director of State Prohibition, Frank L. Boyd, resigned in frustration, stating to the press that enforcement in New York was "a hopeless and thankless task."[11]

This was indeed music to the ears of the speakeasy and nightclub operators. However, the smaller speakeasies preferred to keep their payoffs to a minimum in order to keep more of the money in their cashboxes. The nightclubs, however, needed all the customers they could pull in and publicity of any kind would draw new customers. Into this nightclub environment in the early 1920s entered one of the most colorful, boisterous and indeed gifted promoters and club operators in New York City, and she went by the name of Texas Guinan. Mary Louise Cecilia Guinan moved to Manhattan in 1906 from her home state of Texas and landed a job as a chorus girl. Ten years later she was discovered by an independent film producer, and Guinan headed west to become the quintessential cowgirl in more than 30 B-movies with titles like *The Hellcat*, *The Gun Woman* and *Little Miss Deputy*. She became so popular she had President Harding and the Prince of Wales among her list of admirers. Eventually she tired of the stereotyped roles she was playing, and she was not getting any younger in a town where youth was always king. She moved back to New York City in 1922.

A chance invitation to a party changed the course of her life and fortune. That party proved so lifeless she decided to liven things up and she broke out into song. She soon had others participating, and suddenly she found herself the life of the party. Word quickly spread about the gal from Texas and her ability to get a place jumping. She was asked to run the King Cole room at the Knickerbocker Hotel, and soon it was pulling in celebrities like Rudolph Valentino and John Barrymore as customers. Even New York society matron Mrs. William K. Vanderbilt herself would drop in just to see what all the excitement was about. Texas Guinan clearly had a gift.

In 1924, Guinan chose to cast her lot, for better or for worse, with club owner Larry Fea. He was owner of the El Fey Club on West Forty-Fifth Street that was backed by mobster money. He made her a financial offer she could not refuse, and she in turn promised him to make the El Fey Club the most famous speakeasy in the United States. It could be said that the seeds of Café Society, at least in part, had its start in this club. It drew the likes of Damon Runyon, Dorothy Parker, and Robert Benchley. Playwright George F. Kaufman enjoyed visiting the club, and eventually even Mayor Jimmy Walker was a regular. It was here she coined her trademark greeting for her favorite customers: "Hello, sucker!" Being a former chorus girl, she had an eye for beauty and talent and made sure she had the best—and best behaved—girls performing in her shows at El Fey Club. After several years, however, Guinan desired to have a club of her own, seeing how much El Fey pulled in on a weekly basis.

With the money she had bankrolled from helping to run El Fey Club, she opened the 300 Club on West Fifty-Fourth Street. The place was even bigger than that of her former boss; she commanded a chorus of 40 dancers and she brought in singers and musicians as well. She knew how to keep the liquor flowing and law enforcement at bay—most of the time. Gossip columnist Walter Winchell made the 300 Club a frequent stop on his nightly rounds of the city. Guinan strove to furnish and decorate the place with taste and provide excellent service and the best possible entertainment. This formula pulled in Walter P. Chrysler, Al Jolson, Reggie Vanderbilt, Gloria Swanson, Harry Payne Whitney— the list of customers was truly glittering and they often found themselves mentioned positively or negatively by Winchell in his next day's column. Guinan competed very successfully with other high-profile clubs in Manhattan.

Opposite: **Texas Guinan was a Hollywood B-movie actress in the 1920s but later moved to New York City to become the queen of the speakeasies. With the repeal of Prohibition, speakeasies became nightclubs, and Guinan welcomed Café Society and those who wouldn't consider themselves as such (Library of Congress).**

2. Prohibition, the Speakeasies and Nightclubs of the 1920s 35

The New Yorker *and the Speakeasy Culture*

In February 1925 Harold Ross launched a new magazine targeting the city's most sophisticated residents with a sense of humor to match. That magazine was *The New Yorker*. Ross had only a vague idea of the format for the magazine and struggled in its first year to define what that format should be, and who would write for it. One thing he definitely wanted in his magazine was a weekly review of notable clubs readers might enjoy visiting. Ross brought in Charles Baskerville to write this new column, titled "When Nights Are Bold." Baskerville used the byline Tophat. The first article appeared in the April 25, 1925, issue. Baskerville chose as his first profile the Trocadero Club and he was in luck, as Fred Astaire and his sister Adele were performing with a mix of elegant and humorous dance numbers. "They have a deft touch and create delightfully absurd illusions with a twist of the neck or a crook of the elbow. Their zest and apparent enjoyment captivates the audience early and enthusiasm increases with each dance," he wrote.[12] He also reported the couple were reputed to be earning $6,000 a week. Several other clubs were profiled in his first article and this was the format for the remainder of the series.

Once this issue of *The New Yorker* was on the newsstands, the editorial office was inundated with mail containing membership cards and invitations to visit this or that club in hopes for a review. Baskerville had many to choose from. Two months later, Baskerville dropped in on Texas Guinan's club, and he was impressed with her ability to not only keep the show and its performance moving smoothly, but keep the vocal customers in line as well. "The cuties of the show are well rounded on their corners," he wrote, "and full of pep and Charlestons. One entrancing young person, named Ruby Keeler, sings with a lisp that makes ordinary diction seem colorless by comparison."[13]

A favorable review of one's establishment in *The New Yorker* became highly coveted. The following is just an example that was guaranteed to pack them in: "For dining in a leisurely manner there is no place in New York more delightful than the Crillon. Not for grabbing a quick bite as you dash to a play do we recommend it, but as a restaurant in which you dine comfortably and tastefully in a pleasant setting."[14] A detailed description of the décor of the place followed, as well as the entertainment one would find there, and very soon patrons would be lined up outside the door of the Crillon.

Prohibition resulted in numerous speakeasy and club closings, but many times these were not permanent. The closing by agents of the Prohibition Bureau was referred to as a "padlocking." It was something of a formality to close for roughly 30 days, whereupon the club or speakeasy would reopen with much fanfare. Not to announce the closing would be a missed opportunity, so Baskerville would routinely get such invitations landing on his desk. "The restaurants are sending out announcements that they are to be padlocked and accepting reservations for the gala evening before the doleful event," Tophat wrote in one issue. "These affairs are characterized by much levity and the air of a localized New Year's Eve."[15] These closings and reopenings were conducted much like the prosecution of repeat offenders who plea-bargained down to a lesser charge, paid their fine or bail, and were returned to the streets. Attorneys for these nightclubs and speakeasies did a landslide business in Manhattan. With so many in the city, many law offices performed theses services exclusively.

The New Yorker was still losing money by the summer of 1925 and Ross was anxious to get writing talent that could boost circulation. He hired Ralph Ingersoll to be managing editor, Peter Arno and Helen Hokinson to contribute cartoons, Katherine Angell to review unsolicited manuscripts before she later moved on to fiction editor, and Lois Long as a contributor. All these proved vital to improving the magazine. Bringing Long, a graduate of Vassar, over from *Vanity Fair* proved one of Ross's best hiring decisions as publisher of the magazine. She was placed in charge of writing "When Nights Are Bold," and Tophat became Lipstick. Later she would be permitted to sign her pieces "L.L." and Ross expanded her duties to include a new column titled "On and Off the Avenue." She must have convinced Ross that "When Nights Are Bold" was rather limiting, for that column was replaced with "Tables for Two" in the September 12, 1925, issue.

Long had been reporting on various places she visited for only three months when she was witness to a full-blown police raid. She had much to say about it and she was not at all impressed. It was, however, standard operating procedure experienced by many nightclubs and speakeasies in the 1920s. She reported how events unfolded in the style that endeared her to the readers of *The New Yorker*:

> It wasn't one of those refined, modern things, where gentlemen in evening dress arise suavely from ringside tables and depart, arm in arm, with head waiters no less correctly clad, towards the waiting patrol wagons. It was one of those movie affairs, where burly cops kick down the doors, and women fall fainting on the tables, and strong men crawl under them, and waiters shriek and start throwing bottles out the windows. It was very exciting, and, to me, anything but funny until a particularly big Irish cop regarded me with a sad eye and remarked, "Kid, you're too good for this dump," and politely opened a window leading to the fire escape. I made a graceful exit.[16]

Around Thanksgiving of that year, Harold Ross received an unsolicited article from Ellin Mackay titled "Why We Go To Cabarets—A Post-Debutante Explains." Her father was a multimillionaire and held his share of society balls that his daughter had found so disappointing, primarily for the selection of men who invariably formed what she called the "stag line." She explained she had found these New York society parties woefully wanting for many reasons, and preferred the company of men she liked and admired in the welcoming environment of the cabaret. The article was published in the November 28, 1925, issue of the magazine, and it was something of a bombshell, at least to her "Elders," as she referred to them. The article actually found its way onto the front page of a New York newspaper, and suddenly *The New Yorker* was hip among the city's upper crust. Advertisers came knocking too, and circulation grew. Ellin Mackay later married Irving Berlin. The ingredients of Café Society were being added to the eclectic mix of speakeasies, nightclubs and, as Miss Mackay wrote, cabarets.

Somewhat belatedly, Ross decided that speakeasies themselves deserved space in his magazine for readers so interested. This posed a quandary for him and *The New Yorker*, however. The establishments' exact whereabouts had to remain a mystery, and the magazine had to appear not to overtly support lawbreakers. Ross wrestled with this for some time before deciding reporting on such establishments was just an extension of what the magazine had been doing from its first issue: advise New Yorkers on where to dine and spend an enjoyable evening, regardless of whether or not liquor was served. Tophat and Lipstick had been the pathfinders.

With that settled, "Speakeasy Nights" first appeared in the July 2, 1927, issue, then somewhat irregularly over the next several years. The roving writer charged with gleaning the good ones from the dross was Niven Busch, Jr. The writer had his work cut out for him. By 1927, there were thousands of speakeasies in Manhattan and the surrounding boroughs. As with the column on nightclubs, "Speakeasy Nights" was meant only to be a sampling, as Busch cast his critical eye on an establishment's furnishings, hospitality and quality of its liquor. A speakeasy's atmosphere could run the gamut of simply an apartment-turned-speakeasy to those that bordered on nightclubs; sometimes the establishment lay in the gray area between a speakeasy and nightclub and could not be categorized. Former restaurant owners often provided dining in the "speak" and sometimes even entertainment. Speakeasies were owned by stockbrokers, doctors, lawyers, small businessmen, and of course bootleggers—practically anyone. Due to the high-risk nature of the illicit business, those businesses prone to raids had discardable furnishings, cheap glassware and china if food was served, and a lack of expensive decorations because in all likelihood, a raid would result in the destruction of practically everything in sight. Speakeasies had their broad appeal because, while those wanting to drink could do so in their own residence, it was the lure of frequenting a secret place serving illegal alcohol and being in the company of others doing the same thing for the same reasons that proved alluring. This was all heightened by the use of peepholes in doors, passwords, and in some cases, hidden storage facilities that could make the liquor supply disappear into walls.[17] The clandestine nature of it all was truly seductive. There were so many speakeasies one never had to visit the same one twice.

Busch's reporting on speakeasies caused much the same sensation among readers and business owners as did the ongoing series on nightclubs. The mailbags delivered to *The New Yorker* bulged with offers of free liquor and food if Mr. Busch would only stop by. The magazine took pride in being literary and each column describing the speakeasy was enjoyable to read, so one experienced the speakeasy vicariously. Busch would describe the relative location of the place as being a few doors off Fifth Avenue and somewhere in the Sixties, for example. Another, which went by the descriptive Musical Comedy Speakeasy, was next door to a theater not far from a newspaper office just around the corner. Police officers and enforcement agents found no clues in Busch's articles that would help them in their efforts to pinpoint places to shut down.

The totally eclectic nature of the New York speakeasy made each article a fascinating journey that placed readers in the very rooms with people who took as much risk in being there as the owners did in running the place. Many of the less flamboyant places operated in discreet quiet in an effort to remain undetected. Others operated more openly, particularly those that provided entertainment and food. Some of the speakeasies were even lavishly decorated and furnished, with uniformed waiters and barmen that heightened the pleasure of being in the place. Many of these could be found along Park Avenue and in Sutton Place. Such places had cover charges and drink prices that could only be paid by wealthy patrons. Premium name brand liquor—that was of the same quality of pre–Prohibition liquor—was served in these speakeasies. The shoestring-budget speakeasies in lower Manhattan, and particularly Greenwich Village, often served bootleg liquor with questionable distilling and processing, and it behooved the patron to ask what was available to avoid ingesting something truly ghastly.

Then there were those speakeasies which operated quite openly and were in fact family institutions with a long history in New York. One such place was the Rheingold Speakeasy, which was not a speakeasy, Busch stated, but actually a German hotel with the proper name of the Zukor's Rheingold Hotel, located across the river in New Jersey. The drinking room looked like it was lifted from a Munich beer hall with a magnificent mahogany bar and numerous taps just waiting to serve beer. Busch wrote, "You can get a glass of Rhine wine or an old-fashioned cocktail only if you know August Zukor, the round-headed, barrel-bellied man who inherited the hotel from his father...."[18]

Some of Busch's writing about the speakeasies he reviewed almost waxed poetic. The J.P. Speakeasy on the 29th floor of an office building near Broad and Wall Street provided one such example for him. "At five-thirty," Busch wrote, "six young men who have been shooting craps in the back room of their office come in to let the winner treat. Out on the river a violet mist has risen, making the terraced roofs mysterious. The Woolworth Building, which a minute ago seemed close enough to touch with your hand, has shrunk away, grown taller. Gardens hang in the sky; pyramids of light glitter in the electric evening."[19]

There were theme speakeasies. The Transatlantic Speakeasy had appointments accurately mimicking those of an ocean liner, and the bar itself was a copy of the one in the Ritz Bar in Paris. The place was a two-story affair and apparently no expense was spared to make it an experience one would not forget. It was owned and operated by Irving and Herald Kohn. It was located somewhere on the West Forties. Patrons who were feeling ethnic could visit the Gypsy Speakeasy somewhere on Second Avenue. The owner and all the personnel were descended from Gypsies and they all dressed the part, or what one imagined a Gypsy should dress like. The food was marvelous and the drinks were on par with the ethnic food. There were speakeasies with, appropriately, gangster themes. There were speakeasies with antebellum themes or those where all the people working there dressed as pirates and spoke accordingly. The number of speakeasy themes was a varied as the imagination.

The Failure of Prohibition

The persistence and enduring success of the New York City nightclubs, speakeasies and cabarets in the face of relentless raids made a mockery of the well-intentioned goals of the drys. During the entire decade of the 1920s, Prohibition was met with resistance and even defiance that was cultural and political. The army of wets made up of millions of drinkers, and the clubs and speakeasies that supported them overwhelmed the diminutive force of

Prohibition enforcement agents and New York City policemen who labored to uphold the laws on the books. New Yorkers, and Americans as a whole, were going to have their liquor, beer and wine as they had for hundreds of years, and they would not be denied.

The high-profile court cases of speakeasy and club closings, followed days or weeks later by the establishments' reopening, just mirrored the hundreds of other, lesser businesses which followed the same path. Every time Texas Guinan's place was raided, it made the front page of the daily newspapers and the articles were always read with a smile. By the late 1920s, Guinan had a team of lawyers who knew the system well and knew precisely how to get their client cleared of all charges. Everyone knew Guinan would reopen and it would be business as usual. She was charged in two criminal cases and nine civil cases but was never convicted of a crime. She was a hostess, not a club owner, and she never served liquor herself, as she argued before the judges and witnesses.

The corruption of Manhattan politics exacerbated the failure of Prohibition enforcement. Emory C. Buckner, the United States Attorney for the Southern District of New York, which included Manhattan and the surrounding boroughs, could act unilaterally and bypass the city's police department and agents of the Bureau of Prohibition, collect evidence on the sale of liquor in nightclubs and speakeasies, and then file injunctions on the places to have them padlocked. However, it was rough sledding for Buckner and his attorneys. He discovered the fifth floor of the Manhattan Federal Building was made up of "a seething mob of bartenders, peddlers, waiters, bond runners and fixers," where sympathetic lawyers worked tirelessly to get their clients off with the minimum possible charges and the lowest possible fines.[20] This did not change for the remainder of the 1920s.

The Eighteenth Amendment and its enforcement under the Volstead Act proved to be laudable in its moral impetus but nevertheless ill-conceived by criminalizing a formerly legal activity conducted by millions of Americans every day. In fact, Prohibition exacerbated the backlash of what the dry forces were trying to achieve. People who formerly did not drink, such as writer and humorist Robert Benchley, chose to take up drinking as a form of legislative rebellion, and those who drank chose to drink more heavily. Prohibition proved completely counterproductive and dramatically crippled the dry cause that had been the driving force of the movement for decades before ratification of the Eighteenth Amendment. Liquor was even more prevalent all over Manhattan during the 1920s, not less, which effectively decriminalized it. Early in the prohibition efforts in the city, Joseph Madden, the son of a horse breeder with considerable financial means, spoke to the press about his arrest for simply carrying a hip flask of liquor. Outside the courtroom, the bewildered man stated, "Well, I'm still a gentleman, I suppose. This Prohibition offense seems to be the only law you can get arrested on and still retain your self-respect."[21]

The pendulum of Prohibition began to swing the other way in the late 1920s. Wet forces started to amass, slow at first but growing rapidly. This took organization and the first group to rise to prominence was formed by Pauline Morton Sabine, a New York socialite whose wealth came from Morton Salt. She had initially backed the prohibition movement, desiring a better future for her children, as many parents believed at the time. Then she saw the widespread criminalization of otherwise law-abiding people and how Prohibition actually compounded the problem by increasing the consumption of liquor. She had also seen the rise of organized crime in the control of liquor as a result of Prohibition. The tipping point for Sabine came in two phases. When Ella Boole of the WCTU told Congress in 1928, "I represent the women of America," Sabine resented the proclamation. The second came when newly elected President Herbert Hoover, in his inaugural address in March 1929, made it clear the Eighteenth Amendment needed to be strongly enforced and those who disregarded it were contributing to the disrespect for the rule of law, among other harsh comments. That did it for Sabine. She resigned her position on the Republican National Committee and within a matter of two weeks had formed the Women's Organization for National Prohibition Reform (WONPR). The choice of "reform" over the word "repeal" was carefully chosen. She drew from among her social ranks the women she knew who could help formulate policy and garner support.[22]

With complementary and even flattering profiles in magazines like *Vanity Fair*, *The New Yorker* and *Vogue*, the WONPR grew rapidly in prominence and political clout, growing from 30,000 members in 1930 to over ten times just one year after that. The anti–Prohibition forces now had a voice and others were joining the chorus. Cracks were also starting to form in the Prohibition edifice within Congress. The most vocal opponent in Washington to the Eighteenth Amendment had been New York Representative Fiorello LaGuardia. In his congressional office on Capitol Hill in 1926, he had called in reporters to demonstrate how one could legally make beer by mixing "near beer" with malt tonics. He formulated various types of beverages including a Pilsner and even a stout. The event made the papers across the country. Rep. LaGuardia brashly stated, "If the Prohibition people think it is a violation of the law to mix two beverages permitted under the law and that a person doing so can be arrested, I shall give them a chance to test it."²³ The Capital police refused to do so, because LaGuardia was absolutely correct. This event did much to endear him to the advocates for repeal of the amendment and contributed to his popularity that eventually resulted in his election as New York City mayor after Jimmy Walker.

Nightclub, speakeasy and cabaret owners looked on all these events as the new signs of the times, and that the Eighteenth Amendment might actually one day be repealed. That day was several years away, and once it came, Café Society flourished into a cultural phenomenon unique to New York City alone. However, the economic engine of America was racing out of control by 1929 and what happened next also contributed to the emergence of that same group, who lived and played in stark contrast to many others who struggled to get by.

Chapter 3

The Cult of Personality

The cornerstone of Café Society's appeal starting in the 1930s was laid in the 1920s with the focus in newspapers, magazines and radio on noted men and women across the gamut of professions. They might be politicians, sports figures, industrialists, actors of stage or screen, adventurers, or even gangsters, among many others. What they all had in common was the public's fascination with their lives and, in turn, their lives were the source of countless articles and books, movie clips and radio spots. In short, these personalities were commodities and like any commodity or product they were marketed. This cult of personality truly emerged in the 1920s as an expression of the general public's adoration of the individual and embracing of the concept of individual success or infamy. A college education was held in high regard as a passport to middle- and upper-middle-class success, but oftentimes that college degree was never an issue for those intrigued with personality. The men and women written up the print media often did not have degrees, but they certainly had notoriety, and that was seen as success.

This adoration of personality was also fueled by a technological change—the emergence of radio. Among the first companies to market a wide range of radios was the Radio Corporation of America, formed in 1919. Of necessity, the company was also involved in radio broadcasting, and in 1921 broadcast the Jack Dempsey and George Carpentier boxing match. Over 300,000 people listened to the broadcast. This not only helped to launch the fascination with personality, but listening to an event in real time fueled the desire for the majority of American households to own a radio. Radio manufacturing companies by the dozens sprang up all over the United States to build this new product, ranging in size from small desktop units to massive floor-standing console units.

The Radio Corporation of America, RCA, was soon surpassed by other manufacturers in terms of production. By 1925, the Crosley Radio Corporation was the largest manufacturer in the country, with 1000 employees manufacturing and shipping 5000 radios a day. Crosley also pursued broadcasting licenses and built broadcasting facilities at several locations around the country. The broadcasting studio in Cincinnati, Ohio, boasted 50,000 watts of broadcasting power. Other radio networks were created during the 1920s and radio listening became a national pastime. Many American homes made listening to the radio after dinner a nightly ritual. It was almost exclusively an entertainment medium, with music, short serials, humor, and of course the occasional product advertisement. Any news items were often broadcast at the top of the hour, after 5 p.m.

Those who performed on the radio—and all performances then were live broadcasts—often became celebrities whether they were singers or performers. They became as popular as the stars of the silent screen. This fascination by the masses with radio personalities became a part of the general cult of personality that middle-class Americans found fascinating. Radio was just one leg of communication that spread the mystique of talented but otherwise unremarkable people; the radio performers were simply working people themselves, but they were nevertheless personalities and radio gave them that aura. Radio also publicized the already famous, which only enlarged their mystique. The second branch of the media that promoted the shameless cult of personality was the print medium of magazines and newspapers. Third, film—the movie stars of the day were cultural icons.

New York's Mayor—Jimmy Walker

New Yorkers lived in a city that pursued their fascination with personality with verve. They had to look no further than their own mayor, Jimmy Walker, who was elected to the office in November 1925 after a decade in New York state politics. Walker was born in Manhattan's Greenwich Village in June 1881. In 1886 his family moved to a townhouse on St. Luke's Place and Walker would call that home well into the 20th century. After graduating from high school he attended the New York Law School at the urging of his father, but Walker, true to form, had other ideas. He was musically inclined and wrote several pleasant songs during his twenties, but in 1908, he wrote and published a catchy tune that put him on the Manhattan map. That song was "Will You Love Me in December (As You Do in May)?"

When it was clear the song would be published, and with visions of wealth and fame in the offing, Walker got a $500 advance against royalties for the song from his music publisher and promptly went on a clothing spending spree. Here he displayed his penchant for dapper dressing and bought three custom-made suits, twelve silk shirts, four pairs of shoes with an array of appropriate socks, three new fedora hats that would become his particular fashion trademark, and a walking stick. Walker made a definite fashion statement, and with his charismatic personality, he soon came to the attention of the powerful controlling interests at Tammany Hall. In particular, he drew the admiration of Charles F. Murphy, who chose to back Walker in a New York state Senate seat. Murphy knew Walker had many contacts on Broadway and the Manhattan entertainment industry, and these might prove very useful politically in the future. Walker also married a Broadway singer who had done him the favor of singing his songs. With such a political machine behind Walker, he won that Senate seat handily, and then served the next 11 years in the New York State Senate in Albany. During that time, he built a powerful network of supporters, and at the same time built a noted reputation for his oratory that bordered on brilliant acting.

Always sporting a three-piece suit, flawlessly-shined shoes and a minimum of jewelry, he was the most flamboyant of New York state legislators. Many of his fellow politicians enjoyed watching and listening to Walker as he defended or denigrated a piece of proposed legislation. He had a battery of movements, voice inflections and facial gestures that soon built the Walker legend. The Broadway playwright, producer and director David Belasco would admonish his most promising actors to travel to Albany to observe Walker in action and witness a master of the craft.[1]

When he ran for mayor of New York City in the fall of 1925, his unlikely Republican opponent was Frank D. Waterman, president of the Waterman Pen Company. This unfair political contest was a foregone conclusion, and Walker won the November election in a landslide. There being no mayoral mansion to speak of in those days, Walker acquiesced to his wife's demand they live in the St. Luke's Place townhouse, drab though it was. A political benefactor, of whom Walker had many, offered more than $20,000 for the complete remodeling of the dwelling, and the newly-elected mayor and his wife were quite pleased.

Walker's working habits paralleled those of newspaper columnist Maury Paul, known to his followers as "Cholly Knickerbocker." Like Paul, Walker slept in and often would not awaken until 10:00 a.m. He would read his morning paper in bed, make several calls, eat his breakfast, and have his valet lay out his clothes for the work day. The new mayor was slow out of the gate, but once at City Hall, he was nonstop productivity. After he had been in office 45 days, the *New York Times* ran an editorial that quoted those who knew Walker that he got more done in two hours than most could accomplish in an entire day. All the New York daily newspapers had something to say about the resplendent and hyperactive mayor. His official duties were duly covered, but it was what he did after hours that also got their attention, and that of columnists like Maury Paul.

Walker had been a vocal opponent of Prohibition while in Albany and strongly felt it would be a totally unenforceable law. Countless others agreed, and yet the law passed nationwide. Saloon owners and dining establishments simply got creative in how they ran their businesses and they wanted assurances from the mayor that they could continue to remain open. Walker certainly had no intention of closing down those establishments. He frequented many of the speakeasies himself.

He became the object of more attention in both his personal and political life. In 1927, he was invited to a musical at the Imperial Theater. One of the lovelies on stage definitely got Walker's attention. Her name was Betty Compton. After the show he was taken backstage and introduced to her. Walker poured on the charm, nervously spinning his hat between his fingers. She knew he was married and rebuffed his advances. He persisted. He was smitten. After she accepted his offer of a ride home from a large private party in his gleaming Duesenberg—a gift from yet another political benefactor—she succumbed. Walker and Miss Compton were seen together more and more frequently and their comings and goings were often chronicled in Maury Paul's column, and the others who imitated that column. His extensive and expensive overseas travels filled many column inches in the papers and no one seemed to know or care where all the money to do this came from.

Walker was comfortable in the political favors he handed out and no doubt felt impervious to any investigation into corruption charges. He was careful to steer lucrative contracts to those who had funded his mayoral campaign and helped to suppress scrutiny into those same contracts. There was, apparently, a nebulous connection between Walker and racketeer Arnold Rothstein, who had fixed the 1919 World Series and became one of the most powerful New York gangsters to profit immensely from Prohibition. On an evening in November 1928 when Walker was dining with Compton at a suburban night club, one of Walker's aides came to his table and in hushed tones told Walker that Rothstein had been murdered. The mayor instantly knew this would create problems for him and, in fact, Walker would battle investigations of political payola and corruption well into the next decade.

The Queen of New York's Opera

The fascination with accomplishment and persona in New York City knew no cultural boundaries, and the seemingly most unlikely people were the object of fanatical pursuit. While opera was always the entertainment of the upper class and the desirous middle class, several performers in of the 1910s and 1920s often found themselves the recurring subject of columnists, magazine editors, and of course enraptured readers. One of those opera stars was a beautiful young woman by the name of Geraldine Farrar. She became a celebrity before the word could be defined. She was a darling of newspapers and magazines, and with the emergence of radio, her operatic voice could be heard across the United States. She was also a star of numerous silent films, but she retired from her singing career before "talkies" became popular.

Farrar was born in Melrose, Massachusetts, in 1882. She began singing informally at the age of seven. When her mother saw her potential talent, she sought out singing coaches who told her Geraldine's voice quality and range suited her to operatic music more than popular music. A noted singing coach at time, Mrs. J.H. Long of Boston, accepted an appointment to hear the young Geraldine sing in order to learn her capability and whether she could be coached. In her autobiography published in 1916, Farrar wrote: "Her great brown eyes looked into mine and inspired me with such confidence that soon I was warbling as freely as if I were at home alone.... To my delight I was accepted at once as a pupil, and it is to this excellent and thorough teacher that I can give thanks for proper guidance in my early years."[2]

At the age of 14, she began giving recitals, and three years later traveled to Europe with her mother to perform there. She also was tutored by other well-reputed singing coaches. In the spring of 1898, she and her mother were invited to the White House to visit with the wife of President William McKinley. She was asked to sing "The Star Spangled Banner" to the president and Mrs. McKinley, and Farrar accompanied herself on the piano. Clearly, Geraldine Farrar was destined for great things.

In her early twenties, the management of the Metropolitan Opera, after hearing her audition and knowing her already impressive reputation, offered her the role of Juliet in the 1906 production of *Romeo and Juliet*. The following year she wowed audiences with her performance in Puccini's *Madame Butterfly*, singing opposite the brilliant Enrico Caruso. Interestingly, Puccini himself was at the New York premiere of his opera and was not overwhelmed by Farrar's performance, but he was definitely taken by her looks and charming personality. Farrar helped to take opera mainstream, and as more and more articles, reviews and columnist blurbs appeared during the 1910s, her following by legions of women, and more than a few adoring men, grew.

In 1915, Farrar began her unlikely film career. With no sound, how could a singer possibly shine in a silent film? She could shine for the same reason other silent stars could shine. She was also a performer, not just an opera singer. She picked film subjects that appealed to her. Her first film, understandably enough, was *Carmen*, and was directed by Cecil B. DeMille. DeMille knew what he had in Farrar; she positively exuded sensuality, without any provocative gestures or revealing clothing. The film was a commercial success, and Farrar's film career was launched, bringing her to an even larger audience and expanding her fan base. To help her get into character, he insisted a small music ensemble play during her scenes. She averaged three and sometimes four films a year, working around her Metropolitan Opera season performances.

She lived the life of a star, and per contract she was provided a private railroad car to permit her to travel from New York to California for filming, and back again for her performances at the Met. While in Hollywood, the studio provided her a fully furnished home and a chauffeur to drive her to and from the studio.

Farrar's private life was far from private, and her romances, affairs and short-lived marriage were the subjects of editorial writers from coast to coast. Most notorious was her affair with the very-married Arturo Toscanini, conductor at the Metropolitan Opera. They met at the start of her career at the Met. Their personalities clashed at first, but soon Toscanini was overwhelmed by her seductive power. Naturally, Farrar never mentioned this in her autobiography. Toscanini's wife Carla endured the blatant affair and in fact stayed with him their whole married life, giving him several children. Family ultimately came first with Toscanini, and when Farrar demanded he choose between her and his wife, he fled to Italy in 1915 to break off the affair.

That year, while filming *Temptation*, she met a handsome actor by the name of Louis Tellegen. That was his screen name. He was born Isidore Louis Bernard Edmon van Dommelen. They began dating, but considering Farrar's considerable fame, it is curious why she would take up with a less-than-premier movie star, unless it was Tellegen's performance in bed. The couple married in 1916, much to the attention of the entertainment press. Theirs was a star-crossed relationship. While she was in Hollywood, her hours at the studio rarely coincided with his, and their hours together at their home were the exception, not the rule. The couple never had any children during their seven-year marriage; they were separated in 1920 and divorced in 1923. Her last film was *The Riddle: Woman* of 1920.

Farrar had stated she would retire from the Metropolitan Opera at the age of 40, and in 1922, she did. That did not end her performance career. She continued to perform select recitals to packed theaters. She was independently wealthy and did not need to perform for financial reasons. Her many "Gerryflappers," as they were called, followed her singing performances around the country, if only in print. She remained an operatic star of the first order throughout the 1920s and into the 1930s.³

An Aviator's Exploit

Perhaps no person symbolized the cult of personality in the 1920s better than aviator Charles Lindbergh. There was no postwar boom in the development of commercial aviation after World War I, but aviation did improve delivery times for U.S. Mail. Air Mail was born, and Congress did eventually pass the Air Commerce Act. One of the pilots who hauled the mail in big canvas bags was a young pilot by the name of Charles Lindbergh. Born in Detroit, Michigan, in 1902, when he became old enough to read, he became fascinated with the new technological invention of the airplane. He dropped out of college in 1922, moved to Nebraska, and attended a flight school there to learn to be a pilot. He picked up odd jobs as a barnstorming pilot and wing walker to raise cash and buy his own plane. The long arm of the U.S. government reached out and informed the young pilot he was to report for U.S. Army Air Service training in March of 1924. A year later he graduated first in his class and received the rank of 2nd lieutenant and his pilot's wings. With no war requiring his flying skills, he was hired by the Robertson Aircraft Corporation to lay out airmail routes and deliver mail.⁴

Lindbergh had read with interest about the attempts of pilots to fly across the Atlantic Ocean between North America and the British Isles and Europe. In June 1919, two British pilots, John Alcock and Arthur Brown, flew their twin-engine Vickers Vimy World War I bomber from St. Johns, Newfoundland, and headed for the Irish coast. The harrowing sixteen-hour flight fighting snow, sleet and fog finally ended in a peat bog in Clifden, Ireland. Having succeeded in crossing nearly 2000 miles of the Atlantic, they claimed the *London Daily Mail* cash prize and were even knighted, but their names are but a footnote in aviation history. That year, New York hotel owner Raymond Orteig announced the $25,000 Orteig Prize for any single pilot or pilots who could successfully fly between New York and Paris nonstop. This was an unprecedented technical and human endurance challenge and for more than five years was not accepted. In 1926, Igor Sikorsky built a massive tri-engined plane to be piloted by World War I ace René Fonck and a crew of three. The plane had been successfully test flown several times, but on September 15, the day of the official flight from Roosevelt Field on Long Island, the plane was overloaded and weighed over 15 tons. The plane never got airborne. It crashed on the takeoff attempt, two of the crew perished in the resulting fireball, and Fonck and a fellow pilot barely escaped with their lives.[5]

Lindbergh read of the aviation disaster and reasoned the multi-engine big plane with several crew was not the best approach. The long fight from New York to Paris of nearly 40 hours naturally dictated at least two crew members who could alternate flying duties while the other pilot rested, but Lindbergh embraced an unconventional vision. His contrary view was that the purpose-built plane should be as simple and light as possible in order to carry the requisite fuel and oil, and the engine—only one—had to be utterly reliable. He started formulating the design of the plane and approached potential backers who would foot the cost of building it. He also saw a very limited future flying U.S. Mail between St. Louis and Chicago and eyed the potential $25,000 Orteig Prize as understandable motivation. He was doggedly persistent in getting both financial backers and in securing an aircraft builder to make a plane to his specifications, but by January 1927, time was running out. Others were also pursuing the dream of fame and fortune. Pilots with more flying experience, greater reputation and formidable financial might behind them troubled Lindbergh's thoughts, but he stayed focused.

Finally, a group of St. Louis investors agreed to provide the money and the small firm of Ryan Aeronautical Corporation of San Diego, California, agreed to help design and build the single-engine plane for the shoestring budget of $6,000, but without the engine or instrumentation. Lindbergh already knew the engine he wanted—a nine-cylinder Wright Whirlwind with a superb reputation for reliability. He struck the deal with the aircraft company, which agreed to deliver the plane in less than three months. At the request of his backers, the plane would be named *Spirit of St. Louis*. The plane was completed by the end of April 1927 and Lindbergh flew it from San Diego to St. Louis to show the investors the plane, then flew to Curtiss Field on Long Island, landing there on May 12 while breaking the transcontinental flight record in the process.[6]

Lindbergh nearly lost his place in history, but a tragic air crash by two other Orteig Prize contestants intervened. Two Frenchmen, both veteran World War I pilots by the name of Charles Nungasser and Francois Coli, had left Paris on May 8 with much fanfare surrounding them and their plane,

L'Oiseau Blanc (The White Bird). The pilots and their airplane never arrived in New York, and it was assumed they had crashed in the Atlantic or somewhere over Newfoundland. More than a few newspaper editors speculated the neophyte pilot and his single-engine plane were soon to suffer the same fate as the other attempts, and that Lindbergh was not just audacious, but perhaps foolhardy. The drama of Lindbergh's epic flight was building to a fever pitch as he prepared on Long Island for his flight.

On the morning of May 20, with journalists, investors, and well-wishers standing in the rain-soaked Roosevelt Air Field, Lindbergh pushed his plane's engine to full throttle and it picked up speed, finally lifting off and clearing the telephone wires at the end of the runway by a mere 20 feet. The reporters raced to available phones to call in the historic moment for the afternoon papers. He had gotten little rest in the preceding 48 hours, but he was alert, ready and confident in his plane. He flew up the eastern coastline and over Nova Scotia. This proved a critical test of his instruments, and they were accurate, proving he could rely on them over the Atlantic for a true heading to France. He observed massive icebergs in the north Atlantic. Then in the darkness of night he encountered his first storm, with potentially deadly ice forming on the wing and the struts. Hailstones pelted the fabric-covered aircraft.

Descending to a warmer altitude allowed the ice to melt and reduced the weight on the plane. More than 15 hours into the flight he was feeling fatigue and drowsiness, and he periodically directed cool air from the side window into the cockpit and onto his face. The night would try to lull him to sleep, but he knew if he performed certain tasks, stretching and other tricks to shrug off the dangerous desire to close his eyes, he might make it to the sunrise that would help him stay awake. The marvelous engine droned on assuringly but also hypnotically. During this phase of his flight Lindbergh sensed the presence in the cockpit of ghostly phantoms who conversed with him, and he wondered years later if they had been real or a creation of his sleep-deprived state. Perhaps they were angels. They eventually disappeared, and he worked on focusing on the wave forms he could barely see below and on the smell of the ocean. He found if he could lower the *Spirit of St. Louis* close to the ocean surface, the ocean spray refreshed and revived him, but the risk of a large unseen swell limited the number of these descents.

The first sighting of a group of fishing boats convinced him he must be near land. A short time later, he spotted a bay ahead of him. Checking his map, he recognized it as Dingle Bay on the southwest coast of Ireland. He was right on his planned route. He continued on over the Emerald Isle and the Irish Sea. He spotted the coast of Britain and as he flew over its towns, spotters relayed the news of the plane's sighting, and this was wired to Paris and back to the United States. There was jubilation, but Lindbergh would not hear any of this for several more hours. As he flew on to France, he eventually spotted Paris as the sun was setting and he actually circled the Eiffel Tower as thousands pointed to the sky. He then turned toward the direction of Le Bourget airfield. The points of light seen coming from the ground at first confused him, but then he realized they were the headlights of countless automobiles. After a total of 33 hours, 30 minutes and 30 seconds, the wheels of his plane touched down on French soil.

Lindbergh had prepared for practically every possibility during his flight and had obsessed over almost every detail of the plane, but he had given little thought to what the reaction of the French would be once he landed. As the French mob surged toward his plane, he cut the engine to stop the propeller from killing someone. As he lethargically got out of the plane, he was enthusiastically lifted up and carried prone on countless hands toward the hangar. Two pilots finally brought him to the ground and walked next to him with French police doing their best to shield the aviator to the sound of cheers and tears of joy. Lindbergh did not realize the exultant moment was also a time of healing for the French, who had lost their own airmen in the attempt. Lindbergh's flight was not only an aviation milestone, it was about to become the greatest media event of the decade, and he would become one of the most famous men in the world.

Every newspaper in Paris and throughout France devoted a flood of ink to Lindbergh's heroic exploit. Every picture obtainable of him was published, along with detailed articles of the plane's design; every moment of the flight was described—much of it fabricated by the editors—as well as the numerous failed attempts that had preceded his successful flight. Millions of radios across Europe received news stories of his flight and landing. Banner headlines appeared in every New York newspaper and across the United States. No one had seen an uproar like this since the end of World War I. The French were reluctant to let their new hero go, but Lindbergh eventually flew his plane to Belgium and later on to England. The British gave him a reception much like the French, and as much royal pomp and circumstance as they could muster.

The plane was returned to the United States aboard the USS *Memphis* in June, along with Lindbergh himself, but that was not his desire. He wanted to fly back to the United States; the State Department insisted otherwise. The ship would steam up the Potomac River and Lindbergh would make the rounds in Washington, D.C. Eventually, the plucky pilot made his way to a very expectant New York City, which was ready to give him the welcome mat. Manhattan gave Lindbergh a hero's welcome unprecedented in the city's history. The adulation poured on him left him amazed; indeed, Lindbergh had remained amazed ever since he was swept off his feet in Le Bourget.

After the ship, the *Macon*, docked at the New York Battery, he was taken by motorcade accompanied by a marching guard of thousands of men north to City Hall through an almost blinding cloud of confetti and streamers, with hundreds of thousands of New Yorkers lining the streets. Every New York newspaperman and woman was either along the parade route or at a desk typing the latest news of America's greatest pilot. Mayor Jimmy Walker and his fellow politicians waited expectantly for Lindbergh. The massive city's inhabitants crowded all the sidewalks and spilled out into the streets off the parade route. Lindbergh reveled in the outpouring of pride that left him totally humbled. The events melded from afternoon into evening and the largest banquet in New York City was held in his honor. The following day, every column inch of the *New York Times* for the first sixteen pages was devoted entirely to him and the historic flight. Every other newspaper did likewise. *Time* magazine would eventually vote him Man of the Year in its first issue of 1928. Curiously, *The New Yorker*, already known for its in-depth profiles, never published one on Charles Lindbergh.

Was Lindbergh an aviation hero or a celebrity icon of the media? He was both. America, and Europe, had at that time what seemed like a pressing need for such cultural icons. What fueled this overwhelming response was not just Lindbergh's magnificent accomplishment but his self-effacing modesty and resolute focus on what his fight would do for commercial aviation. He was not brazenly in it for the money, for he was an aviator first and foremost. He was no World War I ace, but simply a young man who learned to fly on his own nickel, mustered the financial and manufacturing support he needed to achieve his dream, then did it. He was the prototypical Horatio Alger story and America went wild over him for reaching his dream.

There were other New Yorkers who also shared in this almost inexplicable adulation.

Baseball's Master of the Bat

St. Mary's Industrial School for Boys might seem an odd school to send one's seven-year-old son, but George Herman Ruth had a penchant, even at that age, for sailing baseballs through neighborhood windows. Historians later wondered whether this was disciplinary or benevolent on the part of his parents. Disciplinary, because St. Mary's was a reformatory, but possibly benevolent, because the school could channel the youth's love of the sport in a constructive manner. It was there that the future baseball legend learned not only the requirements for an education, but through the tutelage of Brother Matthias Boutilier, for the next ten years Ruth also learned pitching, fielding, and most of all, hitting that baseball with power and precision. After graduating from the school, Ruth signed with Baltimore Orioles and played for them just one year before moving to the Cincinnati Red Sox, where he remained for five years. The day after Christmas 1919, Ruth, with the nickname "Babe," was providentially sold to the New York Yankees. He was 24 years old.

Ruth had not yet hit his stride as a slugger, performing pitching duties as much as driving in runs. However, with the move to the Yankees, the coach of the team eventually moved him off the pitcher's mound and focused Ruth's efforts on home plate, where he might do the most good. In his 1920 season with the Yankees, Ruth slammed 54 home runs and his reputation began to grow. The following year, he topped his personal best with 59 home runs.[7] The ranks of Yankees fans began to swell, and every time Ruth came to bat there was anticipation that the familiar crack of his bat making brutal contact with that ball would send it beyond the outfield into the seats. The team had been playing at the stadium located on the Polo Grounds shared with the New York Giants, but construction was begun on a new stadium for the team, and the Yankees moved to their new home in 1923.

Ruth was already a highly paid player, and by 1926 his contract stipulated a season salary of $52,000—more than any other player in the major leagues. This was bumped to $75,000 in 1927. Apart from his income from the Yankees, he pulled in fees for his syndicated (actually ghost-written) articles, endorsements, speaking fees and other sources of income which brought the total to over a quarter of a million dollars. However, Ruth had spending and gambling habits that matched and exceeded his income. He bet over $25,000 on a single horse—which lost. In Cuba, he ran up a $65,000 tab with bookies and could not leave the island until his wife Helen had sent the funds from a secret account she had established for such emergencies.

His performance on the baseball field had been declining along with his wealth. Knowing he needed help if he was to regain first his health and then maintain his earning power, he met with Artie McGovern, who ran an elite fitness gym in New York. His clientele were some of the wealthiest and most famous people of the day. McGovern achieved results with a combination of diplomacy and firmness and an exercise and diet regimen that succeeded in whipping his clients into much-needed shape. They included band leaders Paul Whiteman and John Philip Sousa, Helen Clay Frick (wife of industrial baron Henry), and numerous others who had the means to pay for following McGovern's orders. By mid-1926, Ruth had dropped much fat and replaced it with toned muscle, he was eating properly, and his physical endurance was much improved. He later chose to invest in McGovern's dream of expanding his holistic health concept to several other gyms on the east and west coasts.

Ruth was not the stuff of the gossip columns. He was, however, a constant source of news and stories for the many New York daily sportswriters and of course sports magazines, above all *Baseball* magazine. Even those who had no earthly interest in baseball or knew anything about it knew of Babe Ruth and his legend. Ruth became one of the many achievers in their chosen professions who also became celebrities and whose mere presence walking down a Manhattan street drew smiles, handshakes, waves from cars and eventually crowds. Ruth helped to make the Twenties roar, right along with the stock market. The separation from his wife Helen in 1926 and his season record of 60 home runs in 1927 were read by fans and simple admirers with almost equal interest. Not all eyes were on Ruth, however. Lou Gehrig had joined the Yankees in 1923, and he distinguished himself as a formidable hitter as well, holding down the position as an infielder. The two impressive Yankee hitters often outdid each other in their record of hits and home runs during the latter 1920s. During the 1928 season, Gehrig and Ruth tied each other for runs batted in (RBIs) at 142.[8]

However, it was Ruth who seemed to get most of the ink in the papers and magazines. Gehrig was not flamboyant; he was more of a straight arrow, but he had his devoted followers as well. Nevertheless, Ruth's legend had grown to such an extent by the early 1930s, *Vanity Fair* put him on the cover with a color illustration by Miguel Covarrubias for the September 1933 issue. With that distinction added to his many sports achievements, Ruth technically fit the description of a member of Café Society, but he felt uncomfortable in the 21 Club and even more so in El Morocco. He felt more at home in Sherman Billingsley's Stork Club.

In April 1929, Ruth married Claire Hodgson, several months after the death of his first wife, Helen. His second wife was very involved in the health and maintenance of her husband, and lovingly made numerous changes to his lifestyle in order to keep him healthy, at the top of his game, and a happy husband. No longer did Ruth burn through his income like there was no tomorrow, with unknown amounts of cash in various pockets; whenever he needed money, Claire got out the checkbook and made out checks to him for no more than $50. He good-humoredly went along with his new allowance, because he knew the wisdom of rationing the money was necessary in maintaining their present and future lifestyle. Mrs. Ruth had no desire for them to one day be forced to life in a style that was far below their present means.

Another area of managing her husband was in the area of diet. Ruth had always struggled to get and keep his weight down, and his regimen with McGovern eventually went by the wayside. Claire stepped in and made sure those fat-laden steaks Ruth was so fond of became a special treat instead of a staple. Ruth also went along with his wife's admonitions for getting to bed earlier than he was used to doing in order to be properly rested. Guests to their home were promptly shown the door at 10:00 p.m. In this she was adamant. Ruth good-naturedly went along with this with a chuckle. Those same guests knew better than to make jokes about who wore the pants in the relationship; if they did, Ruth quickly straightened them out.

When the New York Stock Market crashed in October 1929, starting America's plunge into an incomprehensible economic depression, Ruth's wealth was shielded from the massive losses others experienced. He was not invested in stocks but in annuities for the most part. If this had not been the case, he could have been wiped out financially. He was aging and gray hairs were starting to appear. Ruth loved the game and wanted play for as long as his health and the favor of the fans permitted it. Despite the impact of the economic collapse on the incomes of so many of those who attended the Yankees' games, Ruth still managed in March 1930 to get another raise in his salary to $80,000. It turned out to be a good investment. Ruth continued to perform wonderfully, packing Yankee Stadium, and allaying the concerns of the team's management. Babe Ruth was a sports phenomenon at a particular moment in time when people from all walks of life looked to someone who could help them take their mind off their troubles and experience excitement and joy, and vicariously escape their own unremarkable lives.

The Ladies of Broadway

The Great White Way, as Broadway was known for the countless marquee lights that lit up the night, launched many a notable career in the 1920s. Among the most famous of producers on Broadway was Florenz Ziegfeld. Styled after the reviews performed in Paris after the turn of the century, the *Ziegfeld Follies* was first staged in 1907 and ran continuously thereafter, taking on the year the performances took place. Two of the performers in these revues during the 1920s who rose to stardom were Marilyn Miller and Fanny Brice. Miller was an all-around performer who sang, danced and acted both in stage productions and in the *Ziegfeld Follies*, while Brice became known for her comedic performances and singing. Their looks were polar opposites. Miller was a blonde beauty, while the brunette Brice eventually had surgery performed to alter her prominent nose.

Miller had performed in several theater productions during the 1910s and honed her talent during this time. However, when Ziegfeld discovered her, he hired her away to star in the *Ziegfeld Follies of 1918*. She performed along with Eddie Cantor, W.C. Fields and Will Rogers, with music written by Irving Berlin. The producer showcased Miller's talent and beauty in the various production scenes, and she became the star of the show.

Fanny Brice had starred in the variety productions in 1910 and 1911, then left to pursue opportunities in other Broadway productions, as well as London theater briefly, before eventually being lured back by Ziegfeld to resume performing in the *Follies* in 1921. In between these years, she had a relationship with Nicky Arnstein, whose run-in with law enforcement eventually landed him in Sing Sing Prison. Brice visited him weekly and upon his release they were married in 1918. All this drama made Brice a lightning rod for tabloid journalists, but it did nothing to tarnish her own image in the minds of theatergoers. Arnstein had a criminal mentality, and continued to be involved in one nefarious operation after another. It seemed he was constantly dodging criminal charges of one kind or another. Arnstein also found he was interested in other women and Brice eventually discovered this fact. His infidelity coupled with his criminal activity ultimately doomed the marriage, and they were divorced in 1927.[9]

Miller had a professional disagreement with Ziegfeld in 1924, and she signed a contract with producer Charles Dillingham to do the show *Peter Pan*. The following year, she performed in *Sunny*, with Jerome Kern providing the music and Oscar Hammerstein the lyrics. The show had the ingredients of a box office smash, and with Miller's sparkling performance, it was. Enthusiastic audiences packed the theater nightly and helped to make Miller one of the highest paid performers in Broadway theater.

Brice was in constant demand in the late 1920s. She ventured into films and continued to do a variety of theatrical productions. She was never idle. Her film career did not take off, however, and the few films she did make were not well reviewed. She was unfazed and returned to New York to seek new theater opportunities, and new performances in the ever-popular *Follies*.

3. The Cult of Personality

Brice and Miller were a constant theater draw in the 1920s and lent star power to a wonderful form of New York entertainment. But not all the entertainers were in the performing arts. Jimmy Walker proved politics could be most entertaining, especially when he was performing as New York mayor. Geraldine Farrar lit up the operatic stage like no one else in that era. Charles Lindbergh blurred the definition of hero and celebrity, and this product of the media was a reluctant actor on the stage of the 1920s. Babe Ruth grew the sport of baseball in New York like few ball players before or after him. Fanny Brice and Marilyn Miller lived their performance careers both on stage and in the newspapers, tabloids and magazines. These were among the many who fueled New Yorkers' and Americans' desire to follow the lives and accomplishments of men and women. It all set the stage for the fascination with those men and women who would one day form New York Café Society.

Chapter 4

Café Society's Writers, Journalists, Editors and Playwrights

On November 17, 1917, F. Scott Fitzgerald wrote to his mother to say he had received his commission as second lieutenant in the U.S. Army and had gone to Brooks Brothers to order some equipment for his military service. He would receive his basic training at Ft. Leavenworth, Kansas, and an additional six months' intensive training once in France. He was assigned to Camp Sheridan, outside of Montgomery, Alabama. During this time, he met the 18-year-old Zelda Sayer. He regaled her with the novel he was writing with the working title *The Romantic Egoist*. With expectations high, he mailed it off to Charles Scribner's Sons in New York City. Not surprisingly, it was rejected by the editor who read it, but Fitzgerald was encouraged by the suggestions the editor made to improve it. While still waiting to be deployed, Fitzgerald worked on the revised draft, and sent it off a second time. Zelda was sympathetic in listening to Fitzgerald's disappointment at the manuscript's second rejection, and he vowed he would rewrite the entire manuscript, but his regiment received their orders to depart in October 1918.

The months of seeming delay proved a blessing to Fitzgerald and tens of thousands of others. His regiment transferred to Camp Mills, Long Island, and later boarded the troop transport that would take them to Europe. While still in port, the end of hostilities and the Armistice were announced. With mixed emotions for many of the troops, they returned to Camp Mills. Millions of soldiers had died in the conflict, while countless others were maimed, blinded by poison gas or traumatized by the horrors of the war. Fitzgerald would not be one of them. The troops were not immediately demobilized. Fitzgerald finally received his honorable discharge on February 18, 1919. He made plans to move to Manhattan to be near the center of book publishing, and to hold down any worthwhile job while once again rewriting his novel. To Zelda, Fitzgerald's prospects did not look promising, and she rebuffed his proposal of marriage until he could get established. Fitzgerald finally landed an advertising copywriting job. While he found the job unrewarding and boring, he thrived on the pulse of New York City that was the creative lifeblood of so many there.[1]

Many U.S. troops did not see front-line action in the theater of war; they worked in other capacities in support of the troops. One of the publications that contributed to troop morale was *Stars and Stripes*. This paper had first been published for the Union Troops during the Civil War. During World War I, the small editorial office of this welcomed periodical was in Paris and under the auspices of the American Expeditionary Force. At only eight pages, it was a stretch to call it a newspaper, but news it definitely carried. For the most part, *Stars and Stripes* was staffed by writers who had worked in various literary capacities before enlisting. Capt. Franklin P. Adams was the assistant editor; he had worked at the *New York Herald Tribune*. Pvt. Harold Ross had been a reporter in San Francisco before enlisting in 1917 in the Eighteenth Engineers Regiment. He went AWOL, then made his way to Paris and the cramped offices of *Stars and Stripes*. When Alexander Woollcott went to *Stars and Stripes* to discuss a position and met Ross, he was asked his writing background. He proudly told Ross he was a drama critic for the *New York Times*. Ross burst out laughing, and Woollcott was immediately offended and defensive. Part of Ross's reaction was due to Woollcott's bespeckled face and rotund appearance, the antithesis of the lean fighting man on the battlefields of Europe. After getting past the original affront, Ross and Woollcott developed a mutual admiration that would later become a professional respect.

Adams, Ross and Woollcott took their writing at *Stars and Stripes* as seriously as they took their play after hours at the sidewalk cafés, and in the restaurants and theaters of Paris. None of them could have asked for a more culturally rich environment, and they took advantage of it to the hilt. Many sights could be enjoyed for free or very little expense, and their uniforms were often a calling card to having small fees waived. However, the men were not desk-bound, and were often on troop trains to gather stories from the front, or heading off to villages in the French countryside to gather vignettes of how the French were dealing with the deprivations of the war. When the German Army was finally defeated and the Armistice was announced, the editor and manager Guy Viskniskki was reassigned to Germany, and Ross was made editor of *Stars and Stripes* during demobilization.[2]

The pace of reporting at the paper naturally declined, but there was still plenty of related news regarding the aftermath of the war, above all dealing with the pace of demobilization and when specific Army groups could expect to return home. It was during this time that a representative from Butterick Publishing Company stopped by the newspaper and spoke with Ross about starting a stateside magazine for returning troops, to have the name *Home Sector*. Ross accepted the position as its editor at a substantial $12,000 per year and signed six other reporters, including Woollcott, to join the magazine's staff. The magazine's office would be in New York City. While in Paris, Woollcott had introduced Jane Grant to Ross, and the couple admired each other's literary interests. She would prove an invaluable support in Ross's publishing efforts in New York City.

Vanity Fair *Magazine*

In 1909, publisher Condé Nast purchased *Vogue*, a weekly fashion and style magazine, and he proceeded to improve its layout, directing the content to a more upscale female readership. His next acquisition was a magazine called *Dress*, which Nast clearly saw as a rival to *Vogue*. In 1913, he purchased a British literary publication, *Vanity Fair*. He decided to combine the content of the two publications, but for lack of a catchy title, he simply gave the merged magazine the awkward title *Dress and Vanity Fair*. The first issue left him dissatisfied and he wondered what could be done to improve it. Nast decided to call on one of the most cultivated editors in Manhattan, Frank Crowninshield, and get his opinions and suggestions. Crowninshield was the editor of *Century* and had been the publisher of *Bookman* from 1895 to 1900, editor of *Metropolitan* from 1900 to 1902, and then editor of *Munsey's* from 1902 to 1907. Surely, Nast had an ulterior motive in calling on his friend, Crowninshield. He would not go there to pick the editor's brains on how to improve his new, oddly-named magazine and then leave. Nast had an offer to make.

No doubt Crowninshield, for his part, suspected something was up. The publisher of *Vogue* doesn't simply show up to canvass for ideas, so Crowninshield was prepared for the meeting. Nast laid the first issue of *Dress and Vanity Fair* before Crowninshield and explained what he was trying to achieve with the magazine. After perusing the magazine, Crowninshield told Nast that there was no magazine available that covered the topics most discussed at parties, including art, literature, humor, sports, and related subjects, and presented them with undeniable style. Nast immediately liked the idea and offered the position of editor to Crowninshield. He accepted the offer both for the new challenge it would present him, and the fact he had been editor of *Mercury* since 1907. Crowninshield immediately began to formulate his vision for the magazine. While himself quite conservative and the essence of a gentleman, Crowninshield was interested in offering the avant-garde in the arts and letters to stimulate the magazine's readers. Space was made available at the Condé Nast offices and Crowninshield began to assemble his editorial staff. By March 1914, the first issue of *Vanity Fair* was available on newsstands. In his first editorial to introduce the magazine, Crowninshield wrote:

> At no time in our history has the wonder and variety of American life been more inspiring, and, probably as a result of this, young men and young women, full of courage, originality, and genius are everywhere to be met with. This is particularly true in the arts. In our painting and sculpture a highly fertile and stimulating period is at hand. In the world of letters there are evidences of a profound activity, of originality of angle, of an inventive, forward, and reactionary spirit.[3]

Crowninshield was an artistic visionary in arts and letters, and those he brought to work on the staff of the magazine, as well as those he invited to contribute, were the artistic and literary elite, of which there were a great many in New York City and there would be a great deal more in the years to come. Several years after the magazine's start, Dorothy Rothschild came over from *Vogue*; she would become far more famous as Dorothy Parker. Robert Benchley also joined the editorial staff and his formidable wit was routinely displayed in the magazine's pages. Robert Sherwood found employment there, and he, Parker and Benchley were pivotal members of the Algonquin Round Table. Clare Booth Browkah became managing editor, later marrying Henry Luce, founder of *Time*, and she became a literary beacon in New York for the next several decades.

Crowninshield was a near clairvoyant in finding talent to contribute to *Vanity Fair* and be profiled in its pages. Thomas Wolfe, Gertrude Stein, Edmund Wilson, P.G. Wodehouse, Anita Loos, Edna St. Vincent Millay, Noel Coward, T.S. Elliot, William Somerset Maugham, Aldous Huxley, Colette and many others shone from the magazine's pages. Artists whose works were featured included Picasso, Matisse, Gauguin, Rockwell Kent, Tony Sarg and Gluyas Williams. Photography by Edward Steichen, Anton Bruehl, Horst and Cecil Beaton added to the magazine's cachet. However, it was the modern art reproductions in the magazine that had the advertisers up in arms. One advertiser threatened to withdraw its advertising account over the "decadent and distorted" art on its pages, no doubt referring to the work of Picasso.

Crowninshield was at his diplomatic best in deflecting these criticisms by phone or by letter. He could assuage the offended advertiser by saying such criticism was leveled at other great artists of the past, and their work was now considered masterpieces. He would then add that their advertising was viewed by some of the wealthiest and most influential readers in America and it would indeed be unfortunate for them if they chose not to advertise in *Vanity Fair*. Crowninshield usually persuaded the advertiser to stay. Crowninshield was an avid collector of modern art himself and was a tireless proponent of it. In 1929 he helped to found the Museum of Modern Art.

Dorothy Rothschild got her literary exposure at *Vanity Fair* several years before marrying Edwin Parker, a stockbroker, in 1917. Her first poem, "Men: A Hate Song," was published in 1914, and Crowninshield immediately spotted her cutting wit that would be her trademark for years. She worked as an edi-

Town & Country editor Harry Bull, right, amuses his wife Daphne and Lucius Beebe with a story at a private party. *Town & Country, Vanity Fair* and *The New Yorker* were the magazines of choice among Café Society (Jerome Zerbe, by permission).

torial assistant at *Vogue* for several years before Crowninshield brought her on the staff of his magazine. *Vanity Fair* was also the literary launching pad of humorist Robert Benchley. For the most part, the contributors to *Vanity Fair* were often people in their chosen professions of literature, art, theater, and later films. The magazine had its annual Nominated for the Hall of Fame throughout the magazine's publication until its last issue in 1936. From the pages of *Vanity Fair* came many of the charter members of Café Society.

The Algonquin Round Table

After the war, Alexander Woollcott had returned to the *New York Times* as drama critic. As such, he held considerable power in passing judgment on both stage productions and the actors. A positive word from Woollcott could launch a career and a scathing rebuke could destroy it. Woollcott was in demand by publicists trying to get the word out on playwrights, actors and producers of new stage plays. In June 1919, publicist John Toohey contacted press agent Murdock Pemberton at the Hippodrome Theater. Toohey represented Eugene O'Neal and wanted Pemberton to arrange a meeting with Woollcott to discuss O'Neal and convince the drama critic to write a piece for his "Second Thoughts" column in the *Times* that had a hook that would pull the readers in and spread the word on O'Neal. Pemberton had known Woollcott for years and agreed to arrange a meeting of the three of them. Pemberton called Woollcott to meet for lunch the next day at the Algonquin Hotel and Woollcott agreed. Over lunch, Woollcott listened to Toohey's pitch for O'Neal and the rather questionable approach he wanted Woollcott to take, but Woollcott maintained a passive expression. He then informed Toohey neither he nor the *Times* would agree to such a story, because the newspaper had taste, as Woollcott put it.

The subject was then closed and Woollcott immediately launched into one his famed recounts of his exploits during World War I, always prefaced with, "When I was in the theater of war...." Pemberton and Toohey suffered through Woollcott's recollection while they ate lunch. After the nonproductive lunch meeting, Toohey and Pemberton wondered what could be done. Knowing Woollcott never served on the front lines but wrote his articles for *Stars and Stripes* from the relative comfort of his Paris desk, they concocted a sendup of Woollcott before many of the editors of Manhattan's other newspapers and magazines. Pemberton called Woollcott to say he thought the stories of his exploits in wartime France would make fascinating listening for his peers in New York. Pemberton explained he wanted to arrange a luncheon the following week at the Algonquin with Manhattan's newspaper and magazine editors in the audience. This immediately appealed to Woollcott's vanity and he readily agreed. Pemberton prepared the invitations and they were immediately mailed off to editors and theater critics of the dozen major New York City daily newspapers and several noted magazines. From *Vanity Fair* came drama critic Dorothy Parker, writer Robert E. Sherwood, and recently appointed managing editor Robert Benchley. Also present was Franklin P. Adams, his mentor at *Stars and Stripes*, who still wrote his column "The Conning Tower," which he had written before the start of the war; Adams identified himself only by his initials FPA in his column and preferred this in personal greetings. Heywood Broun, drama critic for *New York Herald Tribune*, was also among those invited. Woollcott himself invited Harold Ross and his fiancée Jane Grant; Ross was editor of the *Home Sector*, and his founding with Grant of *The New Yorker* magazine was still six years in the future.

When the festive evening arrived, Woollcott began to describe yet another encounter during his time in France. Before Woollcott could finish his obligatory opening sentence, *Harper's Bazaar* editor Arthur Samuels interrupted by saying, "If you were ever in the theater of war, Aleck, it was in the last-row seat nearest the exit."[4] That brought well-deserved laughter from all but Woollcott, who ignored the remark and continued with his recollection. While enjoying their wonderfully prepared meal, the literary elite of Manhattan listened to Woollcott recount his experiences during the war. Taken with his flair for the descriptive, they all sat in rapt attention. Instead of listening with bemused enjoyment, the editors and writers response ranged from respectful to enthralled. At the end, Woollcott received a hearty round of applause that left him beaming. Perhaps no one present that day found Woollcott's stories more amusing than Sherwood. During the war, he had been shot through both legs and was exposed to poison gas; he lived to tell about it but rarely did. Sherwood had the medals to prove it and Woollcott did not. Pemberton and Toohey were appalled but did not betray their own sentiment. In one respect, it reflected well on the both of them that there had been such a strong turnout of invitees—roughly 35 showed up that day, and Pemberton was complimented on arranging this fine appreciation of Woollcott's contributions during the war.

There was, however, a much more significant development that day. This was the event that gathered some of Manhattan's finest writers, and by serendipity resulted in the formation of what would become known as the Algonquin Round Table. After witnessing the success of the gathering,

Toohey suggested offhandedly that they gather for lunch every day for food and conversation. It seemed like a great idea to most in attendance, but others begged off, saying they would attend as their schedules permitted. Toohey and Pemberton saw it as a means of maintaining professional contacts. Basking in the glow of peer admiration, Woollcott thought it a great idea. Parker, Sherwood and Benchley agreed to make it a daily ritual. All of them were on the cusp of great careers and even greater renown and enjoyed the idea of this mutual admiration society.

FPA was a key member of the group but rarely made it to the daily luncheons. He did, however, manage to meet with members in their less frequent evening gatherings that could go on for hours at a time and provided much material for his column. This also provided more time to permit the verbal brickbats to fly. That was part of the attraction of the Algonquin Round Table. It often became a battle of wits and sometimes the verbal barbs were vicious. This probably had its genesis at the first luncheon put on by Toohey at the Algonquin Hotel, but with the personality types present, this was the natural environment. Woollcott became the *de facto* arbiter of who could enter the Roundtable and who was not welcomed. Few had a second opportunity to make a good first impression.

The winter of 1919 did not go well for Parker, Sherwood or Benchley. Their trial period at *Vanity Fair* was over and Crowninshield was not in a charitable mood. Neither Parker nor Sherwood received raises that Christmas and they were not paid all that much, anyway. Sherwood was informed that he would soon be replaced by an acquaintance of Condé Nast. When Parker wrote an unflattering review of Billie Burke's performance in *Caesar's Wife*, Burke's husband Florenz Ziegfeld, who advertised in the magazine, phoned Crowninshield to complain. Crowninshield called Parker into his office and told her that was not the smartest bit of writing on her part. Parker defended herself by saying a drama critic had to be just that, but it fell on deaf ears. Some sources say Parker resigned over her disagreement with Crowninshield; others say she was dismissed from the staff. When Sherwood and Benchley learned Parker's fate, they made a pact. They threatened Crowninshield with their resignation if Parker was not reinstated. It backfired and Crowninshield informed them to not let the door hit them on the way out.

Sherwood was the first to land on his feet. Artist Charles Dana Gibson was editor of the humor magazine *Life*, founded by John Mitchell in 1883. Gibson had submitted his first illustrations to *Life* in 1886 and had contributed to the weekly magazine ever since, as well as numerous other periodicals. Gibson's fame and wealth grew from his work as an artist of iconic illustrations of beautiful women in all manner of situations. When Mitchell died in 1918, Gibson took over publication of the magazine and Edward Martin was made editor. Sherwood's father and Martin had founded the *Harvard Lampoon*. Sherwood met with Martin, and after publishing several of Sherwood's pieces, Martin hired him as a regular contributor. When Sherwood learned of Parker's and Benchley's fate, he recommended to Martin they contribute to *Life* also. By the summer of 1920 they were both hired as regular contributors. This was a natural for the whimsical Benchley, who wrote theater production reviews; Sherwood became the first film critic, in the days of silent films, and Parker turned out a regular stream of poems for the magazine. Gibson proved to be as generous as Crowninshield was tight-fisted and the three all got by rather well.

At that time Manhattan underwent a live theater building boom with a resulting expansion of theater productions. George F. Kaufman and Marc Connelly entered the ranks of the Round Table through the auspices of FPA. Kaufman and Connelly were struggling playwrights whose stage productions between 1917 and 1920 were far from successful. That changed when a talented young actress by the name of Lynn Fontanne entered their lives. Kaufman and Connelly had written a satirical comedy, *Dulcy*. Theater producer George Tyler liked it and it seemed to be a perfect vehicle for Fontanne. Both Woollcott and Broun attended the first week's performance in February 1921 and the reviews were overwhelmingly positive, from the newspapers at large and from Woollcott and Broun as well. *Dulcy* was "a deft and diverting comedy of character—a gay piece written by and for the sophisticated," Woollcott wrote. Broun was taken by the clever dialog and plot twists, saying it was "an ingenious trick play, and the patter which introduces the legerdemain is even better than the stunts."[5] *Dulcy* became one of the most successful productions of the season. The comedy gave a dramatic boost to Fontanne's career, and Kaufman's and Connelly's stars immediately began to rise.

A year later, Kaufman and Connelly's next production, *To the Ladies*, opened, and it starred Helen Hayes. This too was an immense success. For this production, Hayes had to learn to play the piano. After one night's performance, she was invited to attend a gathering of the Round Table regulars. Somewhat flustered to be among the literary lights of New York City, Hayes tripped over her first sentence, saying, "Anyone who wants my piano is willing to it." Before she could correct herself, Kaufman responded, "That's very seldom of you, Helen." That was her first mild exposure to the wit of the Round Table, and over the following years, as the barbs that the others threw at each other grew more painful, Hayes felt uncomfortable. In fact, many of those who came to the Round Table wondered if it was a good idea, but often endured the remarks—often offensive—just to be among the best and the brightest creative minds in the city.

When F. Scott Fitzgerald's first novel, retitled *This Side of Paradise,* was approved by Simon & Schuster editor Maxwell Perkins and published in March 1920, the author's career was finally launched and Zelda agreed to marry him. His second novel, *The Beautiful and the Damned,* was published in 1922. While not a Round Table regular, he was invited to read from his second novel at Woollcott's apartment on 47th Street with numerous others present and Zelda seated nearby. Woollcott smiled like the proverbial Cheshire Cat. Woollcott's expansive apartment became something of an Algonquin Round Table annex, with many attending to introduce their latest work without the press of lunch hour. Edna St. Vincent Millay read her latest poetry. George Gershwin unveiled his new composition "Rhapsody in Blue" there shortly before the debut at the Aeolian Hall in February 1924.[6]

Woollcott was feeling particularly flush because he had been lured from the *New York Times* to the *Herald* by the paper's publisher Andrew Munsey for $15,000 a year—the equivalent of more than $200,000 today. The fortunes of Connelly and Kaufman had also dramatically improved by the mid–1920s. In fact, the Algonquin Round Table had been something of a creative crucible for many of the active and infrequent members as their creative ability, fame and prosperity increased with the passing decade. Author James R. Gaines described the group's evolution, its influence on Manhattan and society at large, and what would become of them in the 1930s: "But far from being arbiters of their driven culture, the Round Table crowd would only mirror it, laughing all the way and little realizing that they too were becoming a craze: first as part of the nation's "smart set," when urban sophistication had become an attractive model in even the smallest cities; later as charter members of the first café society in America, a speakeasy-bred intermingling of the intellect and wealth that enhanced the value of both."[7]

Indeed, the advent of Prohibition helped to fuel the growth of meeting places that served liquor regardless. Most members of the Round Table did not confine themselves to the Algonquin or to Woollcott's lair, but often selected from among the best speakeasies Manhattan had to offer for nightlife as well. Tony Soma's on West 49th Street was a favorite haunt, as was Jack and Charlie's on the same street, and the Park Avenue Club made for a fine evening of dining and drinking. As the 1920s roared on, some of the clubs became more and more sophisticated, with the larger ones having entire themes reflected in their décor. A handful of these clubs would transition to the post–Prohibition era during the 1930s as among the most popular places of Café Society.

The notoriety of the Round Table writers left them open to recruitment from other newspapers. The *New York Herald* cast the biggest net, and the recruiter was executive editor Herbert Bayard Swope. By 1925, Swope had signed contracts with Woollcott, FPA, Broun and music critic Deems Taylor. All were given salaries by Swope of over $30,000 a year. When other Algonquin members joined for an elegant evening dinner at Swope's mansion on Long Island, they were conversing with senators and congressional representatives, Hollywood actors and actresses, and bankers from Manhattan. Zelda and Scott Fitzgerald often attended these dinners when they rented a place there several months out of the year; it was during this time Fitzgerald gleaned much of his material for *The Great Gatsby*, published in 1925.

By 1926, the members of the Algonquin Round Table were growing in fame and responsibilities that took more and more of their time. Benchley accepted invitations to Hollywood to do some writing for films, and this would ultimately become his home; he would later transition into acting, which he particularly enjoyed. Woollcott moved out of the building floor shared with Ross and Grant, who were increasingly upset over his too-close involvement in their lives. Woollcott had become increasingly controlling both at the Algonquin and just about any other gathering, and other members found it oppressive. Prior to leaving for Hollywood permanently, Benchley wrote regularly for *The New Yorker*, and Parker and Sherwood did as well, while spending less time at their familiar hotel for lunch. Parker had published her first book of poems, *Enough Rope*, that year, and it became a best-seller. Woollcott and Benchley published books of their collected writings. Lesser known members of the Round Table were also gaining renown and the lunch meetings at the Algonquin were only achieved by wading through a gauntlet of curious tourists who packed the lobby to catch sight of the famous writers.

Individual responsibilities gradually took a toll on the cohesiveness of the group by 1928. They met less and less frequently; the novelty had worn off. When Woollcott's sister died, he went to see a psychiatrist and his demeanor changed dramatically. It was a guarded secret that Parker, suffering from depression, had made several suicide attempts that had fortunately proved unsuccessful. The stock market crash that came in the fall of 1929 affected most of the Round Table members not at all, since they had little invested in the market. Their careers continued into the 1930s almost unaffected, and they became honored members of Café Society.

Harold Ross and The New Yorker

Harold Ross and Jane Grant had been married on March 27, 1920. Grant was working once again for the *New York Times*, and she chose to keep her maiden name, with Ross's approval. Ross accepted the position of editor for the *American Legion Weekly* just before the wedding. He brought several of his staff from *Home Sector* with him to the *Weekly* offices on West 43rd Street near the Hudson River. Ross and Grant became regulars in the Algonquin Round Table, but within their own group they referred to themselves as the Vicious Circle. Vicious it often was. Despite being very much a literary group, they rarely talked shop. They were there for fellowship, the jokes, the sophisticated banter, and the inevitable outrageous barbs. One had to sling them as well as receive them. Their notoriety grew in the face of charges of logrolling; they frequently referred to themselves in their writings, particularly in the newspapers which some of them wrote for. The couple enjoyed their life among these peers during the early years in meeting, but Ross longed to launch a magazine of his own.

Among the occasional attendees to the meetings at the Algonquin and Woollcott's cooperative were Raoul and Ruth Fleischman, who often enjoyed the frequent card games played during the evenings. Ross had been saving money from his earnings to put toward the prospective magazine while living off Grant's income. That proved challenging, and Grant branched out into syndicated features and became a contributor to the *Saturday Evening Post*, one of the highest-paying periodicals in America. Ross had gotten increasingly discouraged by the work at the *Weekly* by 1924 and longed to make the leap to magazine publishing. There were a number of things in his favor. Fast rotary printing presses, advances in multicolor reproduction, and new conveyor systems all helped to lower the cost of printing and were instrumental in the success of the *Saturday Evening Post*, *McCall's*, *Liberty* and *Collier's*, among the large circulation magazines, and numerous periodicals published in Manhattan, among them *Vanity Fair*. In addition, postal rates were favorable for mailing magazines.

In surveying the national circulation magazines, Ross had a very different view and it was specific to New York City. He wanted to publish a sophisticated humor magazine written for New Yorkers with advertising, for the most part, of local businesses of interest to residents of one of the most populous cities in the world. What was the cost of launching such a magazine? Grant went to her managing editor at the *Times*, Carr Van Anda, and told him of Ross's idea. She asked Van Anda what he thought it would cost to get such a magazine off the ground. Grant was stunned when she was told it would cost upwards of five million dollars before ad revenues would put the magazine in the black. This was out of the question, but Grant reasoned this was just one opinion.

The others in the Circle thought the notion of successfully publishing such a magazine was a naive notion. To add to the risk, Ross viewed his yet unnamed magazine as an independent publication in order to ensure editorial autonomy. Ross did not entertain the idea of publishing the magazine under the Condé Nast umbrella, and Woollcott for his part would not introduce Ross to Mr. Nast. Bank loans would probably prove fruitless. Circumstances soon pushed Ross further toward his goal. The company that published *American Legion Weekly* acquired the humor magazine *Judge*, and asked Ross to be coeditor. Ross agreed, but after only several weeks decided this had been as mistake; the humor was sophomoric and the cartoons even more so. Ross struggled to get the magazine into shape, but after five months he gave up and resigned as editor in August 1924.

Funding eventually came from a source Grant and Ross had not considered. They attended an evening party of the Fleischmans. During the course of conversation, Ross's idea for a magazine came up. Fleischman expressed interest in helping to get the magazine launched because he hated the baking business in general and his household-name yeast product (still sold today) that was the basis of his wealth. When he asked Ross how much he felt was needed to get the magazine published and editorial offices running, Ross said he felt $25,000 from him, plus a matching amount Ross and Grant had set aside, would do it. That was the hope; it did not prove to be the reality. What was the editorial board? Ross was asked. He actually did not have one, and Ross stalled as he came up with an answer. To get Fleischman to sign on, Ross assembled the names of ten of his constituents in the Circle. This proved a blatant fabrication, as few of them actually would work on the magazine or even contribute, and years later Ross admitted this was one of the most dishonest things he had ever done.[8]

Nevertheless, Fleischman agreed to help fund the fledgling magazine, and Ross moved into an office on West 45th street in the summer of 1924 and set to work. What to name it? The name came from Toohey, who had been instrumental in the formation of the Algonquin Round Table. He suggested the obvious: *The New Yorker.* For the first issue, Ross had his handful of writers do reviews for goings-on that covered current theater, moving pictures, music, art and other events, introduced "Talk of the Town" along with a profile of a noted person, some rather lame humorous cartoons, a column titled "In Our Midst," and other contributions signed at the end of the article usually with a pseudonym. There was no masthead of the editorial board because there really wasn't one. Even Ross did not list his name. Aside from the local advertisers that were Ross's requisite, there were several national advertisers that included Elgin Watch Company and United States Rubber Company for its U.S. Royal Cord Balloon Tires. The issue appeared on the newsstands on Tuesday, February 17, 1925. It proved the publishing nonevent of the year.

Upon examination, the issue proved less than well thought-out. After reviewing the premier issue, Crowninshield at *Vanity Fair* stated they had nothing to fear. The editor of the *Saturday Evening Post*, George Lorimer, had a more violent reaction; he threw the issue across the room. The first issue was universally panned, and Fleischman began to panic. He realized if the magazine was to survive and definitely improve, he had to bring in experienced professionals. Over Ross's grudging protests, Fleischman brought in John Hanrahan, who specialized in revamping and improving periodicals. A forceful marketing campaign was implemented, along with securing advertising clientele that could support the financial demands of the magazine. Ross brought in Rea Irvin to be his art editor, and worked to bring in experienced contributors. Dorothy Parker contributed theater reviews and a poem, and Woollcott contributed a profile. Robert Benchley contributed numerous humor pieces. Other Algonquin regulars also would get into the magazine. Ross improved the writing of the magazine decidedly until it hit on the right formula that would be its identity. Fleischman would eventually have to infuse hundreds of thousands of dollars to keep the magazine afloat until the accounting books moved from red to black.

The New Yorker evolved during the late 1920s into exactly the publication Ross had envisioned but could not initially articulate. Besides the clever cartoons (they were drawn by artists, not cartoonists, Ross insisted) that became a foundation of the magazine's appeal, the listings of music performances, nightclub acts, and other entertainment for each week was a big draw for its readers, who relied on the magazine for honest reviews to make decisions for going out on the town. *The New Yorker* was instrumental, in this respect, in the evolution of Café Society. In turn, the theaters, clubs and other venues coveted the write-ups in the magazine as the chief means of getting positive reviews and bringing patrons in to watch the performances and enjoy dining and dancing. *The New Yorker* became distinguished by the caliber of the writing by its contributors. Even established writers would often have to endure numerous rejections before final acceptance. At the same time, many of the great names in prose and poetry would make it into the magazine to make it one of the finest literary magazines in the United States, and one with a devoted readership. Ross was most surprised to find subscriptions soon were coming from around the country and even overseas. He also found security as the editor for more than a quarter of a century.

Maury Paul Takes Manhattan

There was one man who preceded all this literary activity during the 1920s, and he was a writer of a very different type. He was an observer of New York at large and New York Society in particular. His name was Maury H.B. Paul. Before his arrival, readers of New York City newspapers learned about the activities of the New York 400, which itself had been chronicled by Ward McAllister, merely in the form of wedding announcements, formal descriptions of cotillions, the debutantes being introduced each season, and where the Vanderbilts, Astors and Goulds might be traveling in Europe. Maury Paul changed all that and helped to usher in the transition from the New York 400 to what became Café Society. His sword was not the pen but the typewriter.

Paul was born and raised in Philadelphia. As he grew up, he liked to point out the initial B. stood for Biddle, of whom his mother was reportedly a distant kin. The Pauls had no family wealth and did not put on airs, but Maury Paul always sought for a better life. He attended the University of Pennsylvania, but after his third year he grew impatient or bored, and left before completing his studies. His biographer, Eve Brown, surmised he may have left for other reasons. Brown wrote Paul may have been uncomfortable in the strongly heterosexual campus life where he felt out of place. One evening at a party in Philadelphia, Paul met Alice McGill, who wrote a society column for the *Philadelphia Press*. McGill was not alone in the local press, however. Mrs. Cornelius Stevenson, writing as "Peggy Shippen," wrote a column for the *Public Ledger*, and her column was a far better read. During the course of her conversation with Paul, McGill asked him if he would be her mole after he assured her he could find out what she needed. Any and all news bits he gathered at the many parties and other functions he attended, he relayed to her. He was not compensated for this information, but his day job as a seller of jewelry put money in his wallet. Paul eventually realized if he was gathering this writable information, he could just as well write it himself. He approached George Shor, managing editor of the *Philadelphia Times*, published by Frank Munsey, for a job as a society reporter for the paper, which had no such thing. Shor turned him down and Paul had to come up with another plan.

He chose to embarrass Shor into hiring him. Paul sent roughly a dozen society announcements of fictitious people—some intentionally misspelled—and their incorrect addresses over a period of a week. These were all delivered to Shor, who printed them unquestioningly. Paul bought each issue of the paper, clipped out the error-laden announcements and after he had collected them all, paid Mr. Shor another visit. Paul informed Shor of the embarrassing errors in every announcement, saying if Paul had been on the staff, this would not have happened. Shor was suspicious, but saw the wisdom in hiring Paul to filter all these things which were of no interest to him anyway. Paul was hired at fifteen dollars a week, and with this cunning stroke, he was in the newspaper business. The year was 1913.[9]

For the next year, Paul contentedly attended every society function, significant party, theater production or related event and reported on them in the *Times*. In mid–1914, Munsey chose to close down the *Philadelphia Times*, and Munsey transferred Shor to his New York paper, the *Press*. Shor felt Paul had been an asset to the paper and persuaded Munsey that Paul should go with him. Paul moved to New York City. Paul, thrilled at this new development, already had visions of the New York 400 dancing in his head. He was disconcerted to learn that much of New York society had left the city for Newport, Rhode Island, and the mansions on Long Island. He spent the hot and humid summer learning all there was to know about the wealthy and the connected of Manhattan.

The start of the Metropolitan Opera season was Paul's first big foray into one of the favorite entertainments of the 400. Paul intended to report not only on the performance that night but on those who were in attendance in their private seating areas within the golden horseshoe, as it was called. Well before the start of the performance, Paul noted the name on the brass plaque outside the door to each seating box on his notepad. He took his seat and noted each notable individual as he sat in his respective box, and checked them off. He left before the close of the last performance to avoid the crowds and get to work on the article for the next day's paper. A photographer had been there to take photos of the performance, which appeared in the article. As Paul was admiring his first major piece for the paper, he was told to report to Mr. Munsey himself. Once in his office, Munsey leveled his gaze at Paul and informed him he had just received a call from Mrs. Stuyvesant Fish. Paul smiled expectantly. Munsey then told Paul he had succeeding in opening half the graves in Woodlawn Cemetery. Paul shook his head, baffled. Munsey told him the names on the doors of many of the boxes at the Metropolitan Opera were of the original owners who purchased the boxes years before and had passed on. Paul endured this humiliation with all the grace he could muster and promised it would never happen again. He returned to his desk much wiser.

During the first formative months on the paper, he developed his conversational style of reporting that helped to define the phrase "gossip column." It is not recorded if he wrote under his own byline or a fictitious one, but it was soon to come to an end. In another one of his arbitrary decisions, Munsey merged the *Press* with the *Evening Sun*. Paul was offered the position of society reporter, but working under one Frank Leslie Barker, who was the society editor. Paul bristled at this, not wanting anything he wrote to be edited by anyone. He turned down the offer and cleared out his desk. Fishing around for a job, he took the position of a bond salesman at a Wall Street firm. This was only temporary, while he surveyed the newspaper landscape for turf he could call his own.

He landed a position of anonymous reporter of society doings for the *Evening Post*. While he was selling bonds, and writing for the *Post*, he was called by one of the 400 to salvage a potentially embarrassing occasion. There were only hours to avert calamity, but with cool head and smooth diplomacy, Paul succeeded in averting this woman's potential disaster and the evening event in question went off without a hitch. In gratitude and as reward, the prominent hostess gave Paul an introduction to the very upper crust society he hoped to enter. At one such function, he met Paul Brock, part owner of the *Evening Mail*. Seeing a prime opportunity laid in his lap, Paul asked Brock for a position writing about New York society and giving every good reason why he should do so. Brock liked Paul's elegant manner and his having written for several papers before, and agreed to hire him. He would work under no one. He was permitted to keep the position with the *Post* and the bond sales position as well. Triple dipping netted Paul ninety dollars a week. He was only 25 years old.

Paul chose to adopt a pen name for this new column in the *Evening Mail*; he selected "Dolly Madison," and even registered the name. When his father died in 1915, Mrs. Paul moved to Manhattan and Paul found a two-room apartment on East 83rd Street. The address location was deliberate, because Paul had every intention, now that he was an official reporter of the New York 400 and the countless hangers-on, to live in the fashionable Upper East Side. Paul was moving with amazing speed. For the next four years, Paul

4. Café Society's Writers, Journalists, Editors and Playwrights 77

reported on every sensational yet absolutely true activity of note among the wealthiest of New York's residents in a chatty style that resulted in a steady stream of fan mail as well as rebuttals and denials from those written up in the column. He was always careful to corroborate every bit of information before writing about it, sometimes, to avoid claims of libel, in a nebulous way that became his hallmark. Paul was also writing under the registered name "Polly Stuyvesant" for the *Morning Telegraph*. It seemed there could never be too many outlets for Paul's gossipy outpourings, and he was soon to add one more.

In February 1915, Paul had something of an epiphany. He was dining at the Ritz-Carlton in midtown Manhattan. His ever-watchful eye caught something that he had noticed on a number of occasions before but which really struck him for the very first time. At one table were a group of men and women whose last names were all familiar to him but who typically never socialized with one another—but this new younger generation did. He decided to write about it in one of his columns the next day.

"This place!" Paul remarked. "Society isn't staying home and entertaining any more. Society is going out to dinner, out to night life, and letting down the barriers. Heavens—that I should see a Widener, a Goelet, a Corrigan and a Warren all together. It's like a sea-food cocktail, with everything from eels to striped bass!"[10] In that day's column, he coined a new phrase for what he had witnessed. He called it Café Society, its first mention in the press.

One of the readers of "Dolly Madison" was Marion Davies, who was William Randolph Heart's romantic interest. He asked her one day in her New York apartment what she was reading with such riveted attention and she mentioned the column. Hearst owned the *New York American* and *Evening Journal*. He became irritated she was reading a rival paper but realized it was because he did not have anything comparable in his own. The *American* owned the name "Cholly Knickerbocker," but that column had no steady reporter, and it had degenerated into nothing more than event announcements and some passive attempts at reporting. After suitable inquiries about the true identity of "Dolly Madison," Hearst called city editor of the *American*, Victor Watson, and told him to get Paul into his office and sign him onto the paper's staff.

When Watson offered Paul the position of "Cholly Knickerbocker," he did not immediately accept. Paul had numerous intellectual properties; he wanted to retain rights to those and continue writing for them because they were syndicated and provided him a very nice income. Paul had done some inquiries of his own and he told Watson he had heard Hearst employees were unceremoniously fired after only a few years with the paper. At random, Watson had numerous reporters come into his office to report how long they had worked on the paper. None had been with the paper less than fifteen years. With that, Paul agreed and signed his employment papers. He was now writing for four newspapers and decided to move from the comfort of his apartment to rent an office on West 23rd Street. He hired a secretary to assist in keeping all the columns unique.

Maury Paul was an obsessive-compulsive as a newspaper columnist. He made it look easy but the demands of putting out various different columns for several different newspapers six days a week taxed even his seeming endless reservoirs of creativity and energy. Hours were spent every day cutting out and tracking rival newspaper columns and relevant magazine articles, making phone calls and answering the phone, following up leads to find out if they were true or not, performing countless other related tasks, and finally typing up the various columns he was responsible for. He rarely had an eight- or even ten-hour work day. Paul could not have done this all by himself, and he didn't.

Standing in front of the Salmon Building, Eve Brown looked at the sheet of paper that told her to report to 11 West 42nd Street and go to room 908 at 10:00 a.m. Brown went to the ninth floor, rang the doorbell for 908, and in seconds the door was opened by a handsome young man by the name of Berwyn Hughes. She was taken into Paul's cluttered bedroom/office, where he sat behind his desk. She introduced herself and handed Paul the letter from the employment agency. Paul looked at her approvingly and stood up, realizing too late he had forgotten to put on a belt. His pants fell to the floor, revealing his blue silk boxer shorts. Brown's face reddened in embarrassment and she turned away. Paul scooped up his pants unfazed and, holding them up, walked from behind his desk to survey Brown. She was attractive, tall and reed-thin. As he looked her up and down muttering approval, she began to wonder what she had gotten herself into. He circled her several times and she noted he walked on the balls of his feet. Finally, the short and pudgy man waved his hand and said she was hired. She was not sure what she had been hired for. Before finding out, he issued her a warning saying she better not get fat or she would be fired, saying he hated fat people. Brown learned that morning the second of the many quirks of the man who would be her boss for the next two decades.

When Brown admitted she had no idea who "Cholly Knickerbocker" was, Paul was surprised but did not hold it against her. He informed her he was also "Dolly Madison" and "Polly Stuyvesant" and described patiently the subject of his columns. Her duties would be numerous and varied. She would be paid

4. Café Society's Writers, Journalists, Editors and Playwrights 79

$25 a week. That would not leave her much after rent and other living expenses, but she would get by.

To meet the almost insatiable demands of multiple lines of copy needed every day, Paul cut a wide swath through Manhattan night life. Paul's mind was receptive to practically any news or corroborated rumor with respect to notable engagements, weddings, divorces, charitable events, debutante balls, opera performances, Broadway doings and worthy bits regarding films—in short, anything he deemed notable and worthy of copy. Increasingly, his columns required photographs of all these things; the days of the reliable but dated file photo had lost favor. Marty Black was hired as Paul's photographer and the responsibility of booking Black's services and scheduling the photo shoot fell to Brown. She spent several hours of her day calling prospective photo subjects to schedule the photo shoot for the "Cholly Knickerbocker" column. The photo shoots were often involved. Debutantes, for example, had to be photographed in casual daytime clothes, sportswear, and evening wear with particular emphasis on the gown, as well as with friends and family, and so on. Brown rarely went on the photo shoots with Black; she was too busy setting up other photo shoots, typing copy for Paul, and digging up facts he asked her to chase down.

However, Paul and Brown often went to events together so they could double their fact-finding, and the notepad and pen were always kept at the ready. Memory could not be relied upon. Paul had to supplement Brown's income with a modest expense account to purchase appropriate evening attire. After Paul and Brown had attended an event they would return to the office to record furiously all the facts gathered because material for the columns had to get to the copy desk as soon as possible for the morning papers or next day's evening papers. After a period of several years, William Randolph Hearst himself forced Paul's hand and demanded he write exclusively as "Cholly Knickerbocker." He would be paid $250 per week, making him one of the highest paid columnists in New York City. Paul moved to his new office at the *American* near Columbus Circle in 1922.

"You'll probably have your hands full with me and my column," Paul told Hearst during that contract signing ceremony, "and you'll be besieged with complaints. I won't pull my punches. But this I promise: I'll never write one word of news that is not the truth, and you will never have a libel suit as a result of my column."[11] Hearst admired Paul's bold declaration and believed Paul would make good on it.

In 1925, Paul started a series of new Sunday features that added to his workload and Brown's. Saturday evenings were the longest in order to get the special Sunday copy out in time. Often the two would not leave the office until midnight, not having even taken a break for dinner and hungry for something to eat. With few eateries open at that hour, they would abandon the idea of a sit-down meal. They would hail a cab and sit with eyes closed until Brown reached her apartment building and said good night, and Paul rode on to his apartment in the Salmon Building.

Paul had, by now, a well-developed sense of his own style. Indeed, he could not write any other way. His thousands of readers loved his descriptive phrases that he alone coined. The truly wealthy had "oodles of ducats." If Paul was among the most attractive of New York, they were "Sweetie Sweets." Long Island was, of course, "Longuyland." Whenever he referred to Mrs. O.H.P. Belmont, he was referring to the "Social Sultana." Those attending their first night at the opera were the "Turreted Tiara Set." Paul was nearly incapable of writing a simple declarative sentence adhering to the *Manual of Style*. He created a language of his own, and for most of his readers, no translation was necessary.

With Prohibition in force, more or less, Paul was personal witness to New York Society's disdain for the law. They were scofflaws every bit as much as the middle and lower classes. For example, how could a debutante have a coming out without champagne? The proud parents ordered cases of the most expensive Moet and Chandon, and looked the other way when all the invited young ladies and gentlemen started bobbing and weaving. Paul took note, however. The young women in particular behaved like nothing more than flappers in evening gowns. With raised eyebrow, Paul would record how the men and women behaved like drunken sailors and danced most lasciviously to the latest jazz compositions. Champagne was no respecter of persons, and Paul would take furious notes upon returning to his apartment for him to take to his office the following morning.

Paul thrived on scandal because it provided grist for his mill. In 1922, when Evan Burrows-Fontane sued Cornelius Vanderbilt Whitney in a paternity suit, Paul rubbed his hands and then dug for all the dirt he could to give his readers. "Cholly Knickerbocker" made sure the rapt readers of his column had the most inside information available because the standard news articles wrote the sanitized version. All the while, he steadfastly observed his vow to write only the truth. Paul was a not-so-private detective who made sure he corroborated the most inflammatory information before writing it down in his unmistakable prose for his column. How could he continue to receive invitations to the most exclusive events and private parties while baring the soul of New York Society for all to read? For one thing, his reporting of the facts was not always exclusive; news reporters wrote essentially the same information in very dry form, while Paul conveyed it in the most entertaining way possible. And that was Paul's secret. His column was entertainment, not news reporting. It blew the lid off the 400's attempt to maintain its civility and haughty air.

At the same time, Paul could be most complimentary in his column toward those he favored and admired. His respect for the wealthy was not a blanket respect but varied from family to family. He wrote his column as a mix of the good, the bad, and sometimes the ugly of New York City's wealthiest. In fact, it was precisely because he only reported the truth that his subjects could hold nothing against him and he could continue to be received by the moneyed elite of Manhattan. An example of the respect in which Paul was held among New York's most famous families was the story of George Gould and a woman who had remained a mysterious secret for years.

The Goulds' wealth had been established in the late 19th century by Jay Gould, who had amassed his fortune in the establishment of numerous railroads across the United States and in many other financial dealings which earned for him the nefarious title of robber baron. He became one of the wealthiest men in America. His first child was George Jay Gould, and three brothers and two sisters followed before Jay Gould died in 1892. George Gould followed in his father's footsteps in operating various railroad interests. He married Edith M. Kingdon and they would have seven children. Edith died in 1921. However, Gould had another love interest. Maury Paul learned firsthand the secret life Gould had lived and he would be given the rare privilege of having an exclusive to write about it in his column.

In May 1922, Paul was typing away in his office at the *American* one afternoon when his phone rang. He answered it and was startled to learn he was speaking with George Gould. The railroad tycoon told Paul he wanted him to come up to Westchester the next day and baited the hook by saying Paul would be given an exclusive scoop. The following morning, Paul drove his Rolls-Royce Silver Ghost up to the Gould residence. Once inside, he was taken to a large study. Several minutes later, George Gould walked in with a tall blonde beautiful woman on his arm. Gould introduced Paul to Miss Guinevere Sinclair. Paul said he was delighted. Gould then stated, smiling, she was the mother of three other children he had fathered. For an instant, Paul was speechless. It had been rumored Gould had a mistress, but she had been, understandably, a mystery woman. Sinclair, born in South Dakota to Irish parents, eventually made her way to the Great White Way just before World War I. Her beauty made her stage presence striking and George Gould took immediate notice. He provided her a mansion directly across from that of steel titan Charles Schwab on 74th Street. Gould also built another mansion in Mamaroneck and it was here Sinclair raised her son and two daughters by Gould. When Edith died, Gould planned to have a respectable mourning period before marrying Guinevere.

Gould stated he was going to marry Miss Sinclair and he wanted Paul's cooperation in making the announcement. Gould wanted Paul to witness the marriage ceremony in New Jersey and drive the happy couple to a nondescript ship moored on the North River in Manhattan. He escorted them to the ship and wished them bon voyage. He had to withhold news of the event for 24 hours. Then, it was not only front page news in the *American*, it was the main event in the "Cholly Knickerbocker" column. However, Gould did not get to enjoy the company of his second wife for very long. He died one year later in France from pneumonia. Guinevere Gould later married Viscount Dunsford. She was embroiled in court battles over the Gould estate by other members of the family, and Paul duly noted these events in his column as well.

Paul was on equally good terms with the Vanderbilts of the day. Reginald Vanderbilt, great-grandson of Cornelius Vanderbilt, was better known for his freewheeling sportsman lifestyle than for any business acumen. Paul had been fascinated with Reginald's nonstop living and once he got to know him personally, the two men became good friends. Vanderbilt had married Kathleen Nielson in 1903 but the couple divorced in 1920. Of course, their friendship notwithstanding, Paul gleefully wrote about Vanderbilt's comings and goings, and the Commodore's great-grandson just smiled. In February 1923, he called Paul to come up to his East 77th Street mansion for dinner because he had an announcement to make. This sounded like a repeat of the Gould story, so he visited his wealthy friend with great expectation.

When Paul arrived, Vanderbilt told him to sit down, because he would need to. Paul listened as the 43-year-old Vanderbilt informed him he was going to propose to the 17-year-old Gloria Morgan. Paul just blinked and nodded. Vanderbilt told Paul he wanted the columnist to announce the engagement. Gloria Morgan did not come from a wealthy family, and Vanderbilt himself was living off a $5 million trust fund. Paul knew the Morgan family and had met and even danced with Gloria and her sister Thelma. Despite their age differences, the couple was genuinely in love with each other. There was another fact that Paul did not and would not disclose in his column, and that was the fact Reginald Vanderbilt was a dying man. His health had been declining for the last several years. He wanted a young love as his wife in the last years of his life.

The ever-so-young Gloria Morgan arrived and Vanderbilt sat her down at the dinner table and then proceeded to pour out his heart, emphasizing he was not a man of great wealth like his predecessors, and in the future whatever she inherited would be entirely dependent on the children they had. He assured her the chances of their having a child was probably one in a hundred. Paul listened to the heartfelt proposal with respectful silence. When Vanderbilt asked for her hand, she gave him the words he wanted to hear. Paul went home that evening and wasted no time composing what would appear in the next day's "Cholly Knickerbocker" describing the engagement of Gloria Morgan to Reginald Claypoole Vanderbilt. They were married March 6, 1923, in the apartment of a family friend in the Hotel Marguery on Park Avenue with 50 friends and family attending. Vanderbilt whisked his bride up to Newport, Rhode Island, and his Sandy Point Farm estate for their honeymoon. Vanderbilt defied the odds and the couple had their only child, a daughter named after her mother. Gloria Vanderbilt became the most-photographed Vanderbilt in history, known for her fashion design sense later in her life as well as her numerous husbands.

By the mid–1920s, Paul had confirmed a shift in the social life of those he wrote about. There was less emphasis on the grand receptions, formal coming-outs, and over-the-top dinners in the vast dining rooms of Manhattan's most famous residents. A new, younger generation was going out to theater productions and frequenting the finest clubs and speakeasies. To get the news bits he needed most, he followed the transition and a whole new world opened up to him. Paul's reputation was so great, he was often given a table at these establishments and all meals—but no drinks because he never drank liquor and rarely drank wine or champagne—were on the house. It was just smart business for the proprietor to do this, for it invariably meant that the place would be mentioned in Paul's column.

As the 1920s roared, Paul had no lack of people and events to write about. For him the challenge was what to eliminate. His mind was constantly going, making notes of what he would write about tomorrow, the next day, next week and next month. He was a master of organization and of the filing cabinet. He had many in his office. His writing volume was prodigious, but in reading his columns, he made it look easy. Imitation was the sincerest form of flattery, but there were few who competed on the same level as Paul. Partly that was simply a result of his persona. In the New York press, there was simply no one else like him. He invented the genre. The only one who could be considered competition was Howard White, writing for the *Herald Tribune*. There was Walter Winchell, who during the 1920s began to be read by an ever-expanding readership, but Winchell wrote on a somewhat different plane while developing his own distinctive style.

Paul had amassed considerable clout writing at the *American*, along with either fawning or grudging respect among the New York's upper crust and Café Society. He also had some sense of obligation to those far less fortunate. It is not clear if Paul himself came up with the idea of the Cholly Knickerbocker Ball as a perfect charity fund-raiser, or if it was the brilliant idea of one of his opposite numbers in the paper's advertising department. In either case, Paul completely embraced this benevolent function, and the first one was held in 1923 at the Plaza Hotel. It was originally planned as a one-time event, but the first came off so successfully, it became an annual charity function until the early 1930s. Ensuring the ball came off without a hitch was a testament to Paul's inherent organization, attention to detail, sense of diplomacy, ability to delegate and basically micro-manage the entire social event. For once Paul would do the inviting: it was he who was inviting the most illustrious families in New York to *his* ball, and invariably they all came. Besides, it was all for a good cause and the invitees would be seen as benefactors as well. He managed to work the phones, arrange invitations, coordinate with the hotel on the menu and all seating arrangements and other details, all the while churning out his daily column. He naturally had much to write about in the days after the ball, but it did not end there. He made sure several prominent women who attended the ball also assisted in handing out the food baskets to the poor at the Lexington Avenue Armory. Most of these women had never encountered the truly destitute and underfed. It was a humbling experience for them. Paul took particular joy in seeing the grateful smiles of those accepting the food.[12]

Paul was always concocting how he could expand the scope of "Cholly Knickerbocker" with spinoff columns. The generous Sunday issue of the paper allowed much more room to expand, and in 1925 he launched his "First Families" column that was of particular interest to Paul because of his obsession with genealogy. He would spend hours researching the background of these families at the New York Genealogical and Historical Society, but one requirement was that the family had to have a coat of arms. Like some corporation establishing new divisions, Paul created new columns to run in the paper. There was "Cholly Knickerbocker Says," a variation of the main column. Then he added a department, "Cholly Observes," which ran on Sundays and seemed to dish out information that did not fit anywhere else. There followed "Ask Cholly," which was not drawn from questions from actual readers, but were questions Paul himself derived and which he also answered. With all the inside information he gathered regarding the legitimate and furtive relationships in the city, he introduced "Leaves from Dan Cupid's Diary." For Paul, the possibilities were practically endless, but no one questioned him that perhaps he was spreading himself too thin. He was pulling in readers to the *American* like no other columnist, along with the advertisements that filled the paper's bank accounts, and Hearst gave him full reign. Paul made good on his pledge to Hearst, and neither Paul nor the paper were ever sued for unsubstantiated or untruthful information. By the end of the 1920s, Paul and his alter ego were a newspaper institution nationwide, and he would seamlessly proceed into the 1930s and the Great Depression without slowing down. There was only one other newspaperman who could challenge Paul in the number of readers, and he would become one of the most famous in both print and in radio.

Walter Winchell's Broadway

Maury Paul had been writing columns for several years as "Dolly Madison" and several others names in 1920 when an obscure traveling vaudeville entertainer by the name of Walter Winchell began writing a column for the *Vaudeville News*. Winchell's column was "Newssense," a chatty column about the goings-on of the vaudeville entertainment industry. He was just a contributor, and was not compensated for his column. He traveled with his wife, and together they performed in vaudeville theaters around the country. Winchell had been born and raised in New York City and he longed to get back to Broadway. He wanted to get out of performing on stage and write fulltime. The *Vaudeville News* was edited and published in an office next to the Palace Theater on Broadway. He was finally hired as an editor of the *News* to write a new column, "Broadway Hearsay," and since the paper was published on a break-even basis, he also delivered the paper to every subscriber, mostly agents and managers, but some entertainers as well. The paper was free to the industry with advertising covering expenses.

After working to get out his column for the paper every day, he would frequent the National Vaudeville Artists' Club on 46th Street at night and well into the following early morning. Winchell's nervous energy did not require much sleep to recharge. The atmosphere at the N.V.A. was eclectic and invigorating to Winchell, who wrote that it surpassed the Bohemian mood of other entertainer gathering places. Winchell hungered for this contact, and many entertainers, knowing he wrote for a paper, ingratiated themselves to him in the hopes their names would appear in newsprint. Winchell not only yearned for the attention and respect the vaudeville entertainers and managers gave him, he also wanted something much more. He wanted true recognition and a much more secure living financially. He and his wife Rita were just scraping by. After eight months as editor he was given a raise to $50 a week. He was soon collecting an additional $100 a week in advertising commissions.[13] If anyone could secure advertising is was the persuasive, smooth and fast-talking Winchell.

The pace Winchell kept, with little of his time spent with Rita, put a strain on their marriage. In 1922, she left to go on the road again to get away from their empty marriage, and she continued traveling and entertaining the following year. They were martially and literally separated. In 1924, he received an offer to join the staff of a new newspaper that was forming and would start publication in September, the *Evening Graphic*. By this point, Winchell was well-known to actors like Al Jolson, Eddie Cantor, Fred Stone and even senator and soon-to-be New York Mayor Jimmy Walker. At 27 years old, Winchell was cutting a wide swath in Manhattan.

The publisher of the *Evening Graphic* was multimillionaire and health eccentric Bernard Macfadden, who published *True Story* and *Physical Culture* magazines. Winchell was not entirely sure he wanted to join the ranks of the *Graphic*, knowing the sensationalist format the paper would take. This was not the first tabloid newspaper; that distinction was held by the *Illustrated Daily News*, which debuted on June 26, 1919. The *Evening Graphic*, however, would succeed in becoming the most lurid tabloid, with shocking headlines and even more shocking photos. Winchell made an appointment with Herbert Swope, editor-in chief of the *Herald*. Perhaps Winchell hoped Swope would make him an offer to join his newspaper after he heard Winchell's questions. The offer was not forthcoming, but Swope did tell Winchell that he was a specialist in his field and had written that column for four years. It would be good experience for him to work on a city newspaper staff, and he could always leave the paper if it didn't work out.

Winchell finally made the leap and signed with the *Evening Graphic*. Macfadden approved the final layout of the first copy, which hit the newsstands on September 16, 1924. The September 20 issue introduced Winchell's column, "Your Broadway and Mine." Despite Winchell's reputation in the field of reporting on Broadway, the layout of the desks at the paper revealed where he ranked in the pecking order. Higher-ranked editors had cubicles toward the back of the main room. Winchell's dilapidated desk was near that of the sports editor, just a few steps away from the elevator, which constantly opened and closed as people got on and off. At the end of the day, he bolted for the nearby elevator and made for LaHiff's, which was a restaurant that catered to Broadway performers. There he did what he did best, which was gather the latest news of whatever kind as it related to the Great White Way. His greeting there was always, "What do you know that I don't know?"

Winchell knew much about the field of entertainment he loved, but he didn't know all of it. There was an entire world out there he had bypassed that could prove a rich resource for his column. He knew the world of the vaudeville theater like no one else in New York, but the world of the speakeasy clubs was alien to him. One of the columns came to the attention of Sime Silverman, founder of *Variety*. Winchell had reported that the bouncers at El Fey Club, run by gangster Larry Fey, used excessive force to subdue unruly customers. Silverman called Winchell and said he knew the hostess at the club who could give him the truth, and he would be happy to introduce Winchell to her. Silverman picked up Winchell one evening and drove him to El Fey Club. Walking inside, they were greeted by a blonde and gregarious hostess, and Silverman introduced Winchell to Texas Guinan. She gave him her trademark greeting, "Hello, sucker!" Winchell took an immediate liking to Guinan. After getting the truth about the unruly customer in question—he had been drunk and had pulled a gun on the bouncers—he wrote a retraction.

Guinan offered Winchell the opportunity to visit the club as often as he liked, and she in turn would introduce him to a whole new world of clientele from the business world as well as the entertainment world he had not been exposed to. She would even give him his own table where he could cast his net to gather information for his column. She would often sit with him at his table and give him commentary on the notable customers at the club and what was of particular interest to Winchell. Guinan and Winchell became friends from that moment on. Silverman also introduced Winchell to others with contacts who could also give him vital facts to relate in his daily column. In fact, Winchell's column was perhaps the most legitimate copy in the *Graphic*, which would specialize in reporting grisly murders and their subsequent sensational trials, kidnappings, and other bizarre human events that had a perverted interest among readers.

Winchell wrote on an entirely different plateau than Maury Paul, but they actually wrote about the same folly of human behavior and the fascination of the personalities of the day. Winchell had as much audacity as Paul in writing about the foibles of his subjects, and he also wrote in a jargon that was as unique to him as "Cholly Knickerbocker" was to Paul. As proof of the literary divide between Winchell and Paul, Guinan one night related to Winchell that Mrs. Vanderbilt was going to have twins. Winchell had no idea who she was talking about. Guinan was incredulous, but she filled him in on a short history of the family.

With his ignorance of Mrs. Vanderbilt, it is doubtful Winchell ever read "Cholly Knickerbocker," but he borrowed a page from that column when he launched a new column to supplement his "Broadway" column, to be published on Mondays. "Mainly About Mainstreeters" was Winchell's foray into the very personal lives of those outside the Broadway community. Often inflammatory, Winchell skirted libel by adopting his own slang, which one biographer called "slanguage." In basic terms, it was gossip. Winchell was fascinated with it and he became especially animated when discussing it. In June 1927, the column name was changed to "This Town of Ours."

In writing these columns, Winchell became a personality himself. He also learned how to wield power and what a sentence could do to boost a performer's career or send it into the abyss. Winchell shared something else with Paul—they were both driven to be the best in their profession and both enjoyed the adulation they received. To be among the most successful and the wealthiest in the entertainment field helped to assuage Winchell's insecurity that had its roots in his vaudeville performance days. Winchell became known as the Boswell of Broadway.

Winchell had endured an adversarial working relationship with editor Emile Gauvreau ever since starting with the *Graphic*. His boss was often belligerent, blocked a raise to $300 a week with attendant 50 percent of gross revenue from syndication, and frequently disallowed Winchell's expenses. By the late 1920s, Winchell was receiving and entertaining substantial offers to go to other papers. After legal battles regarding his contract with the *Graphic*, Winchell moved to William Randolph Hearst's *New York Daily Mirror* in 1929. With it came a weekly salary of $500 and 50 percent of the syndication revenue.[14] Winchell was running with the big dogs.

That same year a very tall, distinguished-looking and degreed graduate of Harvard reported to editor Stanley Walker at the *New York Herald*. The man was Lucius Morris Beebe. He too would very soon make a name for himself and later would have a column of his own. Maury Paul, Walter Winchell and Lucius Beebe would become, during the 1930s, the most widely read columnists in New York City. The stock market was at its peak and on the verge of its historic plunge. These men would ride out the Great Depression writing about life in the great city as many struggled to survive and a relatively small group known as Café Society lived very large indeed.

CHAPTER 5

Boom and Bust: Music, Skyscrapers and Wall Street in the 1920s

There was another key element in the emergence of Café Society in the 1930s, and that was the financial buildup during the 1920s, the eventual stock market crash, and the subsequent Great Depression. During the 1920s, many of the characters who would become prominent in Café Society were working to build their careers and learn their craft, and were making names for themselves in doing so. Most of these players did not invest heavily in the stock market. Instead, they invested in themselves and in careers that, unknowingly, insulated them against the economic calamity that was to come. The vast majority of them kept their jobs and incomes and were able to ride out the economic depression in much the same lifestyle they had in the 1920s. Nevertheless, countless businesses struggled in Manhattan during the 1930s, particularly the nightclubs, fine restaurants and other elite establishments, and in many cases it was Café Society that helped them keep afloat during the worst economic downturn of the 20th century.

Certainly, the 1920s were a confluence of societal change, expansion of institutional and individual investment in the stock market, the emergence of jazz as a cultural shift, and something of a building boom in skyscrapers as their architects and financiers strove to outdo each other. In 1920, millions of phonographs were playing recorded music in homes across America, and radio was also spreading hundreds of new compositions in live broadcasts from major cities like New York, Chicago, St. Louis, Dallas, and Los Angeles. Live bands emerged during the early years of the decade, from quartets to full orchestras. Paul Whiteman was an up-and-coming composer and band leader, and he signed his group to a recording contract with the Victor Phonograph

Company. His band had played in Los Angeles and had a very successful stint at the Ambassador Hotel in Atlantic City. Finally, substantial offers were coming from club owners in New York. In September 1920, the Paul Whiteman band signed a three-month contract to perform nightly at the Palais Royal restaurant for $1,600 weekly. The management essentially wanted Whiteman and his musicians to be heard but not readily seen, and wanted them on the second floor mezzanine of the restaurant. White objected politely, saying dancing customers enjoyed reasonably close proximity to the band and enjoyed seeing the band perform. Whiteman had logic on his side.

"Most of my boys are college guys," he reasoned. "We dress well and we know our p's and q's. We met a lot of New Yorkers in Atlantic City, and they'll probably be your customers. They're used to talking with us. We've got to be close to the people, the dancers."[1]

The managers of the Palais Royal were very pleasantly surprised when the publicity announced in the newspapers resulted in a full house that saw New York City's most notable arriving for their reservations with every table taken and customers crowding the dance floor. In the first week performing, Whiteman and his band were a sensation, and reservations now had to be booked weeks in advance. Many had to be turned away. The band's success also drove sales of their Victor recordings. In less than a year, Whiteman and his band became among the most famous musicians in Manhattan, after performing in relative obscurity in California and other venues. New Yorkers had a thing for the music the band was performing—a mixture of popular dance hits as well as newer jazz compositions. There were certainly other bands performing in Manhattan at restaurants and clubs all over the city, but Whiteman's group and their renditions of tunes struck a chord with sophisticated club and restaurant goers.

Whiteman established a business office in the city and began hiring musicians and forming ten man ensembles to perform at other venues in the city and even on cruise ships. By the end of 1922, he had nearly twenty bands performing. He later received an offer to have his orchestra—actually a large band—perform in London. Whiteman still had a fear of performing before large groups, ironically, and he debated taking his musicians to Britain. William Morris, the talent agent, urged him to go, and to take a break from his successful stint at the Palais Royal. He booked passage aboard the SS *President Harding* and the ship steamed for Liverpool. Even before the Whiteman band arrived, there had been debates in Parliament about the band's arrival. Whiteman, in fact, encountered problems regarding work permits and other complications, such as having British musicians perform in his band, which took considerable time to resolve. Finally, the Whiteman band performed in *Brighter London*, and in predictable fashion, they won the British listeners to the sound of jazz, which was alien to them. The band performed before Lord Mountbatten and the Prince of Wales, and the contract at their venue stretched from weeks to months. The Whiteman band finally returned to New York in August 1923.

"The Whiteman Orchestra did not play jazz, as the ODJB (Original Dixieland Jazz Band), Armstrong's Hot Five, or Jelly Roll Morton's Red Hot Peppers played jazz," author Arnold Shaw wrote succinctly, "but its recordings of the day's popular tunes involved arrangements that traded on sounds, harmonies, and rhythms derived from jazz."[2]

In establishing his unique sound of jazz, Whiteman was assisted by a talented arranger and composer by the name of Ferde Grofé, who met the bandleader while performing in Los Angeles before the band moved east. There were many new popular musical compositions pouring forth during the early 1920s, and Grofé took the most popular and created his arrangements of them for Whiteman. Invariably, the arrangements made the tunes even more popular and helped Whiteman sell more recordings, and new pieces were invariably attributed to Whiteman himself—that is, the tunes became identified with Whiteman and his band. There were, indeed, other band leaders performing many of the same hits, and these included Ben Selvin, Vincent Lopez, Art Hickman and Isham Jones among others, but Paul Whiteman became the premier band leader of the 1920s. And greater triumphs were soon to happen for him.

In November 1923, Whiteman attended a concert at Aeolian Hall in New York performed by Eva Gautier. Among her performances of compositions by Bellini, Bartok, Hindemith and Purcell, Gautier performed some jazz songs as part of her repertoire. Accompanying Gautier on piano was George Gershwin. Whiteman was impressed and intrigued, and began to formulate an idea for a similar concert. He knew Gershwin was a composer as well and planned to have him write something specific for the concert. Whiteman put together an eclectic list of compositions he wanted his musicians to perform, not just as a band but as a larger orchestra. Whiteman approached Gershwin and commissioned him to write a new orchestra jazz piece along the lines of "Blue Monday Blues" that Gershwin had recently composed and Whiteman had heard. Gershwin began composing it in January 1924, and over a three-week period, he intermittently composed "Rhapsody in Blue."

Grofé was closely involved in the arrangements of all the selections for this concert, and he spent considerable time on "Rhapsody in Blue." Grofé spent hours at Gershwin's Manhattan apartment as the composer and the arranger worked on polishing Gershwin's jazz epic. Meanwhile, Whiteman worked on selecting the musical numbers he wanted to include in the concert. It was a very eclectic mix. It included "The Livery Stable Blues," "Yes! We have No Bananas," "Whispering" (one of Whiteman's hits from 1922), "Kitten on the Keys," "Alexander's Ragtime Band," "Pomp and Circumstance," and other selections totally outside the realm of jazz. Whiteman billed the concert at "An Experiment in Modern Music." The date was set for February 12, 1924, at 3:00 p.m. and Whiteman estimated it would run for four hours. His recording company, Victor Records, cranked up the publicity machine. Whiteman's band rehearsed the numbers relentlessly to achieve perfection.

The publicity was a success and every seat in the Aeolian Hall was taken

Paul Whiteman was the premier bandleader during the Café Society golden era of the 1930s. Despite the Great Depression, Whiteman and his orchestras were kept busy playing primarily in New York City but also traveled the United States. His musical renditions appealed to a broad audience, but Whiteman enjoyed venues frequented by Café Society (Library of Congress).

that afternoon, and it then became standing room only. The concert started off with "The Livery Stable Blues" and this set the tone and the mood. Over the next several hours, with appropriate intermission, Whiteman and his band played the advertised selections, some which received just polite applause. Finally, the 22nd composition, "Rhapsody In Blue," was up. Gershwin walked briskly from offstage to the piano, sat down and looked at Whiteman. The bandleader turned to clarinetist Ross Gordon, who started the slow, sultry wailing opening that caught everyone's attention. Gershwin came in with his piano and all eyes were upon him. The audience, which had become somewhat restless in the previous hours, were swept off their feet with Gershwin's composition and Grofé's arrangement. Whiteman was in his element and his 21 musicians performed brilliantly. With the climactic ending, the audience exploded in a wave of applause. Whiteman beamed at Gershwin, who was all smiles himself as he took his bows. The last composition, Edward Elgar's classical march, was practically anticlimactic and strangely out of sequence to end the concert. Nevertheless, the concert was well-received by the audience, if not all the critics, and Paul Whiteman, right or wrong, was dubbed the King of Jazz in the newspapers. It was perhaps more correct to say Whiteman was now the king of symphonic jazz. And it was this genre that would become so identified with emerging Café Society that would reach its fruition during the 1930s.

The concert was not a commercial success; Whiteman personally lost thousands of dollars he invested in putting on the performance, despite many being turned away. Nevertheless, what the bandleader lost initially was actually the best investment he could have made in his career and those of his musicians. To placate those who could not enjoy the original performance, Whiteman scheduled another one three weeks later, and the second performance was sold out as well. Whiteman now sensed he had inadvertently touched a nerve with people with his particular renditions of compositions, and he chose to maximize this newfound interest in his musical performances. Booking agents sent Whiteman's office phone ringing off the hook. Whiteman accepted an offer to perform at the Philadelphia Academy of Music in April. Later that month, Whiteman and Gershwin gave a benefit concert at Carnegie Hall for a music scholarship fund, and this too sold out. While the audience realized they were listening to great performances, they may not have known they were witnessing the performance of a composing legend in the making—George Gershwin. Many years, even decades later, those who attended the Whiteman-Gershwin concerts would recall their attending these historic performances and watching Gershwin perform in person. "Rhapsody in Blue" became Whiteman's signature composition, which he almost always performed at every venue.

An agent at the New York Metropolitan Musical Bureau succeeded in signing Whiteman and his orchestra to a concert tour guaranteeing $10,000 per week. Gershwin even agreed to perform with Whiteman's orchestra on as many scheduled performances as he could during the spring of 1924. Concerts were held in upstate New York, Pittsburgh, Cleveland, Indianapolis, and St. Louis among a fifteen-city tour, but Gershwin had to return to New York before the band left for Canada so he could compose for George White's *Scandals*. That June, Whiteman and his orchestra met with Gershwin for the historic first recording at the Victor studios of "Rhapsody in Blue."

The remainder of 1924 was spent recording in the studio in Camden, New Jersey, which boasted of the new Orthophonic recording technique, and making numerous concert tours further and further from Manhattan. It seemed every state wanted to see and hear the Paul Whiteman Orchestra perform, and they were not limited to major cities. Smaller cities in Nebraska, Missouri, South Dakota, Wisconsin and Illinois, for example, were finally able to experience the famed Whiteman sound. It was a hectic career for all the musicians, and those men who could not bring their wives along learned of the strain it put on their marriages. In 1925, the concert tour schedule expanded, as the hottest jazz orchestra in America crisscrossed the country. Whiteman traveled in his own Pullman railroad car, while his musicians rode in sleeper coaches, but none of them were complaining. They were living the life they wanted to as musicians.

Whiteman was very discerning about the technical skill of his musicians. He wanted the best for his orchestras and he had more money than any other band leader to get them. One of his saxophonists was paid over $40,000 a year, and this was in the mid–1920s. Whiteman himself was earning over a quarter of a million dollars a year at this point. His perfectionism in selecting musicians was discernible to other professionals. None other than Serge Rachmaninoff, who had listened to Whiteman's orchestra perform, was incredulous at their performance. "Who does this?" Rachmaninoff asked in disbelief and admiration in hearing the musicians. "Who has taught them? An orchestra of virtuosos."[3]

Whiteman recognized the roots of jazz were clearly based on black composition and performance, while all of his musicians were white. Whiteman saw jazz as a non-racial issue while acknowledging its true roots. When Duke Ellington began a long run with his small group of musicians at various clubs in midtown Manhattan, Whiteman and Grofé went to listen as much as their hectic schedule allowed. Whiteman saw the genius in Ellington's performance on the piano and listened carefully to each number, trying to glean the essence of the true jazz they were listening to. Whiteman wanted to embrace more of the essence of jazz in his performances, and he and Grofé struggled to achieve this. Whiteman and Ellington had a mutual respect for each other, and years later, Ellington wrote of his impressions of Whiteman and what he was achieving in jazz music. Ellington felt Whiteman's music was taking the snobbishness out of jazz and providing opportunities for musicians.

In 1926, Whiteman made a discovery in the voice of Bing Crosby. Actually, it was Crosby, along with another performer, Al Rinker, who sought out Whiteman. The band leader liked what he heard and signed the two to join his orchestra. Their first performance with Whiteman and the orchestra was in Chicago in December of that year. While in Chicago, Whiteman made several new recordings and included the first collaboration with Crosby and Rinker, who sang "Wistful and Blue."

Whiteman had been entertaining the idea of having an exclusive club of his own in New York City. Past experience told him he could keep it packed night after night. After months of planning and negotiating with investors, the Whiteman Club on 48th Street just off Broadway opened in February 1927. The first weeks the club was indeed packed with eager listeners and dancers, but interest could not be sustained for the months that followed, and the Whiteman Club eventually closed. It was his first business failure, but Whiteman quickly recovered.

His success during the 1920s spawned many competitors. These included Fred Waring, Ben Bernie, George Olsen, Ray Miller, Art Landry, King Oliver, the pair of Ohman and Ardon, and Miff Mole. However, Whiteman topped them all when it came to recording. The famous bandleader spent almost 70 days in 1928 in the recording studio. However, the Victor recording company was looking for ways to save money, and his musicians were facing lower recording session payments, and Whiteman was competing with Victor music director Nathaniel Shilkret. What this came down to was a professional conflict of interest. In simple terms, Whiteman was losing his power in the recording studio. Whiteman seriously began considering going to another recording label, and Columbia looked like a very good possibility. In addition, Columbia was pioneering the shift from cylinder to 10-inch and long-playing 12-inch flat disc 78 rpm records. Whiteman met with Columbia executives and they soon came to a contractual agreement. His contract with Victor was soon to expire, and now he and his musicians were prepared to make the switch.

It seemed to many in Manhattan the pace of life was picking up. The prosperity was palpable. The number of stage productions, musical performances by bands like those of Paul Whiteman, movies, and in fact all forms of entertainment seemed endless. Now, Manhattan was witnessing changes to its own skyline. This was fueled by the fortunes of New York's key moneymen and ambitions which seemed to have no bounds. It would result in some of the most famous buildings in New York—and the world.

The Race to the Sky

The prosperity of the latter 1920s also initiated a building boom in New York City. The financial district was perhaps the first to benefit from this as banks and insurance companies chose to expand, and have an impressive structure that spoke of the institution's solid reputation, confidence, trust and corporate prestige. Soon, however, the building of skyscrapers moved to midtown Manhattan and to heights only previously imagined. The financing of such structures hinged on the number of floors and the ultimate rentable square footage that was calculated by a rather straightforward formula. During this time, however, there was a new incentive to be first with the tallest. This incentive had nothing to do with dollars and cents; it was personal.

In the spring of 1928, real estate developer August Reynolds unveiled the renderings and drawings of a 67-story skyscraper having a total of nine hundred thousand square feet of rentable space.[4] The architect of the building was William Van Alen. It was initially identified as the Reynolds Building, but within a year, it would be known by another name: Chrysler. What Reynolds was selling was not a building but an idea. Reynolds was a consummate salesman, and he sold Walter P. Chrysler on the idea of underwriting the expense of building Van Alen's design. Chrysler was definitely interested. The automotive titan had acquired the Dodge Brothers as a brand and he was launching a new low-priced brand as well: Plymouth. Chrysler was intent on taking on Ford and General Motors to challenge their positions in the automotive marketplace. Walter P. Chrysler had vast visions, and a sparkling new skyscraper in the heart of New York City was the right idea at the right time.

Although the Chrysler Corporation was based in Detroit, Walter Chrysler had his New York offices at 347 Madison Avenue, and he spent a great deal of time there. In November 1928, Chrysler met William Van Alen for the first time. The two men spoke a great deal about the vision of the building and they had a meeting of the minds. Van Alen certainly sensed this commission would probably be the biggest of his architectural career. However, after looking at the renderings and drawings of the building as originally conceived, Chrysler was not enthusiastic. He had a much different idea, and he wanted to sound out Van Alen to see if the architect was married to the design. He listened to Chrysler carefully and weighed his responses with as much care as he paid to vital building details. The architect was indeed flexible, but then, after all, Chrysler was now the client.

Chrysler told Van Alen he wanted a taller building and unlike anything ever built before. The automaker wanted the architect to travel the world, if necessary, to get the inspiration to design a building that would be a marvel of the world and lend untold prestige to Chrysler Corporation. The two men had a gentlemen's agreement. Incredibly, Chrysler and Van Alen did not sign a contract. They had a mutual trust in each other. All Chrysler demanded of Van Alen was his very best effort.

Van Alen and his junior architects and draftsmen labored for the next several months on the design of the building. Chrysler and his architect conferred routinely over this period, refining aspects of the building to the automaker's wishes. Finally, on March 7, 1929, Chrysler issued the plans and copies of the building's rendering to the expectant press. All the New York dailies made it front-page news, if below the fold. The key specifications were: sixty-eight stories, 809 feet tall, a total volume of 13.6 million cubic feet and 900,000 square feet of rentable space. The building could, by code, hold 11,000 people, and they could be moved among the skyscrapers floors by 37 high-speed elevators. It was billed as the world's tallest building—potentially. The Chrysler Building, as it was identified, reflected the spirit and prosperity of the times. However, Walter P. Chrysler was not the only man with aspirations of architectural greatness.

Craig Severance had an inauspicious start in the field of commercial building architecture. Nevertheless, he became affiliated with a number of great firms before launching his own architectural practice. Dropping out of college normally would impede a promising architectural student from proceeding, but Severance chose to work his way up through several firms and get his experience that way. He joined the firm of Rich & Lamb, laboring over a drafting board on a number of commercial projects for several years. One of the most prestigious architectural firms in the country, Carrère & Hastings, accepted his application and the two men recognized, with time, Severance's design ability. He proved even more helpful as a site superintendent, making sure construction was going according to plan and resolving issues as they came up onsite. This was critical to his future ability on a project that took place starting in the late 1920s as part of the building boom in Manhattan at that time.

In 1914, Severance formed a partnership with Van Alen. Most of their commissions were in New York City. Both Severance and Van Alen became quite successful during the first decade of their partnership and into the 1920s. Severance was the more flamboyant of the two, and flaunted his prosperity and success by driving a Rolls-Royce and enjoying his yacht off Long Island Sound. He also frequently traveled to Europe and often brought his luxury car with him to use in his travels. The problems with the firm arose when Van Alen began to miss important delivery dates for plans, for often taking individual credit for the firm's designs, and other issues. At that point, Severance chose to end the partnership and launch out on his own.

By 1925, Severance had a booming practice, several lead architectural designers, and a large office of junior designers churning out drawings. The national economy and that of New York City were booming, and Severance was in the right place at the right time to take advantage of it. Thus, it was of paramount importance for a New York architect to land important commissions for new buildings in the Wall Street district. One of the most powerful real estate developers in the city was George Ohrstrom. In the late 1920s, he shrewdly acquired several lots in the financial district and succeeded in interesting P.A. Rowley, the vice chairman on the board of the Bank of the Manhattan Company, in Ohrstrom's plan for a new headquarters skyscraper building on Wall Street itself. Rowley was intrigued, but more pieces of this expensive puzzle had to be assembled before the bank might be seriously interested. Ohrstrom hired Paul Starrett and William Starrett, two of the most able and accomplished commercial builders in Manhattan, to handle the construction. Once Ohrstrom had secured the necessary financing, involving negotiations with the Manhattan Bank and other lenders, the project was approved by the board of the bank, and Ohrstrom hired Craig Severance as the architect for what would be called, simply, 40 Wall Street. It would be the tallest building in Manhattan and overshadow every other building in lower Manhattan.

Thus began a professional rivalry between Severance and Van Alen. Each architect became aware of the other's project, and there began a race to the sky. But the closely guarded secret of the ultimate height of each building kept changing as each learned of the other's plans. Finally Severance had plans for the bank building reaching 900 feet and the firm worked valiantly to keep this a tightly guarded secret from the public and Van Alen in particular. Then, in August 1929, the architectural world was abuzz with the news that the site of the Waldorf Astoria Hotel at 34th Street and Fifth Avenue was being purchased for the creation of yet another skyscraper. The owners of the legendary hotel had plans for a new hotel in the city, but what would happen to the existing structure? Sadly, it was to be razed in order to make way for a new commercial building. However, this would be a most notable building in its own right, and would compete for the title of the tallest building in Manhattan. This project also had some powerful backers and promoters and this new building had a name in keeping with its grand vision: the Empire State Building.

Thus, in 1929 the citizens of New York City watched three massive buildings rise from street level in a three-way race for the title of the tallest building in the city: the Chrysler Building, 40 Wall Street and the Empire State Building. The head of the consortium for the Empire State Building was politician Al Smith, and he released statements that this building would be the tallest in the city: "It's going to be the largest office building in the world and the largest single real estate undertaking in the history of the country."[5] Smith went on to state this epic building would measure nearly 1000 feet in height, provide office and business space for 60,000 people, and have three million square feet of rentable space.

The pace at which these three buildings were erected was breathtaking, but the Empire State Building had a late start. People working in other, lesser skyscrapers would note the height of the two buildings under construction on a Monday, and absentmindedly forget about them until Friday. They would look out to the Chrysler and Manhattan Building and be startled to see they had risen several floors since Monday. So it went during the feverish summer and fall months of 1929. In fact, the 64th floor of the Chrysler building was completed in September. That same month, the Manhattan Company Building, as 40 Wall Street was referred to, was also nearing completion. However, the building that would follow them would end up beating them both.

John Jacob Raskob was the man behind the Empire State Building project. During the 1920s, he had managed to amass a personal fortune approaching $100 million. He had devoted practically every waking hour during 1929 to bringing the massive building project together. Those considering financing the project could read the financial reports and news articles, and the bankers were understandably nervous about starting yet another skyscraper with the Chrysler and the Manhattan Company Building due to open in 1930 and the financial markets displaying figurative cracks in the foundations. Raskob became famous as a deal closer, and he was determined to close this one as well. At a lunch meeting with those who would underwrite the project, Raskob had words of assurance.

"Gentlemen, a country which can provide the vision, the resources, the money and the people to build such an edifice as this," Raskob stated, boldly gesturing to the impressive architectural model on the nearby table, "surely cannot be allowed to crash through lack of support from the likes of you and me."[6] By the time he had made that statement, the Waldorf Astoria was being razed so the site could be cleared for the skyscraper that would be built there. The architectural firm chosen for the building was Shreve, Lamb and Harmon.

Even as the Chrysler and Manhattan Company Building were in the later stages of their construction, the two buildings battled for height supremacy as plans were altered for the spires of each building. The *New York Evening Telegram* printed a story in October 1929 stating the Bank of Manhattan Building, with its latest architectural changes, would rank it twenty feet taller than the 905-foot Chrysler Building. Naturally, Walter P. Chrysler would not settle for this, and he got together with Van Alen to see what could be done about it. Even as the battle for the sky continued, the market on Wall Street had already started its tumble.

The Market Peak and Slide

Indications of financial market volatility were witnessed as early as June of 1928. During the first three weeks of that month, the Dow Jones Industrial Average lost all the gains it had made since March. Numerous financial advisors stated the bull market of the 1920s was over. It was not. The market had corrected, and then it was off and running again. The number of shares traded daily on the New York Stock Exchange (NYSE) during that same three-month period went from just over 3.8 million shares to over five million shares on June 12, with stock tickers lagging more than two hours behind when the market closed. While many worried that this was an alarming trend, none other than Andrew W. Mellon issued a statement that there was no cause for worry, and that the wave of prosperity that was washing over the land would continue. Many believed him and eagerly joined in the market.

After the election of Herbert Hoover for president in November, there was something of a boom in share buying just under the June 12 record. Then, on November 16, a new record of 6,641,250 shares were traded. In December, there was a selloff in segments of the financial markets. Radio Corporation of America, for example, fell a shocking 72 points from its high of 420. Nevertheless, other stocks recorded dramatic gains during the year. Du Pont rose from an already high 310 to 525, and Montgomery Ward rose from 117 to

440, as just two examples. During 1928, over 920 million shares traded hands, significantly more than the over 575 million shares during 1927. Brokers' loans to buy stocks on margin boomed during 1928 to nearly six billion dollars.[7] Financial speculation on this scale had not been experienced by Wall Street in its history.

In February 1929, the Federal Reserve Board proposed the rediscount rate for business borrowers should be raised one point to six percent, in an effort to put the brakes on speculation. This was not followed through with until sometime in August. In March 1929, the heads of the Federal Reserve banks around the country were meeting in Washington, it was believed, with the new president and others in the nation's capital. No statements were forthcoming from the Federal Reserve over these behind-closed-doors meetings, and investors, brokers and money managers began to get nervous and worry. Then, on Monday, March 25, significant selling started taking place, and grew during the week. On March 26 over eight million shares traded hands, and the word was out. The Fed was silent, and its silence bred fear in the market. Suddenly, the financial speculators who had seen nothing but a rising market for months were hit with alarming losses and were informed of such in a dreaded telegram demanding more margin.

This momentary panic was stayed not by the recalcitrant Federal Reserve Board, but by one of the country's most powerful and influential bankers, Charles E. Mitchell. In a widely published statement, Mitchell said National City Bank would loan money as necessary to prevent any market liquidation. Within 24 hours, the market stabilized. In Wall Street, perception is often reality, and that directs the buying and selling, and thus the direction of the DJIA.

Following individual stocks, the speculation tool of choice during 1928 and 1929 was the investment trust. Between 1927 and 1929 the value of investment trusts sold to the public rose from $400 million to roughly three billion dollars. Loosely defined, an investment trust was the mutual fund of its day. Those who bought into these investment trusts felt they could rely on the wisdom of the trust managers, and the diversity of the bonds, preferred and common stock held within the trust. To the unsophisticated, investment trusts appeared to be the alchemy of turning some base metal into gold. Those with more wisdom knew that any speculative investment that rose could also fall—sometimes dramatically. Nevertheless, the years of 1928 and 1929 could be seen in hindsight as nothing more or less than a classic mania of the sort history has often been witness to.

In these barely regulated investment trusts, the web of financial vehicles and how they were controlled were often a mystery with nothing more than faith that kept the trusts growing. One such trust was the United Founders Corporation, which claimed to have resources of over $686 million. With numbers like that, it had to be sound, many investors reasoned. Over this fulcrum of trust, much of the invested moneys were leveraged. Dollar signs in the investors' eyes appeared as the value of the investment trust went up. Few gave any thought what would happen if the markets went down. Investment trusts became a burgeoning market in themselves. After all, markets were sound, according to everyone from the president on down. One of the biggest proponents of speculative investment trusts was Goldman, Sachs & Company.

During the summer of 1929, the DJIA knew only continued appreciation. Individual shares also surged. Incredibly, Westinghouse during that summer went from 151 to 286 points, General Electric from 268 to 391, and even the staid American Telephone & Telegraph went from 209 to 303. This was happening across the board. It was not uncommon for investors to conduct their trades even from ocean liners departing for or returning from Europe; the telegraph rooms on those ships were kept operating around the clock so the transactions could be waiting on the brokers' desks when they arrived in the morning. Also, brokers' loans mushroomed during the summer of 1929, increasing by $400 million *a month.*

There were a number of wise voices of warning amidst the cacophony of unrestrained investment speculation. Among them was Paul M. Warburg of the International Acceptance Bank. He issued statements admonishing the Federal Reserve to take on a stronger restraining influence in the markets, for if this was not done, there would be economic calamity, even a national depression. The financial services firms of the Standard Statistics Company and Poor's, which would later merge and become Standard & Poor's, wrote papers cautioning investors about the delusion of ever-increasing common stock values. These voices of reason, however, were drowned out by what was nothing less than a mania, like so many manias of the past.

However, it is a commonly held belief that virtually every American was investing in the stock market, no matter how few shares they held. In fact, only 1.5 million people, out of a total American population at the time of roughly 120 million, were actively involved in stock speculation, a Senate investigative committee learned during the 1930s.[8]

Many wondered when or even if the great bull market of the 1920s would come to an end, or if it would just keep climbing into the 1930s. It has been recorded that, in fact, the bull market of the New York Stock Exchange ended on September 3, 1929. On that day, AT&T reached 304, J.I. Case 350, New York Central Railroad 256, and RCA 505. Those and many other companies never saw such highs again. While historians state the market crashed in October, the selloff began in September; the mood had decidedly changed, and savvy investors and even speculators began to bail out of the market. But not all of them; many chose to ride it to the very bottom in the belief their losses would be temporary and their stocks would rebound.

Financial historians record that America, in fact, was already well into the throes of an economic depression based on other factors apart from the stock market. Production indexes had peaked in June and had already begun to descend. Steel production, a strong indicator of financial health, had been steadily falling since June, for example. Freight car shipments of all goods had also been dropping during the summer. Only those with their finger on the pulse of these vital indicators would sense impending financial disaster. It would appear that some had sensed this coming and had begun to sell during the first week of September. As word spread, like dominoes, the selling spread to individual investors and institutions. And yet, there were those who refused to believe the bubble had burst, and there might yet be a recovery to the rapidly declining stock values.

There would be little doubt regarding this during October 1929. On Sunday, October 20, 1929, the *New York Times* splashed the headline, "Stocks Driven Down as Wave of Selling Engulfs the Market."[9] At that time, the stock market was open on Saturdays, and the headline reflected the previous day's results. On Monday the 21st, massive selling continued, with over six million shares sold—the third highest volume in the market's history to date. There was a curious, surreal lag of information *vis-à-vis* market conditions in this plunging market. More than a few investors and speculators were financially wiped out but did not know it for hours after the market closed because of the stock ticker was backlogged with punching out the tape. Stocks almost across the board were declining daily, and the DJIA continued its steady decline as well. Incredibly, and as a measure of the degree of panic selling taking place, on October 24 nearly thirteen million shares were sold, and sold to those who wanted to buy them. The noise rising from the stock exchange floor was a din that drowned out all but the loudest orders. Only the closing bell prompted the shouting to slowly relent.

The decline in the value of many stocks was breathtaking during the last week of October leading into November. Stocks were going for pennies on the dollar. Whereas many had originally sold for hundreds of dollars a share, oftentimes there were no buyers for the stocks at all. Brokers became bewildered at being unable to find a buyer at any price for a stock that had once sold for over $300 a share. Things would continue to get worse—much worse. The investment trusts in which so many hundreds of millions of dollars were invested were now leveraged in reverse and virtually all of the more than 750 trusts simply collapsed and were wiped completely out with resulting total losses of the "investors." Paper profits evaporated in the face of real losses.[10]

Perhaps the only good news during these dark days was the landslide victory of Mayor Jimmy Walker against his opponent Fiorello La Guardia. At least it gave many reason to celebrate at speakeasies all over the city. But many others commiserated at those same speakeasies for the financial losses they experienced. It seemed the market had no bottom. Stocks continued to plummet. Auburn Automobile lost 66 points in a single day. Otis Elevator, with no pun intended, fell 45 points in a single day of trading. The carnage just continued, despite efforts of market support by the biggest banks. It was during this period that legends grew around the few stories of lower Manhattan hotel clerks asking if the hotel room was indeed for sleeping, or did the person wanting a room plan to open the window and jump out. There were a few actual cases where this happened, but it was not at all widespread. In the most-cited story, two men leapt from an upper story window of the Ritz Hotel holding hands. Some simply put a pistol to their head when their despair of being financially wiped out overwhelmed them.

The collapse of the stock market had little effect on plans to build the Empire State Building. It was projected to cost $43 million to build with $16 million of that for the land alone. Completion of the skyscraper was set for May 1, 1931. Initially, the Empire State Building was proposed to have 80 floors. Before the building was completed, it would go much higher in Raskob's quest to beat the Chrysler Building. And in the midst of the financial devastation in lower Manhattan, hundreds of construction workers who were laboring over the Manhattan Bank Building and Chrysler Building would move on to the Empire State Building and other commercial construction projects. The expansive Rockefeller Center would come to mid–Manhattan later.

Van Alen had come up with an ingenious architectural sleight of hand in order to push the total height of the Chrysler Building as high as possible and keep all contenders at bay—or so he thought. He designed a telescoping spire that would extend the height of the building from the original plans first laid out by an additional 185 feet. After this clever spire was finally riveted in place, the Chrysler Building stood 1,046 feet tall. It was officially the tallest building in New York City, including the Manhattan Bank Building. It was even taller than the Eiffel Tower. This occurred just days before the collapse of the stock market that October. Walter P. Chrysler had bragging rights and his building was one of the most striking and handsome in the city. Being the penultimate auto man, Chrysler knew how to promote his newest creation, and he spent significant advertising dollars to attract tenants to the prestigious address of, according to his definition, the tallest building in New York City.

Naturally, those who had backed the Bank of the Manhattan Company fought back with a plausible argument that the tallest point humans could stand in their building was the observation deck, which stood just over 836 feet from ground level, while the observation deck of the Chrysler Building was recorded at 783 feet—a full 53 feet lower. However, in the arena of public opinion, the Chrysler Building still held the honors for the tallest building.

Walter Chrysler's achievement would be short-lived. After the foundations of the Empire State Building had been poured and the foundation beams secured, Manhattan residents marveled at the speed of the construction of each floor's beams of the city's newest skyscraper. However, as each floor of the building rose into the sky, employment among architects and engineers plummeted. Construction in Manhattan dropped 50 percent by the end of 1930 and industrial morale was at its lowest point in decades. However, what was bad for the nation was a financial boon for the cost of building the Empire State Building. In fact, the Empire State Building would end up costing less than $25 million to build due to rapidly falling prices for the primary building materials and other construction costs.[11] Construction continued at a record pace even in December 1930 and the following two months. The office interiors had been completed floor by floor as quickly as the available crews could move on to the next one. Finally, the Empire State Building was officially opened on May 1, 1931. While Walter Chrysler's record of owning the tallest building was eclipsed by the Empire State Building, the car maker's pride in his building, truly stunning amidst Manhattan's skyline, was undiminished.

As the Great Depression deepened from 1931 to 1932, these three buildings stood in defiance of the economic calamity that had befallen the nation and the great city itself. People wanted to listen to music and dance their troubles away or at least ignore them for an evening out on the town, and Paul Whiteman and his bands and orchestras were there to help them do just that. The means of entertainment in New York City during the 1930s was seemingly endless. And if a couple couldn't afford a night on the town, there was always the phonograph that could play a song that could take them away to a place they could not be. Members of Café Society were needed by the establishments they frequented as much as they needed the nightclubs, restaurants and theaters. This co-dependence began in the 1920s and came to fruition in the 1930s. Café Society would live in stark contrast to the many who struggled to even survive, but the skyscrapers that glittered at night and the music that was heard were available to all.

Chapter 6

Effect of the Great Depression on New York Society and Café Society

If a metaphor can be drawn regarding the New York Stock Market crash and the subsequent impact on the city's residents of all socioeconomic backgrounds, it would be that of the RMS *Titanic* cruising at its maximum speed in a dead black night before striking the ghostly iceberg that ripped a fatal wound in its hull and doomed the ship. As Capt. Smith ordered all engines stop and a damage assessment from Thomas Andrews, managing director of Harland & Wolff which built the *Titanic*, there was little concern by the passengers for their survival or that of the ship. They could not possibly know the danger they were in, since it was commonly perceived the ship was unsinkable due to its very tall bulkheads and means of sealing off each of the ship's compartments from adjoining compartments. For that reason, there were a woefully inadequate number of lifeboats. The iceberg had sliced a breach in the ship's hull nearly 200 feet long and when Andrews learned of this, he realized the *Titanic* was doomed. He also knew with the number of lifeboats onboard, only a few hundred would be saved. Over 1500 of its passengers perished and the luxury liner sank to the bottom of the Atlantic Ocean in a matter of hours.

In like manner, although the stock market crash that took place during October and November of 1929 caused countless millions of dollars in losses, reassuring words were issued by the heads of banks and the Federal Reserve itself that the national economy was basically sound and the markets would recover. That did not disguise the fact that those of the wealthy who were heavily invested in the Market took staggering losses. However, financial historians have stated the fundamentals of the national economy—other factors such as over production and production capacity, subsequent government regulations including protective tariffs, among many other issues—were also contributing factors to the subsequent economic depression.

The members of Café Society, while they may not have lost fortunes in the collapse of the stock market, nevertheless felt the economic oppression from the aftermath. Gloria Braggiotti, while retaining her job as a fashion editor for the *New York Post,* recalled years later what it was like for her during the early 1930s: "The depression years were very difficult for us professionally and thrilling socially. We were out of jobs but in on everything else. We used to charge our breakfasts at the drugstore and then go to lavish parties given by people like Condé Nast and Cobina Wright."[1]

Wealth Destruction and Preservation During the Great Depression

The Gilded Age, which embraced the New York Society 400, had essentially faded from its former prominence by the time of the stock market crash. Such lavish, open spending by families like the Astors and the Vanderbilts on huge mansions was not socially advantageous during the economic events of the 1930s. Mrs. Harrison Williams, wife to a utilities magnate who was one of the richest men in America, greatly enjoyed the wealth in her possession and spent it accordingly. She was known to spend in excess of $100,000 per year to buy the best haute couture for her wardrobe, while she and her husband had numerous homes around the country. Her knowledge, appreciation and discernment of art in all its forms made her one of the foremost experts in art collection in the country. However, over-the-top conspicuous consumption in the manner of the Astors and Vanderbilts was, to her way of thinking, passé. She spoke to Lucius Beebe about the transition from Society to Café Society and why it was significant during this period.

"Birth no longer is the prime requisite of society," Beebe records her saying. "If there is a society, it has leveled to personalities of intelligence or cleverness or interest, or to those who are just well liked and have enough money to maintain with reasonable conventional comforts. And that is as it should be."[2] One can imagine Beebe commenting his approval to one of the wealthiest women in America while endeavoring to keep from smiling. However, Mrs. Williams's remark was the essence of what Café Society was in the 1930s. She was herself of humble origins, born Mona Strader in 1899 in Louisville, Kentucky; her father was a horse farm overseer. She married into wealth and divorced twice before marrying Harrison Williams in 1926. Williams, who was 24 years her senior when they married, had founded the American Gas & Electric Company in 1906 and six years later established a tax-sheltered holding company. He was a widower when he met the stunning divorcee and she knew a good thing when she saw him. Williams was undeniably handsome and very wealthy, with an estimated net worth of $700 million in the late 1920s.[3] Although Harrison Williams lost considerable wealth in the market crash and subsequent Great Depression, the Williamses continued to live in the style to which they had become accustomed, but many others were not so fortunate. One need not survey New York City alone to find men who made a vast fortune and lost nearly all of it as a result of the stock market crash and subsequent Great Depression.

Take, for example, Edward T. Stotesbury. Born in Philadelphia in 1849, he grew up there and received a conventional education. He attended Union Business College and joined the investment firm of Drexel & Co. around 1866. His extraordinary career there would span over half a century. By 1882, he was promoted to the position of partner in the firm. He became quite wealthy in the course of directing the financial investments of Drexel itself and its clients. He and his first wife had lived in a mansion in Philadelphia but she died in 1881 giving birth to their third child. He remained a widower for years. He was a devout Quaker, so when he met Mrs. Eva Cromwell in 1909, all he could do was resign himself to her friendship. However, her husband died later that year, and Stotesbury bided his time. He started courting her in 1910 but it was two years before they were married. He was 62 years old.

Stotesbury had held on tightly to his wealth during his first marriage, and later regretted he had not enjoyed more of it with his first wife. He was now worth tens of millions of dollars and he intended to spend it lavishly on his new wife. Eva was quite content with the magnificent home they lived in in Philadelphia until they were invited to attend a ball put on by Peter A.B. Widener at his palatial estate, Lynnewood Hall, in Elkins Park outside of Philadelphia. Widener had amassed his fortune primarily through urban transport in Philadelphia and other major cities. As their chauffeured limousine approached the Widener mansion, Eva was almost speechless. As they walked through the three-story portico, then the entrance and into the Grande Hall, it was a revelation to her. She had never seen anything so magnificent. Her years living in Washington, D.C., with her first husband and seeing the Gilded Age homes there did not prepare her for this. "Ned," as she called him, just chuckled, not yet of a mind to build such a residence himself. Eva toured the 110-room mansion and marveled at the exquisite art collection Widener displayed in the art gallery that the traction magnate was known for. All this left an indelible impression on Mrs. Stotesbury.

Stotesbury himself prospered even more in the early 1920s and he was also compensated as a board member of numerous other large corporations. As the couple increasingly entertained at their Philadelphia mansion, it appeared their present home was inadequate for their increasing position within Main Line society. They mutually agreed a new, much larger home was needed. Architect Horace Trumbauer had designed the remodeled Philadelphia mansion for the Stotesburys and he had also designed Lynnewood Hall. They commissioned Trumbauer to design a new country residence in the Whitemarsh Valley. It took four years to design and build Whitemarsh Hall, but in 1920 the Stotesburys moved into their 147-room mansion. As the 1920s roared, the Stotesburys entertained on a grand scale there, but only during the spring and fall seasons. During the summer, they lived at their mansion Wingwood House in Bar Harbor, Maine; during the winter months they lived in the Palm Beach, Florida, mansion El Mirasol. By 1929, Edward T. Stotesbury was estimated to be worth $100 million. He was spending over one million dollars a year on the maintenance of their three properties.

The stock market crash and subsequent economic depression ravaged Stotesbury's extensive and diverse economic holdings. After threats were made against the Stotesburys and a possible bomb plot suggested against Whitemarsh Hall, they temporarily closed their three mansions in 1932 and took an extended trip to Europe for an undefined period of time until things hopefully cooled off. They did not return to Whitemarsh Hall until 1933, but Ned Stotesbury had only a few more years to live. He died there in May 1938. It was only after Eva's shocking meeting with the executors of her husband's will that she learned the extent of wealth destruction she was faced with. The preliminary assessment by the executors was that his estate holdings had been reduced to four million dollars, but a more careful evaluation a year later disclosed a figure closer to ten million dollars. Estate taxes would seize much of this. She could not afford to maintain the three mansions, so she put Whitemarsh Hall and the other properties up for sale, but during the Great Depression, there were no buyers. She was forced to sell all her personal jewelry to raise money, donated the paintings in the mansion to Philadelphia museums, and moved to Marly, a mansion in Washington, D.C.

Those wealthy individuals with much invested in the superheated stock market indeed lost a great deal in the subsequent crash and depression of the

1930s. However, this was not universal. Mr. and Mrs. Harrison Williams lived very comfortably throughout the 1930s; they enjoyed their Fifth Avenue mansion in New York City and their winter home, Blythedunes, in Palm Beach, Florida, and spent time cruising on their yacht *Warrior*, among the largest motor yachts in the world. Williams had not come to be worth over half a billion dollars by investing carelessly. His wealth had been significantly more than Stotesbury's. The bulk of his holdings had remained in public utilities. Mona Williams became one of the most prominent members of Café Society during that decade.

In counterpoint, many of those within Café Society who had not invested heavily in the stock market escaped relative unscathed. Maury Paul was among New York's highest paid journalists and he had the devoted "Cholly Knickerbocker" readership to merit his lofty salary at the *Journal and American* newspaper. He could quite comfortably afford to buy a Rolls-Royce and kept it throughout the Depression years of the 1930s. Paul kept his comfortable hotel suite and avoided the large mortgage that came with owning a multi-story townhouse on the Upper East Side. In short, he lived well within his means.

His opposite number at the *New York Herald Tribune*, Lucius Beebe, also sidestepped the financial wreckage of some of his wealthier friends and successfully held onto his job at the paper writing "This New York." Not only that, his presence at any one of a dozen nightclubs, restaurants and bars in Manhattan was welcomed with open arms by their proprietors and in almost every case he enjoyed whatever he wished on the menu and bar list completely gratis. (See sidebar.)

The Vanderbilts and the Astors remained at the pinnacle of New York Society, but determining the effect of the Great Depression and new income taxes on their wealth requires diligent research because these families, while still conspicuously displaying their wealth through their palatial homes, kept the facts regarding their wealth and holdings quite private. By and large, the great Society families, who had worked to build up and maintain their wealth over several generations, held onto much of their wealth during the 1930s, and in some cases prospered despite the dismal state of the economy.

Among the Astors during this time, Vincent Astor was a worthy heir to strengthen and expand the family fortune. He was the son of John Jacob Astor IV and Caroline Schermerhorn; she was known as *the* Mrs. Astor during the Gilded Age. Vincent was born in 1891. He was attending Harvard when his father died with the sinking of the RMS *Titanic* in 1912. He inherited more than $80 million, the majority of it in real estate, and this made him wealthier than William K. Vanderbilt, Jay Gould or even John D. Rockefeller.[4] With the heavy responsibilities of managing the family fortune, he chose to leave Harvard while still a freshman. Young Vincent had financial wisdom beyond his years, and he set about refurbishing the Astor family reputation as New York's slum lords. At the Astor head office at 23 West 26th Street he established plans for revitalizing existing rental properties and conceiving new and better ones. He chose to live at the family twin mansion on the corner of Fifth Avenue and 65th Street.

In 1913, he directed a renovation by Tracy & Swartwout of ten houses between 43rd and 44th Streets near Times Square. Astor directed them to combine the separate residences into a single apartment complex having a common courtyard. This became Westover Court and was applauded in the press for its vision. The following year he started an ambitious project called Astor Court located on Broadway between 89th and 90th Streets. He commissioned architect Charles Platt to design this thirteen-story apartment complex. Perfection is often in the details and this building had many handsome details uncommon for the day, which gave it an aesthetic quality that appealed to many eager tenants. Astor Court became a model for excellent apartment building design.[5] Astor continued to commission renovation and new construction projects into the 1920s and 1930s throughout Manhattan and the surrounding boroughs. His great-grandfather, John Jacob Astor, founder of the family fortune, would have disapproved, but Vincent was an Astor with a conscience.

Vincent Astor, nevertheless, lived like an Astor should. During the 1920s, he spent a great deal of time resting and relaxing on his 264-foot yacht *Nourmahal*, and its tremendous range permitted numerous trans–Atlantic crossings. He bought and sold his personal properties and ultimately sold the mansion at 840 Fifth Avenue in 1926. Vincent Astor did not invest heavily in the stock market; this was just not in the Astor blood. The fortune had been built on real estate, and that is where the bulk of it remained. When the portents of an economic depression were voiced in 1928 and 1929, this had little effect on the reckless stock purchases and investment in unregulated trusts. There were other indicators of a weakening economy before the Wall Street collapse in October 1929. While many investors were wiped out, Vincent Astor's wealth remained virtually intact. He took advantage of distressed property prices, which only increased his personal wealth as the economy slowly recovered during the latter 1930s and early 1940s.

The Vanderbilts were a considerably larger clan and the Commodore's wealth upon his death in 1877 had been disbursed among the second and

6. Effect of the Great Depression

third generation. They had been more intent on spending the wealth by building mansions than preserving it and making it grow. Their mansion building had begun in earnest in the 1880s, concentrated in New York City but with additional homes in upstate New York, North Carolina, and Newport, Rhode Island. Richard Morris Hunt, one of America's premier large residence architects, was commissioned by William K. Vanderbilt to design Marble House in Newport, Rhode Island, which was completed in 1892. George Washington Vanderbilt, who inherited ten million dollars, commissioned Hunt to design the largest residence in American history in Asheville, North Carolina. George W. Vanderbilt called it Biltmore and its completion in 1895 consumed much of his wealth. Hunt's architectural office was kept busy with other Vanderbilt commissions, and that same year marked the completion of The Breakers in Newport for Cornelius Vanderbilt II. The offices of McKim, Mead & White designed Florham for Hamilton McKown Twombly and his wife Florence Vanderbilt, who was the daughter of William H. Vanderbilt and the granddaughter of Cornelius Vanderbilt. Florham, situated in the rather off-the-beaten-track location in Morris County, New Jersey, was completed in 1897.[6]

Through the 1920s, the Vanderbilts continued to live as they always had and trusted their holdings to provide them the money to do so. The last mansion to be built by a Vanderbilt was erected in 1925 when Florence Twombly commissioned a new home on the corner of Fifth Avenue and 71st Street.[7] There, at age 71, she became the *grand dame* of New York Society, even though the Gilded Age had long passed. Competing with her was Grace Vanderbilt, who resided at 640 Fifth Avenue in one of the earliest Vanderbilt Fifth Avenue mansions. Grace and her husband Neily Vanderbilt moved into 640 in 1914 and the mansion received extensive reconstruction in 1916. Both Florence and Grace entertained extensively in their respective Fifth Avenue mansions throughout the 1920s and 1930s, even though their fortunes were damaged by the Great Depression. The Vanderbilts knew no other way to live. Those who could no longer be bothered with dealing with dozens of servants and the staggering cost of maintenance and mounting taxes simply moved into the Plaza or Waldorf Astoria hotels.

Among the most intriguing personalities during the 1930s and the focus of much attention during the era of Café Society was Barbara Hutton, granddaughter of Frank W. Woolworth and heiress to the five-and-dime magnate's fortune and her father's as well. Woolworth had launched the first of his five-and-ten-cent stores in 1879. Woolworth's marriage to Jennie Creighton produced three daughters. Helena, Jessie and Edna Woolworth grew up in privilege and wealth as their father's fortune grew with the expansion of the chain of stores across America and into Europe. Financier Ed Hutton married Marjorie Post (of Post cereals), and his brother Frank, who had co-founded E.F. Hutton, married Edna Woolworth. Edna was the most beautiful of the three daughters and Frank was undeniably handsome; and it was little wonder their first and only child would also be a beauty as well. When she was born in New York City on November 14, 1912, the wealthy couple named her Barbara. Edna learned of her husband's infidelities and committed suicide when Barbara was four years old. Frank Hutton had been an absentee father and little Barbara actually went to live with Grandfather Woolworth in his Fifth Avenue mansion in 1916.[8]

Remembering neither the love of her mother or even the concern of her father, Barbara grew up with her aging grandfather and a grandmother who was suffering from senile dementia. Woolworth died in 1919 and his wife in 1922, and as Woolworth's will had declared, Barbara came into a fortune with a carefully crafted trust. The figures for her inheritance vary according to different sources, but it was in the tens of millions of dollars. She grew up attending elite boarding schools. Edward Hutton and his wife showed more concern and care for Barbara than her father. Nevertheless, Frank Hutton invested much of her inheritance wisely and the fortune grew dramatically during that decade. Hutton also had the financial wisdom to see the vast financial bubble that had grown, realizing it would one day burst. He liquidated Barbara's, and no doubt his own, investments at stupendous profit. When the stock market plunged in October and November 1929, young Barbara's vast holdings were secure, as were those of her father and uncle.

The visits to her aunt, Marjorie Post Hutton, and her breathtaking estate, Mar-a-Lago, in Palm Beach, Florida, were formative to the teenager. Her aunt also had a luxury residence on Fifth Avenue, one of the largest yachts in the world, and essentially anything great wealth could buy. Marjorie Post and her husband continued to live quite unaffected by the deepening economic depression. Having never really known her mother, she patterned herself after her aunt Marjorie, who became her role model. At age 18 she gave a lavish debutante party in New York City in December 1930 at a cost of $60,000 Depression-era dollars, with Astors, Vanderbilts and Rockefellers in attendance. Her very public coming out drew the attention of the eager press and she was never out of the limelight. Barbara Hutton's wealth at such a young age fascinated America, and she was relentlessly dubbed the "Poor Little Rich Girl."

Her father had since remarried and her new stepmother intended to exploit Barbara's notoriety in an attempt to break into American and European society. The Woolworth heiress was introduced to Queen Mary and she was launched into the dying world of the British aristocracy. She danced with the Prince of Wales, among many others, and was taken under the wing of social hostess Elsa Maxwell, who wanted to be the arbiter of Barbara's comings and goings. With Maxwell's whirlwind parties and gatherings in France and New York, Barbara Hutton was known personally to every legitimately and illegitimately titled man. In 1933 she married Prince Alexis Mdivani from the Republic of Georgia. The Paris wedding in June of that year was front-page news in every metropolitan newspaper in America and many newspapers in Europe. However, he was abusive to Barbara and she divorced him in 1935. Prince Mdivani was killed in a car accident just months after the divorce and once again Barbara Hutton was in the news, with the newspapers eager for front-page stories that might boost circulation and offer a distraction from the economic malaise gripping America.

She did not remain a widow for very long. She quickly married Count Kurt von Haugwitz-Reventlow of Denmark and within a year they had a son named Lance. The very attractive couple were in great demand in America among Café Society circles and European courts. The Countess Reventlow was for much of the 1930s apart of the cult of celebrity that was of such interest to Americans, regardless of their financial state. Her wealth remained relatively unaffected by the Great Depression, but her life would be no better or happier possessing it.

Among the most esteemed members of New York Café Society was composer George Gershwin. He had built up an astonishing record of musical achievement by the end of the 1920s and became one of the highest paid composers of the decade. He earned his money from commissions for complete songbooks for stage productions, private commissions, and royalties from the sales of his recorded music. He was without doubt the most prolific of musical composers of his day, and in most cases he collaborated with his brother Ira, who wrote the lyrics for all the vocal pieces. George and Ira Gershwin, in fact, grew wealthy together. George was seen more frequently because he often played his compositions on piano. Ira did not play the piano and was often overshadowed by his brother for this reason.

The perception of George Gershwin was that he composed constantly, and rarely had time for his other personal interests, but this would be a gross misperception. Gershwin's wealth, relative to other composers, permitted him to indulge in his passion for modern art collecting, and in the sports of skiing, hiking, tennis, fishing, swimming, horseback riding and golfing, among other activities he enjoyed doing. He lived his life with panache, taking great joy in all this physical activity, and his comfortable financial position allowed him the means to do so. He also had a very active social life, and in Manhattan, he had a great many talented friends he often spent time with. Gershwin was a skilled dancer, and enjoyed sharing his advice with Fred Astaire regarding dance steps for his compositions for movies. The legendary dancer received that advice with admiration; Gershwin and Astaire were peers in their respective crafts. Gershwin used every minute of every waking hour to live life to the full. Ira, on the other hand, was more bookish, and more of an introvert who enjoyed the comforts of his home while reading his many collected books.

Jazz composer George Gershwin was among the elite within New York Café Society, and he often debuted new musical compositions in the homes of other creative New Yorkers before performing them before audiences. His symphonic jazz compositions like "Rhapsody in Blue" and "An American in Paris" were the quintessence of sophisticated Manhattan music (Library of Congress).

In 1929, the brothers moved into two separate penthouses at 33 Riverside Drive between West 75th and 76th Streets.[9] Gershwin had, by the mid–1920s, maids who prepared his meals and performed other personal tasks for the great composer, and staff assistants to help with his duties related to his work. His staff always followed him wherever he moved in Manhattan. With the demands for composing musicals, both George and Ira needed to live close together since they collaborated on so many commissions. George Gershwin never married, but the handsome and wealthy composer had numerous love affairs during the 1920s and 1930s.

Gershwin did have stock investments, and with the stock market booming in the latter 1920s, there was no reason for the composer not to invest a portion of his income in stocks as well. Consequently, his stock holdings did suffer losses in the market crash in October 1929. However, biographer Howard Pollack, while writing that Gershwin suffered losses in the tens of thousands of dollars, does not say how quickly Gershwin moved to liquidate them. These losses did not affect his lifestyle in the least. Gershwin's popularity and demand by theatrical producers and film studios was so great with current and future commissions after the market crash that Gershwin remained in a strong cash-rich position.

Universal Pictures approached him for the right to use "Rhapsody in Blue" for the 1930 film *King of Jazz*, and for this and other contributions was paid $50,000 that year as well. During the summer and fall of 1930, the brothers Gershwin worked on a new theater production titled *Girl Crazy*. For this, they received an equally large commission, and it was well-earned. After a preliminary opening in Philadelphia September 29, 1930, *Girl Crazy* opened at the Alvin Theater in New York on October 14, 1930. It starred the 19-year-old Ginger Rogers in her theatrical debut, and Ethel Merman, among other new stars. The incomparable compositions by George with lyrics by Ira for "I Got Rhythm," "Embraceable You," "But Not For Me," and twelve others, along with rousing performances by the cast, made *Girl Crazy* the sensation of the 1930 theater season. The show received excellent reviews and performances were frequently sold out. It ran for 272 performances on Broadway and grossed over one million dollars.[10]

With an offer to write the musical numbers for a film, Ira and George Gershwin temporarily moved to Hollywood and naturally rented a home in Beverly Hills. The Fox film studio hired the Gershwins to write the music for a film, *Delicious*. Gershwin earned $70,000 (while brother Ira received $30,000) for compositions for the film. Once again, George Gershwin was in his element because the movie was about New York City. The signature composition for the film was "Second Symphony," which had several working titles, including "Manhattan Rhapsody" and "New York Rhapsody." Ira Gershwin enjoyed the pace of filmmaking, which allowed a more leisurely work schedule and a lot of time to see the stars who were so eager to meet the famous composer and lyricist team. George Gershwin, however, would be disappointed with the result as seen and heard in the film. A number of Gershwin's compositions were shortened in the film. The scope of his work was hampered by the limits of the medium, not the least of which was the low audio quality achievable with film in the 1930s. The film debuted in December 1931 in New York at the Roxy Theater, with crowds lined up even on Christmas day. Interestingly, a number of music critics considered the "Second Rhapsody" less ambitious and satisfying than "Rhapsody in Blue." Paul Whiteman continued to hold his concerts devoted to his Experiment in American Music, with the fourth installment held at Carnegie Hall, where his orchestra performed this new Gershwin rhapsody in November 1932.

Gershwin received more positive and critical acclaim with his music, along with his brother's lyrics, for the musical *Of Thee I Sing* of 1931. The playbook was written by the winning team of George S. Kaufman and Morrie Ryskind. Part musical, part political satire and part comedy, it would prove to be the Gershwins' most successful Broadway production of their careers. The show opened in December 1931 at the Music Box Theater to a sold-out audience. First night attendees included Irving Berlin, actress Lillian Gish, Samuel Goldwyn, philanthropist Otto Kahn, Ethel Barrymore, Mayor Jimmy Walker, and many more. The show was so brilliant and clever, with critics especially praising Ira Gershwin for his lyrics, that Kaufman, Ryskind and Ira Gershwin were awarded the Pulitzer Prize for the best American play of 1931. The continuously sold-out tickets soon resulted in the production's being moved to the larger 46th Street Theater. By the end of its first full year, *Of Thee I Sing* had grossed $1.5 million. Both the Gershwins were investors in the production and profited accordingly. It ran for 441 performances before finally closing on January 14, 1933.

The 1930s would prove a repeat of George's prolific work during the 1920s. Apart from new ambitious compositions, Gershwin continued to support stage productions his New York audiences could not get enough of. The composer embarked on a folk opera, *Porgy and Bess*. Edwin DuBose Heyward, the author of the novel, was hired by Gershwin to write the libretto in a collaboration with Ira Gershwin. The story, taken from the novel, takes place in a black tenement around the late 1920s in Charleston, South Carolina. The cast was entirely African American, and while most of the musical compositions are not known, the signature piece, "Summertime," is a classic of the American stage and was heard by millions. The production opened in Boston in September 1935, and the following month it opened at the Alvin Theater. It ran for 124 performances, but after initial financial success that more than covered costs of the nightly production, ticket sales began to fall and it closed in January 1936 in the red.[11]

Movie musicals had experienced something of a revival in the mid-1930s, with the popularity of the Busby Berkeley productions and a run of films starring the dancing duo of Fred Astaire and Ginger Rogers. In addition there had been technical improvements in the recording of sound and the ability to edit prerecorded music with the soundtrack. George Gershwin, after the demanding work for *Porgy and Bess*, wanted to return to the musical genre, and had his agent put out feelers for potential contract work on such a film. Gershwin's financial demands were very high; he wanted $100,000 for three months' work plus a percentage of the film's gross. All the prospective studios balked at this, countering that even Jerome Kern and Irving Berlin were now composing for films at significantly lower compensation. Kern, for example, signed an agreement with RKO Studios to compose the music for *Swing Time* for $50,000 and a percentage of the profits.

Faced with this reality, the Gershwins agreed to a fee of $55,000 to do the music and lyrics for RKO on an Astaire-Rogers film which eventually was titled *Shall We Dance*. Among the memorable numbers were "Let's Call the Whole Thing Off," and "They Can't Take That Away from Me." The film opened in the spring of 1937 and received excellent reviews from virtually all the film critics, but it was far less commercially successful than *Top Hat*, which had earned over one million dollars at the box office. *Shall We Dance* pulled in $413,000.[12]

George and Ira Gershwin had begun work on another film, *Damsel in Distress*, in January 1937 and continued working on it until May. Gershwin had been complaining of headaches and resulting severe mood swings. Inexplicably, Gershwin was not immediately taken to a specialist to try to determine what the problems was. It was not until June of that year he was admitted to a hospital. In July he collapsed in the home of a friend in Hollywood and was rushed to a hospital, where he fell into a coma. George Gershwin died from a brain tumor on July 11. He was only 38 years old. The composer's death was front-page news in practically every newspaper in the United States. One can only speculate about the body of work George Gershwin would have written over the next forty years had he not died a premature death. Ira Gershwin continued to compose lyrics for many years thereafter.

This eclectic mix of creative people, financiers, heiresses and journalists shows the breadth of the lifestyles not often considered during the 1930s when reviewing the Great Depression. It dispels the preconceived notion that nearly everyone suffered during this time, which was clearly not the case. Even in the midst of economic chaos, New York Café Society prospered, dined, danced and celebrated their life among their peers.

Excerpt from "The Depression Years" in *The Lucius Beebe Reader*.[13]

> I can only say that, while I may be one of a microscopic band of survivors, I lived higher on the hog through the disaster years of 1929 to 1934 than I ever have before or since. Stockbrokers might be tossing themselves from upper floors in numbers making it advisable to walk in the middle of Wall

Street or William Street. The men might be coming for the pianos at the stately homes of Syosset and East Hampton, and the soup kitchen might be going at full blast from the Battery to the Bronx, but I, for one, rode it out tearing at pheasant *en plumage* like Henry VIII lunching with Cardinal Wolsey, and cuffing magnums of Bollinger '26, a particularly delectable vintage, from the Plaza in Fifty-ninth Street to the Bermudiana Hotel in Hamilton. I was repeatedly nominated for lists of the best-dressed and most versatile men about New York. My photo in glad evening attire glared at less fortunate passersby in Radio City, and Carino, the maître d'hôtel at El Morocco and the snootiest waiter captain in town, received me with princely honors.

None of these boons and usufructs cost anything, or if token payment was exacted, it was at the approximate rate of ten cents on the dollar. My weekly salary from the *New York Herald Tribune*, of thirty-five dollars, judiciously portioned out, enabled me to enjoy a way of life associated in more normal times only with Henry C. Frick and Diamond Jim Brady.

The secret of this five-year skirmish among the fleshpots usually reserved for our betters was that young and reasonably attractive people of both sexes were in greater demand as shills in the luxury spots of town

The bar at El Morocco was a popular location for "the names that made news," as Lucius Beebe often wrote in his column, "This New York." Here, Beebe shares some conversation with actress Gloria Swanson and George Schlee, husband of fashion designer Valentina. The couple on the right are not identified (Jerome Zerbe, by permission).

6. Effect of the Great Depression

than may be even faintly imaginable to the current generation. For peanuts I occupied a five-hundred-dollar-a-month suite at the Madison, the only condition being that half a dozen times a day I walk through the lobby looking prosperous, and dine, on the cuff, in the Madison Restaurant, then under the management of the now legendary Theodore Titze of the Ritz. I was supposed to look carefree and bountifully stoked with *foie gras* and forty-year-old Hennessy, which, in fact, I was.

CHAPTER 7

This New York: Maury Paul, Lucius Beebe and Walter Winchell

Maury Paul had a routine to his day and it did not vary despite the worsening national and New York economy. Banks were closing in increasing numbers throughout Manhattan in 1930, shops were being shuttered, and unemployment had more than tripled since the fall of 1929, but for "Cholly Knickerbocker" life and work went on virtually unchanged. He would awaken around 9:00 a.m. in his penthouse apartment bedroom, having moved from his ninth-floor apartment some years before, and inform his manservant he wanted breakfast. Paul would be brought the morning copy of the *Journal-American* first edition and would meticulously comb his column for accuracy and any typos. If he found anything amiss he would inform the copy editor, something the copy editor never relished. Next, he would open the *Herald Tribune* and peruse Howard White's society column. White was among his competition, but that did not prevent Paul from mining the column for ideas.

With this out of the way and breakfast complete, Paul prepared to dress for work. He was a dandy, and he dressed the part. The disheveled Walter Winchell look was anathema to him. His shirts and suits came from London's Bond Street, his ties were silk, he alternated between suspenders and a belt on any given day, his socks were always held up with solid gold buckle garters, and his shoes were either Italian or English. He used hair tonic to control his thinning hairline, and liberally doused himself with his favorite cologne. A final touch was a fresh red carnation in his jacket lapel. He would inform his mother he was leaving, she would wish him a good day, and after the elevator ride to the ground floor, he would hail a cab for the short ride to his cramped office at the *Journal-American*. Once at his desk, he partially reversed the procedure: after placing the carnation in a waiting glass of water, he would hang up the jacket, remove the gold cufflinks to roll up his sleeves, unbuckle his straining belt to make himself more comfortable, light up the first of many cigarettes, sit down to his precious notes on the desk, and hammer the keys of his typewriter as he recorded the events for the next column. He would don his reading glasses for work but he was never photographed at any social function with them on.

Paul's long-suffering secretary Eve Brown had fled to Paris in 1929 with her husband after yet another heated argument with Paul had escalated to a shouting match when the pressures of churning out columns seven days a week had proved too much. Although she vowed to never cover the goings-on of New York Society or Café Society again, she actually wound up at the *Paris Herald* writing much the same material. She returned to Paul's services in 1931 and remained with him for more than a decade until his death in 1942.

During Brown's absence, Paul hired another secretary to help him, but he still was the most skilled on the phone in extracting needed information from primary sources or getting vital bits from his select informant chain. His typing paper had to be a specific shade of yellow, and if the newspaper ever ran out, Paul's mood became less than pleasant when white paper had to be substituted. Paul was not a celebrity at the *Journal-American*. To all the others laboring over their typewriters, he was a newspaperman just like them. In a purely working sense, he viewed himself like that as well. His pay scale did not reflect that viewpoint, as he was the highest-paid of the staff of reporters and columnists at the paper.

Precisely at 6:00 p.m. he would complete what he was typing, turn in his copy, shoot his sleeves, put the cufflinks back on, affix his pants and belt, put on his jacket and return to his penthouse. There he would bathe, shave, select his dinner clothing, and set off for any one of a dozen possible venues for the evening. These might include an opera, a theater opening, a private dinner party, a charity ball or even a debutante event. He could often be seen at his reserved table at El Morocco, enjoying conversation with his few friends and their guests. While this was a relaxing time for Paul, he was still working, pulling in any relevant information he could use in the next column. Paul loved what he did for a living and it could not have been more at odds with a quarter of Manhattan's citizens who could find no work at all.

In the venues that Paul would inhabit practically every night of the week, the worsening economic depression was of little concern to those in attendance, even though many had suffered losses in the Wall Street debacle and the growing aftermath. While Paul increasingly wrote about the Café Society that was emerging in the early 1930s, he still held a great deal of affection for the great family names counted among the 400. Paul knew from memory practically every family tree of the Vanderbilts, Astors, Goulds, Fishes, Belmonts, Goelets, Drexels, Oelrichs, and Biddles—of whom he insisted he was one and had the lineage to prove it—and many other families as well. And in some of those trees he knew of branches that were quite illegitimate, and which only served to provide him more material to write of at the most appropriate time. He had successfully crashed Society as anyone else might crash a wedding, and he comfortably rubbed shoulders with some of the wealthiest people of Manhattan.

A Night at the Metropolitan Opera

The premier event of the social season in Manhattan in the 1930s was the opening night of the Metropolitan Opera. Built in 1883, the original Met was located on Broadway between 39th and 40th Streets. Opening night was of particular interest to Paul because it was often one of the few public appearances of the grand names he knew so well as they arrived to take their seats in the Golden Horseshoe. While the season ticket holders would enter via the main entrance on Broadway, the wealthy patrons always arrived at the carriage entrance on 40th Street. Horse-drawn carriages once brought opera attendants to this entrance, but today it would receive Rolls-Royce, Packard, Cadillac V-16 and Duesenberg limousines.

New York's newspapermen and women always came to this entrance and the adjoining lobby to await their arrival. But in a curious and unwritten code of the Met, these patrons never arrived in time for the opening curtain. Oftentimes they never arrived until the close of the first act. Paul, however, was always there on time. He greeted and was greeted by his fellow journalists and he was joined by his secretary Eve Brown. Both had their notepads and several pencils to note the illustrious people and their attire. The copy for the performance that evening had already been written and they would not be attending the performance. Paul was not a theater and opera critic; he was "Cholly Knickerbocker."

A car pulled up, the chauffer got out and opened the rear passenger door, and out stepped the lovely Mrs. Cornelius Dresslhuys in a white satin Art Deco style of the day, ermine jacket, large pear-shaped diamond earrings and matching necklace. A barrage of flashbulbs followed. Ignoring all others, she immediately spotted Paul, walked up to him, greeted him by his first name, they kissed each other's cheeks, she smiled sweetly then swept inside. The fellow journalists were slack-jawed, but Paul was nonchalant and scribbled on his notepad while Brown tried to suppress a smile. Next to arrive was Mrs. Byron Foy, and the ritual was repeated. She warmly greeted him, they exchanged endearments, and she was off to the opera. Trying to pass through the lobby undetected was none other than Mrs. Hamilton Twombly, but Paul knew his Social Register, and he reported her arrival of this member of New York's upper crust.

The display of visible wealth and luxurious dresses on the women arriving was described diligently. Some of the women arrived wearing diamond tiaras, but nearly all displayed breathtaking diamond or emerald necklaces with matching earrings, while others chose pearls. The dresses were satin and velvet that best flattered the woman's figure—or not at all in some cases. Mrs. George Washington Kavanaugh arrived wearing a gold lame dress with full-length ermine cape and an array of diamond bracelets running up her arms. The photographers were ready and a blinding sequence of flashbulbs followed.

And then Lucius Beebe himself arrived, impeccably dressed as always, wearing his evening tuxedo, top hat, and evening overcoat with white gloves. He now had a column of his own at the *Herald Tribune*. He was not there to critique the performance that evening, but instead to enjoy the festivities during intermission and after the opera at Sherry's Bar inside the Metropolitan Opera building. There was no professional jealousy between Beebe and Paul. In fact, there was mutual respect. With Beebe was Mary Anita Loos who, while not wearing a dress costing hundreds of dollars and jewelry in the tens of thousands, was still a beautiful date for the elegant Mr. Beebe. Paul noted their arrival on his notepad.

But the queen of the evening had not yet arrived, and Paul was getting somewhat nervous. She must be coming, he thought. Then he spotted a stirring out in the carriage entrance and the reporters flocked to see who it was. As though before a ship parting the waves, the reporters made way for Mrs. Cornelius Vanderbilt, wearing a royal purple gown, matching evening wrap and diamond tiara, the requisite diamond earrings and diamond necklace. Bedlam broke out and the photographers snapped fresh flashbulbs in place and fired away. They crowded each other to get closer to Mrs. Vanderbilt, and she was clearly uncomfortable with their proximity. It would be some years before Mrs. Vanderbilt would learn a new protocol whereby she would enter the lobby, smile and pause for a minute or two to allow the photographers to take their pictures, then move to her seat in the Golden Horseshoe.

Paul then looked at Brown and nodded, and the two made for Sherry's Bar. They went up three flights of stairs to one of the highest places in the bar. The soprano of this evening's performance may be in full song, but here was where Paul knew the action would be. This was where they all came to see and be seen, and to drink—some heavily. Paul surveyed the array of people below him. He whipped out his opera glasses to zero in on the notable women and get a closer look at their jewels. Paul had sold jewelry during his days in Philadelphia and he had a better eye than most for what was paste and what was the real thing. He dutifully noted what he discovered on his notepad. However, Paul never revealed the truth in his column of what some of the women actually wore. The diamonds were always glittering, the rubies were always precious, and the emeralds were always exquisite. Paul earned the respect of many a society woman by never exposing an uncomfortable truth— at least about her jewelry.

When the duo of "Cholly Knickerbocker" finished gathering their crucial notes, they said their goodbyes as they left and caught a cab back to Paul's office at the *American*. They would spend the next several hours compiling their notes and typing the story, selecting the photos fresh from the newspaper's development lab, and writing suitable captions. Together, they would not finish this work until three or four in the morning.

The opening night of the Metropolitan Opera in the 1930s was indeed the most lavish public display of New York wealth during the Depression. The collective wealth of box holders in the Golden Horseshoe totaled nearly a billion dollars (down from the peak in 1928) and the precious stones and metals that graced the women's necks and cleavage, dangled from their earlobes and wrapped around their wrists, totaled nearly one hundred million dollars. The dresses were often made for this unique event and sometimes worn only once. Paul would write about this unabashed display in his inimitable style, and it would be read with keen interest by his followers. Sociologists have wondered why this did not result in scorching letters to the editor. Paul's column never ignited class envy. Instead, his columns about such events were read eagerly. There were several reasons for this. In part, it was New York's fascination with the cult of personality. For another, this was evidence the economic depression that gripped New York and the country did not affect everyone, or so it appeared on the surface. It was almost an affirmation of prosperity hoped for. "Cholly Knickerbocker" was entertainment; it was escapism. And for many in the Great Depression as lived in New York, that is how they viewed it.

"Lucius Beebe Depicts Modern 'Café Society'" by Cholly Knickerbocker, the *New York American,* March 1937.

> Congratulations to Lucius Beebe—he of the prolific and extravagant vocabulary—on the interesting opus published in the new March issue of *Cosmopolitan* under the label "Café Society."
>
> "Café Society" is a term I coined back in 1915 while dining one night in the old Oak Room at the Ritz Carlton, then the favorite gathering place of those who preferred to dine in public. "Café Society" of 1915 was a far different article from Lucius Beebe's "Café Society" of 1937—and not nearly so interesting. For "Café Society" of today is, to say the least, "comprehensive"—which is wasn't in 1915.
>
> Many members of my "Café Society" of twenty-two years ago now consider themselves vintage New York social leaders—which immediately stamps them "bores!" There are no "bores" in the Beebe article in the *Cosmopolitan*. Lucius has woven a fascinating tale around the "glamour boys and girls," who much prefer dancing at El Morocco or the Stork Club to dinner with Mrs. Vanderbilt or Mrs. Twombly.
>
> That's all in the Beebe story, from Elsie de Wolfe Mendl, now on her way to Bali Bali, to Mrs. Harrison Williams, who is keeping the social pot boiling down at Palm Beach, and from Libby Holman Reynolds, now in California, to Marion Tiffany Saportas, who typifies, probably more than anyone else I can think of, what is meant by "Café Society."
>
> Even the society "gossip writers" come in for their share of attention from the erudite Lucius. And I hereby thank him for so graciously referring to "Cholly Knickerbocker" as "stoutish and jolly." That's letting me down easily. Others have dubbed me "fat and vicious!"
>
> It's a swell article, "Café Society" in the March *Cosmopolitan*, and if you miss it you will miss a slice of what we are pleased to call "life" in this great metropolis of the purple-robed and pauper-clad.

The Easter Parade

The annual New York Easter Parade was an institution in the city and had been the focus of interested readers of the New York dailies since just after the turn of the 20th century. In its early days, the Easter Sunday worship services in several of the city's most prominent churches like St. Patrick's, St. Thomas's and St. Bartholomew's were followed by a fashion parade down Fifth and Park Avenue. One had to get to one's respective church early or be swept away by the fashionable tide of strollers. The years of the Depression had little effect on the head count, and in fact the numbers seemed to continually rise with each passing year. Paul would complain in his column that the days of former elegance, leisurely pace and abundance of shoulder room of the participants was long gone, replaced by crowded throngs, the flotsam and jetsam of society with a lowercase "s." And yet he continued to cover it each year because it provided more grist for his journalistic mill, and his readers wanted his take on it each year.

Paul would seek out the formidable two Society women who could always be counted on to turn out for the parade, and they were his chief draw to the event. They were Mrs. Cornelius Vanderbilt and Mrs. George Kavanaugh. Paul would first seek them out in the church where they would worship that morning and he made sure to catch them before they departed at the end of the service. He had no intention of confronting them—indeed, Paul spent years avoiding Mrs. Vanderbilt. He was there as an observer and chronicler. What the ladies were wearing was of prime importance, and he documented it in his bombastic, journalistic style.

It was also an annual event for Paul because he was the master of ceremonies and judge for the Easter Bonnet Luncheon. While British women were famous for their hats worn during the Ascot races, this was the annual New York event where the American ladies could really put on a show. Paul and Peter Arno were the judges during the 1930s. The judging event rarely went quietly, as each woman's hat being judged was accompanied by cat calls, whistles and sometimes the uncharitable boo. Paul would work to keep the comments from the gallery in check. At the end of the day's events, Paul and Brown would head back to the office and once again put down their observations of that year's event.

Stoking the Coals of Family Feuds— and His Own

Over the years, Paul had become the master of seeking out familial discord, including the roots of that discord, and the longer it went on the better Paul liked it. It was a form of journalistic soap opera to record the foibles of Society and Café Society names. One such example involved John Jacob Astor and his betrothed, Eileen Gillespie, during 1933. A month before the couple was engaged, Paul had written in his column the engagement was eminent, and in so doing, he beat the other New York journalists in revealing the news. When those writers dutifully announced the engagement, Paul gleefully told his readers that "Cholly Knickerbocker" had let all of them know the month before of this premarital event.

Maury Paul (left), Lucius Beebe with his date Gloria Braggiotti, and an admirer enjoy the atmosphere at the El Morocco Bar. Formal evening attire was required at the club. Men always wore tuxedos and women the finest gowns. While appearing to be enjoying themselves, Paul and Beebe were gathering information for their newspaper columns (Jerome Zerbe, by permission).

However, he sensed something was not quite right between the couple, but played his cards close to his tuxedo shirt. When Astor abruptly broke off the engagement, Paul was on it like a shot, and in his column tried to get to the bottom of Astor's motivation. There were two sides to every coin and Paul worked tirelessly to extract the sordid facts in the interest of truth. Paul had little trouble in gathering the "factoids," as he called them. Paul not only described Astor's reasons for dissatisfaction but also the Gillespie family's reaction. Astor openly insulted Eileen Gillespie and Paul was only too happy to record the vitriol in his column. The Gillespies did not take this lying down but fired their smoking retorts in return. The accusations went back and forth like a tennis ball at a Forest Hills tennis match. A key issue was Miss Gillespie's refusal to return the sizable diamond engagement ring until Astor apologized for his bruising remarks. Instead, Astor threatened to file a lawsuit against the young woman in an effort to get the ring back, and Paul all too eagerly noted the shocking facts to his eager readers. Paul was in his glory. All the while, Paul was fastidious in corroborating the facts; there was nothing speculative about Paul and the stories he wrote in "Cholly Knickerbocker."

Paul did not confine his writings to people and events only in New York. When Paul got word that Edward Windsor, the Prince of Wales, and the very married Mrs. Wallis Simpson were seeing each other, he could forecast a romance in the making but he was prevented from reporting it by his editor-in-chief at the *Journal-American*. The Prince was not yet divorced and neither was she. Paul also grasped the astounding ramifications if the Prince did marry a commoner—the prospective King of England would have to abdicate the throne. A compromise was reached between the editor-in-chief and the noted columnist: Mrs. Wallace would be the Prince's "favorite dancing partner." Paul made this improbable romance his own to the point he considered it his intellectual property, but the international ramifications of the relationship soon took it out of his hands and it was covered in all the New York and national major metropolitan dailies. In an effort to regain control of his subjects, Paul wrote a 12-part biography of Mrs. Wallace Simpson. When the couple married and Prince Edward abdicated the throne, Paul recorded the events with his characteristic spin. Paul, however, nursed several long-running feuds of his own.

Paul met Elsie de Wolfe early in his New York journalistic career. She was a recognized and accomplished interior decorator by that time. In 1926 she married Sir Charles Mendl; she was then known as Lady Mendl. Paul soured on her after that, and every several months, Paul had something caustic to say about her. The motive never became clear. He kept the barbs flying for years, and Mendl had no means of rebuttal. Paul often reported his dislike for certain people and at those times he could be his most insulting. Sometimes the attacks would come and go over a matter of weeks; others could drag on for years. He had the decided advantage of a nationally syndicated newspaper column, while the victims of his derogatory comments did not.

"No woman is beautiful"

Apart from his mother, Maury Paul had no love of or for women. He was an unabashed homosexual and had probably been so since his early editorial days in Philadelphia. While he often spoke with the greatest love and respect of his mother, Paul's father remains a man of mystery who might hold the key regarding Paul's sexual orientation. Eve Brown, Paul's secretary from the early 1920s to 1942, learned virtually nothing about Paul's father. Paul's voice and mannerisms were overt and unmistakable, and this was in stark contrast to Lucius Beebe and Jerome Zerbe, who were far more subdued in this respect. Paul's lexicon displayed in his daily column reflected this. A wealthy individual had "oodles of ducats," Long Island was invariably "Longuyland," when the telephone rang, he would write it "tinkles," and when one of the prominent women of New York Society had put on significant weight, she was "afflicted with embonpoint."[1]

Despite his grueling work schedule, Paul invariably had a companion with him in his moments when he was not on the job at the office or out on the town gathering material. He had his personal residential retreat in Wilton, Connecticut, and it often lent him the privacy he did not have in Manhattan. While *Vanity Fair* remained in print, one of its staff illustrators was Carl Haslam. Where Paul and Haslam met is not documented, but the illustrator differed from Paul in one key respect. Paul was a teetotaler while Haslam was a heavy drinker. However, he never drank in quantity to the point of becoming drunk. Paul found that when Haslam drank, his wit sharpened and his smooth personality became more effusive. When Paul left New York for Wilton or went on the road for a several-week getaway, Haslam usually went with him.

In his later years, Paul welcomed the company of entertainer Dwight Fiske, who performed his routines at the piano at many exclusive supper clubs in Manhattan. He had an avid following among a select few within Café Society and one of his greatest admirers was Maury Paul. Fiske and Paul remained close until the last year of Paul's life.

Brown marveled that Paul could be kissed, albeit on the cheek, by what must have been hundreds of women over his newspaper career and never have a true desire to be with any of them. In most cases, Paul's interest in them was merely gratuitous and part of his job. His flattering descriptions of them were not heartfelt but performed in the line of work. One day while Brown was clipping rival articles at the office, Paul was visited by a striking young woman who had stopped by to divulge some much-needed information for his column. When she left, Brown remarked how beautiful the woman was. Paul's retort was brusque.

"No woman is beautiful," Cholly Knickerbocker responded.[2]

Lucius Morris Beebe

Stanley Walker joined the staff of the *New York Herald Tribune* in 1920 as a reporter and rewrite editor. In 1926, he was promoted to night editor of the paper and city editor in 1928. His was one of the key posts at the paper and in a fascinating city like New York in the late 1920s, there was almost too much news to cover. The feverish stock market was reaching its peak, Prohibition was in full force and yet universally ignored by drinking establishments and brazen citizens, and organized crime was seizing the opportunity to provide and control the liquor that flowed into the city. Jimmy Walker was the dapper mayor of the city who pretty much left the city to run on its own. The Broadway theater district was experiencing a golden age of productions. Into this rollicking metropolitan tableau walked Lucius Morris Beebe in June of 1929.

As night and later city editor, Walker had seen some curious sights and met some curious people in his profession, but he had never met anyone quite like Lucius Beebe. When Beebe was introduced to Walker, Beebe clicked the heels of his highly polished shoes, bowed at the waist, and said, "Sir." Beebe, then 27 years old, straightened to his full six-foot, four-inch height. He was impeccably dressed from head to toe, and this was not first-day-on-the-job attire; as other newspapermen would come to learn, this was very much standard dress for Beebe. Walker, himself only 31, hired Beebe as a general copy writer for $35 a week. His previous position had been with the *Boston Transcript*. The route Beebe had taken to wind up at the *New York Herald Tribune* was a unique one, marked with numerous self-destructive pranks that routinely got him into trouble with two Ivy League college administrations that were happy to see him leave. He curbed those tendencies at the *Tribune*, but it is worthwhile to look at Beebe's family line and earlier years to better understand how he became so accomplished as a chronicler of Café Society in the 1930s and 1940s.

The first ancestors of Beebes landed on North American shores in 1650. The Beebe clan settled in Boston and Wakefield, Massachusetts. The family successfully ventured in various trades, banking and utilities. Beebe's father, Junius, had become wealthy as director of the Atlantic National Bank of Boston and of the Mutual Chemical Company of New York. In 1886, he married Eleanor Merrick, and Lucius was born in December 1902. Beebe's upbringing was conventional, if privileged, and he entered Roxbury School in Connecticut in 1920. After completing Roxbury, he enrolled at Yale to study literature. However, Beebe had a low boredom threshold and his studies were interspersed with both practical and impractical jokes. The worst of them was when he stood up during a performance at Yale's Hyperion Theater and announced that he was Professor Tweedy of the Divinity School, then threw an empty liquor bottle onto the stage. This was too much for the university administration and Beebe was expelled in the middle of his sophomore year.

After a brief stint at the *Boston Telegram*, Beebe succeeded in being accepted to Harvard with some confession of his past indiscretions and assurances that such behavior would not be duplicated at Harvard. Beebe did not hold to that promise for long. The pranks continued throughout his remaining years at Harvard, yet all the while he applied himself to his studies, handing in his assignments and getting acceptable grades. Fellow classmates noted the large wardrobe Beebe wore on campus. He stood out both for his height and his splendid attire, and his welcome ability to acquire all forms of liquor and mix any form of drink his classmates desired. He graduated from Harvard in 1927 with a bachelor of fine arts in literature, and chose to attend graduate school to get a master's in poetry. Unfortunately, Beebe once again crossed the line, this time participating in a brawl that could have resulted in severe charges, and brought embarrassment to Harvard. Beebe was invited to leave, and he did. He worked for a time at the *Boston Transcript*, and formulated a plan to move to New York City to see if he could land a job with one of the city's larger newspapers. Stanley Walker took the bait. A Harvard graduate couldn't be all bad.[3]

Walker kept Beebe, a freshman newspaperman at the *Tribune*, within proscribed limits, editorially speaking. Beebe wrote the average, inconsequential news items, obituaries, and the occasional human interest story—whatever he was asked to do. Even with these pieces, he managed to work into the copy his fanciful style of writing that was subtle at first and grew bolder in his second year on the paper. He got something of a break from this editorial wasteland when Walker assigned him to cover the performing arts, both stage and screen. This was more in his element, and provided him even more creative license. He could also dress the part, and it was common for Beebe to appear at a theater production with top hat, evening cape over evening dress, and carrying a gold-capped walking stick. He carried a notepad and pencil to take down notes on the performance and interview the performers after the show.

Beebe naturally wasted little time finding his speakeasies of choice after joining the *Herald Tribune*. The first one was literally next door to the paper's offices on 40th Street, and was known as Bleeck's Artists and Writer' Club. To the editors and other staffers at the *Herald*, Bleeck's was an institution at the paper and a magnet to other creative types all over Manhattan. It was run by a Dutchman by the name of Jack Bleeck. Besides the staffers at the *Herald*, editors and writers from *The New Yorker* frequented the place. It was not uncommon to see Noel Coward, James Cagney, Tallulah Bankhead and current notables from New York's burgeoning theater district. Even Mayor Jimmy Walker would put in a regular appearance.

Beebe frequented a number of private speakeasies, and he soon knew where most of the better ones were. One of the more public ones he would write about years later was P.J. Moriarity's on East 58th Street. It was ably run by two Irishmen, Dan and Mort. It was a manly bar and no women were welcomed in its early years. The two brothers had the connections with the police and political forces in the city to keep their speakeasy running smoothly during Prohibition. Here, a newspaperman like Beebe could be standing at the bar next to a Whitney, Mellon or Vanderbilt. Such places were the usual stop after finishing copy for the next day's paper, but Beebe would down his last drink, head back to his apartment, shower and prepare himself for his evening out on the town. That might include a private party or a pleasant visit to one of the nightclubs in mid–Manhattan.

Beebe Gets His Column

Then life took a fortuitous turn for Beebe through no effort of his own. Harry Stanton was the powerful manager of the Herald Tribune Syndicate, and in the summer of 1933, possibly smarting from the success of Maury Paul's "Cholly Knickerbocker" column, he pondered the possibility of a new *Herald* column that focused on some of the more outrageous aspects of New York and New Yorkers. When Stanton put the idea to Walker, the city editor knew just who to tap for the job. Walker called in Beebe and he went over the idea with the former Bostonian. Before the as-yet unnamed column ran in the *Tribune*, it would first be tried in the *Philadelphia Inquirer* and several other papers to gauge the response before Beebe would be promoted to having his column run in the *Herald Tribune*. Walker felt a prospective column title "So This Is New York!" would fit for now.

Beebe worked out a formula whereby he would briefly comment on four to six topics having to do with some aspect of the good life in New York City and the notable people in it. His column would be weekly and thus not tax his responsibilities for other material required by the paper. During the first week of September 1933, he worked on the column and turned in the copy to Walker. The city editor approved it and it was sent on to the *Philadelphia Inquirer*. Beebe's first column appeared on September 9, 1933. In it, he commented on New York's finest headwaiters and hotel managers, the absence of Noel Coward from Manhattan and how his memorable parties were missed, Scribner's editor Robert Bridges, and stage actress Pat Campbell. Beebe's column in the *Inquirer* was well-received that month, judging by the letters sent to the editor. It was decided to try the column even further from New York City, and it was actually picked up by the *Wyoming Pioneer*. The *Herald Tribune* was avoiding the other major metropolitan papers for the moment. It was no surprise the citizens of Wyoming found the jottings by Beebe of life in Manhattan of great interest to them.

In the fall of 1933, the column was picked up by the *Cleveland Plain Dealer* to run on Sundays and had been retitled "This New York." The two previous markets kept the original title so as not to confuse the readers, but the copy was the same. Naturally, New York City's newest columnist did not escape the attention of Maury Paul, who made certain to get copies of the *Philadelphia Inquirer* and check to make sure Beebe was not edging onto "Cholly Knickerbocker's" turf. He was pleased to see Beebe was not. Also, Beebe's topics and writing style were distinctly different from Paul's. The *Herald Tribune* was still not comfortable, however, with introducing Beebe as a weekly columnist in its own paper as yet.[4]

Beebe proved he had an ability to gather diverse yet relevant and interesting facts about life in New York City and its environs that would make captivating reading in his column. He was not so narrowly focused as Maury Paul on the doings of Society and Café Society; he cast a far broader net. He reported seats aboard the *Merchant Limited* train running out of Boston for New York were all filled with not an empty one available, the lounge car was populated with prosperous men smoking and reading various newspapers, while the club car had the sound of happy banter, wagers being made over card games, and laughter over winning hands. Stewards were serving drinks and meals in the packed dining car. Beebe's impression was that the *Merchant Limited* was back at full strength from its money-losing days of 1931. National unemployment had peaked at over 23 percent, but certainly 1933 was shaping up to be far better than two years before, if the new Irving Berlin-Moss Hart revue *As Thousands Cheer* was any indication. Beebe reported that attending would prove to be an evening very well spent. Beebe made sure a little-known gathering spot called the Coffee House, founded by *Vanity Fair* publisher Frank Crowninshield and Joseph Choate, made his column because it was the gathering place for the likes of many of those in arts and letters as well as finance. Beebe made mention of one of Manhattan's leading connoisseurs of fine cigars, William Osgood Field, and how he could distinguish a cigar's quality simply by feeling its rolled tobacco leaves and savoring its unlit aroma.

Beebe's column, whether it was titled "New York Speaking," or "So This Is New York!" as it was in a few of the outlying papers syndicating it, "This

New York," revealed a city that was active and a people who were enjoying both their labors and the life New York had to offer. The column was a distinct counterpoint to the general mood both spoken and unspoken, and the disheartening news reported on the pages of New York's dailies. Beebe reported on the closing performance of Archibald MacLeach's *Union Pacific* at the Ballet Russe, and the standing ovation and the many curtain calls that followed its performance that evening. He did not fail to mention the sea of minks and sables worn that evening and the jewels worn which had been fashioned at Manhattan's most famous jewelers. But Beebe also enjoyed writing about the lesser-known artisans such as Paul Flato, who had a client list almost as impressive as Van Cleef & Arpel. His diamond and platinum corsage found eager buyers at $5,000. Another jeweler with a Fifth Avenue address fashioned a diamond brooch of the Three Little Pigs with a price tag in 1933 dollars of $4,500. Months after the repeal of Prohibition, Beebe was writing about the lingering effects of what he called the "great foolishness," as well as how the former speakeasies were now operating as legitimate, licensed drinking establishments.

The first Beebe column to run with a photo appeared on Sunday, January 7, 1934. The previous week, Beebe had decided to hire a horse and sleigh with the first heavy snowfall and be the first to ride to the Central Park Casino to claim the prize of a magnum of champagne. This was meant to revive a New York custom that had flourished during the latter 1800s with two other taverns that had since disappeared. Joining Beebe was Paul Mellon, son of former Secretary of the Treasury Andrew Mellon. With Paddy Rafferty at the reins, they left the Hotel Madison on 58th Street where Beebe had his apartment, and at a leisurely trot, and with photographers stationed all along the route, soon claimed the bubbly prize of Lanson 1921. The photo of the winning contestants accompanied the column and it was the first casual photo op of the fledgling columnist. Beebe took great joy in the activity as it reflected an institution of a bygone era he still admired. However, the Casino had also become a symbol of the corruption of Mayor Jimmy Walker's administration, and in 1935, New York Parks Commissioner Robert Moses ordered it razed. In its place was built a children's playground.

The *Herald Tribune* finally made a commitment to "This New York" and it appeared in the Friday edition June 1, 1934. For New Yorkers and readers of the syndicated column, "This New York" would become a window on a very different world from that which unfolded on street corners with their apple sellers, the many small stores with their "Going Out of Business" signs, and the men in their long coats and hats waiting for their daily bowl of soup.

These are the enduring images of the Great Depression that persist to this day, but Beebe's column showcased the successful, the elegant, and frankly, those who just seemed unaffected by the greatest economic collapse in the history of the United States. Beebe's column was the antidote to the relentless financial malaise that gripped Manhattan and the country. His column was pure escapism, and yet it chronicled a segment of New York life that was entirely real; it was no fantasy.

Throughout the 1930s, Beebe would devote his column to the broader aspects of New York City day and night, while Maury Paul would remain focused on the subject he knew so well. This is perhaps why there was no professional jealousy between the two journalists. In fact, Beebe and Paul could often be seen enjoying a lunch or evening meal at the Colony or sharing conversation during late nights at El Morocco. Rarely was Walter Winchell seen at either of these two elite centers of Café Society. Winchell's orbit of activity involved different venues, and he could more frequently be seen at Sherman Billingsley's Stork Club. Beebe had his own journalistic formula, and the end of each column had a paragraph of miscellaneous news items with a heading that differed from week to week. It could be Boulevard Backchat, Around the Town, Notes at Random, Gotham Trivia, or any of a dozen other descriptive phrases.

Brief mentions in Beebe's column included the fact that there were more symphony orchestra players in Paul Whiteman's band that any other musical ensemble of popular music, that the new bar at the Plaza Hotel had the elegance of a Fifth Avenue club, columnist Hedda Hopper could be seen wearing hats that permit a curl of her hair through the top, Dwight Fisk was packing them in at Lerue, Cobina Wright often gave the best midnight-to-morning parties, and that John Perona, owner of El Morocco, might just as well leave the place open 24 hours a day, as the happy attendees are still going strong into the early morning hours. No esoteric bit of information was too offbeat to be included in his column end notes. Indeed, this was part of the increasing popularity of "This New York."

In 1934, Beebe's boss, Stanley Walker, published his second book, appropriately titled *City Editor*. Beebe naturally made mention of the book in his column. Beebe stated it was an unforgiving look at the state of journalism as personally experienced by Walker, covering the caliber of journalism schools, ethics, freedom of speech, and corporate influence on editorial content, among other topics. In it, Walker revealed a wealth of detail of his profession written in a style that garnered praise from fellow editors and book reviewers. The *New York Times* gave the book a very positive review. Beebe, without being patronizing, stated, "The charm of the job is that the book is the quintessential Walker just as much as he is himself when hoisting them bravely over the mahogany in Jack Bleek's—comprehensive, frequently sardonic and always compelling stuff."5

Beebe also made mention in his column of the first collection of Jerome Zerbe's photographs taken in nightclubs, private parties, at the theater, and wherever Café Society chose to gather. *People on Parade* was published in December 1934 and it was the first photographic tribute to the social phenomenon that was Café Society. Zerbe asked Beebe to write the introduction. The book revealed that Zerbe was no mere nightclub photographer, but that he was very well-traveled and his photo contributions had appeared in *Town & Country, New York American, New York Evening Journal*, and *Stage*, among other publications. Zerbe photographed the names that made news in the early 1930s, including the names that would become news in that decade. Zerbe's style was mostly candid, but he also became known for his formal portraits. The book was a remarkable photographic collection of an era in New York, Greenwich, Detroit, Cleveland, and other cities, of the successful and accomplished and occasionally others who were simply in the right place at the right time. The subject of Zerbe's photography of the time was unique in many ways, but perhaps the most significant was that practically no other photographer did the same thing or so well.

In like manner, "This New York" was a journalistic diary, in a way, of a life in Manhattan that was far removed from *The Forgotten Man* as written years later by Amity Shlaes, and *Hard Times* by Studs Terkel. Beebe wrote about the New York of his day, the people he met, and the places he visited to drink, eat a marvelous meal, or enjoy the company of others. Beebe never wrote about the forgotten man, but about the man who was thriving in the face of economic calamity, about performances on the stage that left one laughing, about some new place the reader would enjoy visiting himself, and about the good life in New York that was available if one would just go there. Of course, there were places where most readers could never hope to go, such as El Morocco with its enforced exclusion. But Beebe wrote about practically the entire gamut of life in New York and left those who read his column wanting to grab the next train for Manhattan.

Clearly, however, Beebe was most at home among the opulence of certain events and was completely in rhythm with his surroundings. His writing at times like this was truly lyric, such as when he described one evening at Madison Square Garden with the annual Horse Show for a column which appeared November 10, 1934:

The week that this hippodrome is in progress at Madison Square Garden sees more broadcloth and ermine, more hundred thousand dollar ropes of pearls and gold plate dinner parties than any other New York festival of tradition. Park Avenue, the more conservative faubourgs [sic], café society and the world of amateurs of horseflesh all unite under a common hallmark of the most formal observances and the effect is one of eye-filling opulence. Opening night found the gangways of the Garden flooded with a tidal wave of sables flecked with a foam of gleaming shirt fronts and white ties. While skating rinks of diamonds gleamed latently beneath the smartest wraps of Paris couturiers, and opera hats collapsed and rumbled like continuous heat thunder on a summer evening.[6]

This was quintessential Beebe, with a descriptive style that became synonymous with his byline. He used this selectively, however, or it would have been tiring week after week. His description of the newly opened Rainbow Room on the 65th floor of Rockefeller Center (with plate glass windows that went down to the floor, permitting dinners to look out over Manhattan, and almost gave the sensation of floating over the city at night), was also pure Beebe. He pulled his readers in and kept them with an eclectic mix of topics that he never seemed to exhaust, because New York City was forever changing. This was particularly true during the 1930s. Indicative of this was the construction of the Chrysler Building, the Empire Building, and lastly Rockefeller Center. These skyscrapers were symbols of prosperity in the face of oppressive economic stagnation and contraction. They were symbols of hope, and Beebe often incorporated them into his columns.

Practically no man looked better in an evening tuxedo with tails than Beebe, as written by Zerbe on numerous occasions, and the only man to equal him wearing a top hat was Fred Astaire. The columnist was often called on to model evening dress as a male model for various women in magazine articles. Harry Bull concurred with this assessment and asked Beebe to help with a layout for an issue of *Town & Country*. He was shown arriving at the Persian Room in the Plaza with Miss Frances Brett wearing furs by C.G. Gunter's Sons, casually leaning against the bar of the Caprice Room in the Weylin Hotel with Miss Gloria Debevoise wearing a Jay-Thorpe evening dress of white crepe with diamond jewelry by Udall & Ballou, and arriving at the Rainbow Room wearing a mink-lined and sable-trimmed coat with Miss Gladys Swarthout wearing an Elizabeth Hawes velvet gown and cape. Beebe enjoyed such photo shoots immensely and each article only worked to build the Beebe charisma as New York's best-dressed man-about-town.

In 1935, Beebe wrote *Boston and the Boston Legend*, which was published later that year. He had written several shorter works devoted to the poems of Edwin Arlington Robinson, but this new book was his first significant publication. It was in this book that his writing style was the subject of review as much as the content itself. James Lane of the *New York Sun* referred to Beebe's writing as "purple," "gleefully trite," and at its worst, "irritating." This was not the first time Beebe's writing was called into question, having also been commented on in numerous magazines almost as much as his wardrobe. However, there were many newspapermen in New York whose identity was a question mark and who made no name for themselves at all. If there was one thing about Beebe's writing that everyone agreed on it was that it was unique in all of journalism. Even Maury Paul had commented on it.

Beebe had on several occasions mentioned the pleasant atmosphere of the gatherings at Harold Ross's apartment home, and by 1937, Ross felt Beebe had achieved sufficient notoriety to merit a profile in *The New Yorker*. Wolcott Gibbs was dispatched to gather information surrounding the growing Beebe legend, perhaps fueled by Stanley Walker's descriptive phase of Beebe as the "millionaire reporter." Beebe was no millionaire, although he might have dressed and lived like one. His father had died in 1934 but had left him no estate. Instead, a trust fund had been set up in the amount of $200,000 with specific terms. Beebe also owned half the family farm in Wakefield, Massachusetts. Although Beebe's column had limited syndication, he earned $7,500 a year from this and he received another $5,000 from book royalties, speaking engagements and magazine articles. He also received income from properties in Key West, Florida, and Mineola, New York. King Features tried to lure Beebe away from the *Herald Tribune* with an offer of $500 a week to write for the Hearst papers plus half of the take from other syndicated newspapers. Beebe turned down the offer, citing the *Tribune* as the logical venue for his writing, out of professional respect to the paper itself, and because he enjoyed working at the paper. Stanley Walker, although having left the *Tribune* in 1935 for other editorial opportunities, was impressed with Beebe's decision.

Beebe was a lifelong bachelor and he would admit he could live quite well with just himself to support. He lived in a well-appointed suite on the seventh floor in the Hotel Madison with a substantial closet and several dressers to house his many suits, shirts, tuxedos and other apparel. Beebe's daily schedule differed somewhat from that of Maury Paul. For one thing, Beebe was up at 7:00 a.m., had his breakfast in the hotel, and would reach his desk at the *Tribune* by 8:30. He would write until 12:30 or 1:00, or go in search of some specific material, turn in his copy, then leave for lunch at Bleeck's with staffers or go to 21. In the afternoon, he would go to the Biltmore Hotel to receive a steam bath and rubdown, and on occasion would entertain the company of Walter P. Chrysler or Alfred E. Smith, among others. Beebe would then return to the Madison for a late afternoon nap to rest up for a long night on the town. He would shower, dress appropriately for the activity that evening, and if not having guests in his suite, would head for 21, El Morocco or the Colony on those evenings he was not going to a first-night performance, an evening at the opera, or a party at the home of a member of the Café Society set. Approximately twice a month, he selected two evenings when he would not go out at all, relax in his suite, and go to bed between nine and ten.

Beebe and the Ladies

Unlike Maury Paul, Beebe truly enjoyed the company of beautiful, intellectual and conversational women. His most frequent lady companion either day or night was Gloria Braggiotti. A Florence, Italy-born and Boston-raised beauty, Braggiotti was saved from an unproductive theatric career by Henry Sell, then editor of *Harper's Bazaar*, with a busy advertising agency on the side. Sell advised her to temporarily take over the "Madame Flutterbye" column written by Molly Thayer, who was leaving for an extended trip to Africa. With Maury Paul's help, she learned what to write and how to write it. As Paul tutored Braggiotti, she had easy entrée to the exclusive circle at El Morocco. When Beebe met her, they immediately established a rapport, and he would often take her to theater performances. Braggiotti also enjoyed the company, panache and wit of Jerome Zerbe. She did not have to be concerned about romantic interest from the two men; their friendship would always be platonic. She would marry artist Emlen Etting in 1938.

"Lucius knew my grandmother was a real Beacon Street Bostonian, and he loved the idea that I was Bostonian," Braggiotti recalled.[7] "That's how Lucius and I hit it off. That was the tie we had. I was probably one of the youngest women that he ever went around with. I was in my early twenties. Even though I had many beaus, I did go out with Lucius and Jerome a lot, and they liked that because so many girls were so rude. They didn't know how to make the break between a boyfriend and someone who wasn't, whereas I acted the same. To me, an attractive evening with Lucius or Jerome was the same as with someone who might have been madly in love with me—I didn't care. It was still a charming evening for me."

One of the higher profile women Beebe escorted of was Libby Holman. She had come to New York in 1919—the same year as Maury Paul. She struggled to break into theater productions and took up singing in speakeasies to make a living. It took her ten years to get a role that gave her the recognition she sought: she performed with Clifton Webb and Fred Allen in *The Little Show*. Her singing performance of the number "Moanin' Low" earned her numerous curtain calls and she became the editorial focus of Walter Winchell and other theater reviewers. During the 1930s, she established her career as a theater performer and torch singer. The death of her husband in 1932 from a gunshot wound to the head was one of the more controversial court cases of the 1930s, but Holman was acquitted of charges. Holman did not confine her romantic interests to men, and she, like Cole Porter, was openly bisexual. Beebe was nonjudgmental of Holman and she was respectful of Beebe.

While Paul would often take a defensive position at his reserved table at El Morocco and shun close female companionship, Beebe would make the rounds and spend time with prolific writer Anita Loos, or strike up a conversation with Gloria Swanson at the bar when she was in New York. Married women welcomed Beebe's company and conversation. Among them were Valentina Schlee, Mrs. Tiffany Saportas, Angela Krimsky (the wife of the producer John Krimsky), and Mrs. Harry Bull (wife of *Town & Country* publisher Harry Bull). Beebe was closed-mouth about his relationship with Charles "Chuck" Clegg, although they were seen together on many occasions. During the thirties, Clegg was leery when photographed with Beebe by Zerbe and in no photo was Clegg ever seen smiling. They would remain companions until Beebe's death in 1966.

As the national and New York economy slowly began to recover from the Great Depression in the latter 1930s, the activity of night life in Manhattan changed not at all. "This New York" remained a weekly column and Beebe did not have to work under the pressing daily schedule that Paul did. Café Society remained a source of material for Beebe, as did New York itself. Beebe cultivated his interest in railroading and his first book on the subject, *High Iron: A Book of Trains*, was published in 1938. He would write and publish many more on the subject during the 1940s and 1950s. But for now, he relished living among Café Society and writing about the good life in New York City.

Walter Winchell and the Power of the Media

Winchell had been with the *Mirror* four months when the economic collapse struck the Wall Street market in the fall of 1929. He read the news himself with bewilderment, as market machinations were not within his scope of reporting, but he did view the events with justifiable fear; neither Winchell, nor anyone, had in recent memory ever seen such a decline in the stock market and such chaotic trading conditions. The bad economic news was coming from all sides, and Winchell worried what it might do to his career. Winchell always harbored a fear of failure, and the market crash only exacerbated his worries. The uncertainty for newspaper advertisers was felt almost immediately, as ad revenues began to decline. As the revenues declined, newspapermen began losing their jobs, but Winchell's position was secure. He was one of the most widely-read syndicated columnists in America. However, the drop in newspaper advertising revenue was also due to the dramatic increase in the popularity of radio and the shift in advertising dollars to this rising medium of entertainment. The radio manufacturing industry grew dramatically in the 1920s and the formation of the National Broadcasting Company (NBC) in 1926 and the Columbia Broadcasting Network (CBS) in 1927 fueled this dramatic growth. The Crosley Radio Corporation was the largest manufacturer of radio receivers in the United States, building and shipping more than 5000 radio sets a day. Powel Crosley was likened to Henry Ford as a captain of this industry. By the late 1920s, there were tens of millions of radios in operation in America. Between 1928 and 1932 sales of radios grew from eight million to 18 million sets a year. The medium of radio would be a new channel of communication for Walter Winchell.

Opportunity came in the spring of 1930 to do a 15-minute program on WABC in New York sponsored by the Saks Department Store. With his vaudeville training of rapid-fire delivery and his distinctive voice, this was a natural for Winchell. "Before Dinner—with Walter Winchell" hit the airwaves on May 12, 1930. With the initial success of this program, it was renamed to the more appropriate "Saks Broadway—with Walter Winchell." This national exposure in radio made Winchell an even greater celebrity—and a personality of greater interest to other, bigger advertisers. One of them was Lucky Strike cigarettes. Radio was a communication medium virtually unaffected by the Depression and the biggest advertising dollars were spent on it.

"The Lucky Strike Dance Hour" soon followed in luring Winchell to radio to supplement his daily column in the *Mirror*. Broadcast on NBC's nationwide network of 50 stations from New York to Los Angeles, Winchell popularity grew even more popular, and much more prosperous. He was now earning over $5,000 a week between his income from the *Mirror* and his new radio program.[8] The musical hits of the day were interspersed with ads for Lucky Strike cigarettes and other advertisers and the obligatory gossip tidbits Winchell was known for. It was one of the most-listened-to radio programs on the air. Radio went a long way in temporarily blocking out the worries of the day. In addition to the music, the commentary by Winchell was a welcomed distraction to millions of listeners.

Winchell, it seemed, was burning his cigarettes at both ends. He was a workaholic and his nervous energy and need for ever more information kept driving him on day and night. He would plow through his mail, which was the source of much of his material for the column, and he was helped in this by two secretaries. Sifting through his public's letters would take several hours, and he would take his notes as he read them. Concerning letters he would wish to answer, he would write a note to the secretaries, and these letters would be sent to his office at the *Mirror* for them to type. He would leave his apartment around 10:30 p.m. and head for the Stork Club and his reserved table in the Cub Room. He was there not to relax but to gather essential information for his column as the king of gossip. Winchell often played fast and loose with the facts, and if something could not be definitively proved, he would word it in his column in such a way that it might mean any of several things so as to avoid libel; the conclusion was left to the reader. However, on most occasions he simply threw out the embarrassing facts as he knew them and damn the consequences for those he wrote about. He damaged countless careers and marriages in this fashion. When threats—veiled and direct—were made against him, he eventually had bodyguards to accompany him. He could afford it. Circulation of the *Mirror* had climbed from 430,000 to 585,000 in the first year his column ran in the paper.

Part of Winchell's news gathering routine was to leave the Stork Club early in the morning and drive around Manhattan for any happening that might be worthy of comment. During the 1930s he had gotten permission to have a police radio receiver installed in the car so he could follow the police calls and maybe get a scoop no other journalist could hope for. Sometimes he would be in on a crime as it was happening, or arrive just after someone had been shot—someone of some importance, he hoped. Winchell liked a crime story as much as a juicy tidbit about a prominent divorcing couple or a Broadway actress with a nasty habit of snorting cocaine. After the threats against him started coming in, he carried a snub-nosed revolver as a defensive weapon in the pocket of his jacket or overcoat. He would cruise the city for several hours before returning to his apartment, get something to eat, and sleep for as long as his nervous energy would allow. He would awaken in the afternoon, review proof copy for his column, make any last-minute changes, and send it off for the next issue of the paper.

By the strict definition of Café Society as defined by Maury Paul or

Lucius Beebe, Winchell could be considered a member, but in fact he was too crass to rub shoulders with the likes of either of his fellow columnists. By the same token, neither Paul nor Beebe ever entertained offers to do radio programs that spread their fame and increased their fortune as did Winchell. The three men had a mutual respect for one another, but only Beebe and Paul could comfortably spend time together. Winchell had the journalistic power to get into any club in the city, but he was out of his usual element in the elegant surroundings and people seated at their small tables in El Morocco. This club was a different world to Winchell, and he was more attracted to the diverse customers and atmosphere of the Stork Club. It could be argued that Winchell's column had more in common with "Cholly Knickerbocker" than "This New York." Both Paul and Winchell trafficked in gossip that could prove most damaging to those who were the subject of copy, and both columnists reveled in the exposure of those they wrote about. However, Winchell had a distinct nasty streak, and he thought nothing of firing off the most insulting or humiliating words toward someone he chose to target. Paul, Beebe and Winchell all had their devoted followers. To use a metaphor, Paul was Park Avenue, Beebe was Fifth Avenue, and Winchell was Broadway.

Winchell was the only one of the three journalists to marry. The couple had adopted one daughter, whose name was Gloria. Winchell had another daughter by his wife June, and they named her Walda. In 1932, Gloria died at the age of 9 and it left the couple devastated. The child's death affected Winchell profoundly and his subsequent columns reflected this. In November 1933, he had a nervous breakdown and was briefly unable to write his column. The same week of his breakdown, he learned his friend and mentor Texas Guinan had died in California. Winchell reflected on the fact that fifteen million people across the nation were unemployed and the evidence was all over New York City. Then, it hit home for Winchell when President Roosevelt ordered a bank closing the week he was inaugurated in order to stem a run on account withdrawals. Winchell never walked around with a lot of cash, and suddenly he found he could not get access to his substantial cash reserves. He admitted in his column he could not tip the waiters at the Stork Club but a fraction of his usual, and he could not pay for other items but put it on account. It was a watershed event for Winchell and it proved to him how fragile the national and local economies were and how vulnerable he was personally. The Depression now affected everyone, not simply the masses of unemployed.

In some respects, Winchell had a distinct advantage over Paul and now Beebe, whose small syndicated column "This New York" was finally rolled out in his own paper, the *Herald Tribune*. Winchell could also report the news as part of his column, and many city and national events were mentioned in it. One of the biggest was the Lindbergh child kidnapping and subsequent trial of suspect Bruno Hauptmann. Winchell was always in search of the scoop to beat his fellow newsmen and this was the biggest story of the 1930s. While he could not scoop this story, Winchell sought to follow trails of clues that would make his column unique. He was relentless in stating Hauptman was guilty of the kidnapping and death of the child. He used every opportunity to state so in his column while other reporters debunked him and pursued other suspects. Winchell was in the courtroom when the guilty verdict was read and the mob of reporters all bolted for the door to get to the phones. Winchell chided the reporters that he alone had called it and implored them to give him credit in their articles. It was yet another display by Winchell of his eternal insecurity and need for attention and even adulation. Many of his friends and acquaintances had witnessed it, and here it was on public display.

Other radio programs were offered Winchell after the Lucky Strike-sponsored program, and Winchell shifted toward a news format that again suited his personality and delivery. The *Jergens Journal* permitted Winchell to report the news, and his ratings continued to rise from 1933 to 1936. Commensurate with these ratings came increases in the payments for each of his broadcasts to the point he made $2,500 per broadcast by 1935. His style was to start with a big news item, followed by six or seven shorter news items and working in his beloved gossip tidbits and opinion. The radio program was the vocal equivalent of his column, but the material for the two rarely overlapped. Every program would end with a trademark comment delivered in the inimitable Winchell style.

During the 1930s, Winchell's circle of friends and acquaintances included some of the most powerful men in the country. He had no aversion to consorting with Al Capone at his Miami compound, or Lucky Luciano in Chicago. Luciano offered Winchell protection with two bodyguards, and he gladly accepted them. He could pick up the phone and call FBI Director J. Edgar Hoover, and America's chief law enforcement officer would visit Winchell at the Stork Club. Winchell knew he had arrived when President Franklin D. Roosevelt drew him aside and said he had some news to give him. Few other journalists in America had that notoriety and power.

Next to Winchell, Paul and Beebe looked positively sedentary. Winchell was constantly talking, smoking, gesturing and moving. If he had ever lost his voice he would have been incapacitated. By 1935, he was nearing 40 but looked nearly ten years older with his smoking-induced gray complexion and silver receding hairline. Despite his nonstop activity and obligations to the *Mirror* and his national radio program, Winchell looked to stage and screen to expand his scope of activity and income. There was no prospect too outrageous for Winchell, and when he entered talks with Darryl Zanuck at Twentieth Century–Fox on a possible movie role that could launch a cinematic career, Winchell believed it within his realm of possibility. He had been a vaudeville entertainer in his twenties and as recently as 1931 had packed in audiences for a limited engagement at the Palace Theater.

Irving Thalberg of MGM and Harry Cohn of Columbia Pictures had been in negotiations with Wichell to star in a film, but it was Darryl Zanuck who succeed in luring the journalist and vaudeville performer to come to Hollywood. In September 1936, Zanuck thought he had the right script to showcase Winchell, titled *Wake Up and Live*. Winchell signed the contract, which would pay him $75,000. Winchell left for Los Angeles in mid–December. Winchell did not simply walk onto a set and give his lines. He had to perform a screen test like any other prospective film actor. Not surprisingly, he did quite well, and Zanuck sincerely praised him after viewing the short clip. Nevertheless, Winchell was anxious and unsure. He welcomed the opportunity to do the film but dreaded failing to perform before the camera. The performing stage was one thing, but filmmaking was a whole new mountain of worries to surmount. Director Sidney Lanfield often had to shoot around Winchell's lateness and visible nervousness, but as production progressed, Winchell relaxed sufficiently to perform all his scenes very well.

When Zanuck saw the final cut of the film he was elated and told Winchell he felt he had found a new star. This fed Winchell's ego but did little to assuage his anxiety and doubts about what audiences would think. The first press screening of *Wake Up and Live* was in Hollywood at Grauman's Chinese Theater the first week in April of 1937. *Daily Variety* gave the film rave reviews, and the *Hollywood Reporter* said the film was headed for record-breaking business. Winchell was relieved and pleasantly surprised by the critical response from the entertainment press; it was ironic for him to be on the receiving end of media praise. The New York premiere was at the Roxy Theater and it set box office records. He received critical praise from the *New York Times* and the other New York dailies. This gratified Winchell and his legend grew even more.

Doing the film had taxed him not physically but emotionally. Film acting was not the cakewalk he thought it would be, and he felt drained. Zanuck was glad the film was doing so well financially; his gamble in giving Winchell his break into acting paid off handsomely, and the very positive reviews confirmed his confidence in him. The contract Winchell signed had an option clause for future films and Zanuck wanted to start another in a matter of months. Winchell wrote Zanuck saying he could not do another film given the demands of his column and radio program, but the real reason was his relentless fear of failure. Zanuck wrote back a blistering letter mentioning all the money the producer had spent to do the film and the significant salary Winchell had received, and all the personal considerations he had given Winchell to accommodate his other work. The film maker had invested heavily in Winchell and he was going to earn a return on his investment. When the agreement to do a second film reached him in New York several months later, Winchell grudgingly signed it. The film was *Love and Hisses*.

Winchell again took the train from Penn Station for Los Angeles. He grew impatient with the pace of filming, with roughly five minutes of acting to every hour of waiting. He smoked constantly as he was forced to wait either on the set or in his room near the set. Again, he performed well, but he was glad when it was over and he could go back to New York. Hollywood for him would never be as glamorous again. He was anxious to get back before the radio microphone and tell Mr. and Mrs. America the latest news and gossip. *Love and Hisses* opened in January 1938 and the reviews were more subdued; some critics even panned it. It marked the end of a very short acting career, and Winchell was glad it was over.

By the close of the 1930s, Walter Winchell was a media icon, read by millions and listened to by tens of millions all across the United States. For many, a day without Winchell was no day at all. He was a force of nature, and among the most famous journalists in the world. Maury Paul worked at a pace almost as manic as Winchell's in churning out his various columns. Lucius Beebe was perhaps the happiest of the three columnists. He certainly was not overworked as the other two columnists were, but Beebe rightly believed that was their choice. His weekly column allowed him all the freedom and time to enjoy the great city and its night life and write cheerfully about the comings and goings of Café Society.

Chapter 8

The Colony, the Plaza, the Rainbow Room and the Waldorf

During the 1930s, there were other businesses which were a powerful draw to Café Society members. Often, these were the finest of New York restaurants within grand hotels. Or one might be a nightclub with dinner and dancing in an exclusive location, such as the Rainbow Room atop the RCA building in Rockefeller Center. Others mimicked the Rainbow Room. There was the Pierre Roof on the 42nd floor of the Hotel Pierre on Fifth Avenue at 61st Street, overlooking Central Park. There was the Starlight Roof at the Waldorf Astoria Hotel on Park Avenue between 49th and 50th Streets. And there was the St. Regis Roof in the Hotel St. Regis on Fifth Avenue at 55th Street; the hotel's Iridium Room opened in 1938. Each of New York's finest hotels naturally wanted its guests to dine within the hotel, and in these cases, no expense was spared to make the atmosphere as exclusive as possible and the food five-star—or as many stars as the restaurant could muster. Among these was the Persian Room in the Plaza Hotel. However, a few of these upper-crust restaurants were independent businesses.

At the apex of these elite eating establishments in terms of its unsurpassed cuisine and service was the Colony Restaurant. It was opened in December 1920 at 667 Madison Avenue and operated by Joe Pani, who also owned and operated the successful Woodmansten Inn and the Knickerbocker Grill. Pani recruited Ernest Cerutti to be the Colony's first headwaiter. Cerutti, born in Savona, Italy, into a family of innkeepers, was skilled in the arts of the profession and proved an excellent choice. Pani and Cerutti, in fact, had worked together at the Palast Hotel in Berlin many years before. Cerutti had honed his craft at the Savoy Hotel in London, where he eventually became headwaiter in 1908. It was there around that time he met Eugene "Gene" Cavallero. He was also born in Italy, in the town of Mantua. Although Cavallero worked under Cerutti at the Savoy, the two Italians became best friends. While their paths occasionally crossed over the next twelve years, they would become working partners in the successful establishment of the Colony. Pani selected Alfred Hartmann, who came from Alsace and had the culinary skills of the highest order, as the principal chef. He had worked at the Vanderbilt Hotel in New York before World War I, survived the carnage in numerous battles, and returned home to the States physically and mentally in one piece. He then went to work at the Knickerbocker, where, after two years, Pani tapped him to be the head chef at the Colony. Along with the additional staff of assistant chefs and waiters, the combination of this personnel at the Colony would make it legendary.[1]

Joe Pani nearly ruined the fledgling reputation of New York's newest restaurant before it got started. There was an abortive attempt to turn it into a nightclub, which Ernest in particular protested vehemently. Pani ignored Cerutti's complaints, though Cerutti was so upset with the situation he was transferred to the Knickerbocker Grill. Gene Cavellero, who had joined the Colony in 1921, was promoted from captain of the waiters to headwaiter, and kept the Colony running smoothly. But clearly, Cavellero was not entirely happy with the entertainment format of the restaurant either. The restaurant struggled to break even during 1921 and the early months of 1922, despite the fact the food was perhaps the finest served in Manhattan. Cerutti returned to the restaurant, rejoining Cavallero and Hartmann, and the three men held private meetings to see if they could buy the Colony from Pani and make the restaurant what they knew it should be. Through a third party, they put forth their proposal. Pani came back with an offer of $25,000. They managed to raise $18,000 among themselves and signed a note for the balance. In March 1922, the Colony was theirs.[2] The musicians and performers left to perform elsewhere in New York.

One of the Colony's problems in the early 1920s was it was not being frequented by the right crowd. The customers were, many times, wealthy criminals who were operating liquor cartels. With them came their women, who were not their wives. Had *The New Yorker* existed at the time, the magazine would have proved to be an ideal advertising medium to the correct targeted readership, but Harold Ross would not launch the magazine until 1925. Nevertheless, not all the customers of the Colony were rumrunners. The reputation of the restaurant spread by word of mouth and gradually New York's elite were discovering 667 Madison Avenue. One evening, the phone rang;

8. The Colony, the Plaza, the Rainbow Room and the Waldorf

Cavallero answered with his well-rehearsed, smooth greeting, and was surprised when Mrs. William K. Vanderbilt made a reservation. He remained calm, said he looked forward to her party's arrival and slowly put down the receiver. The atmosphere among Cavallero, Cerutti, Chef Hartmann and the staff was electric. When Mrs. Vanderbilt and her party arrived, the service was no different or the food any less superb. At the end of the sumptuous meal, one of the greatest names in American and New York Society complimented Cavallero and Cerutti and said she would return. Of course, she told her friends of the wonderful food and service at the Colony, and its fortunes were secured. Now they knew they could make the restaurant a success.

It was not long before the dining room saw the likes of the Astors, the Wideners and others from the remnants of the former 400. Joseph E. Widener, heir to the Widener fortune and known around the country for his horse breeding and racing, raved about the food and impeccable service. Reginald Vanderbilt soon decided it was his favorite restaurant. Mr. William K. Vanderbilt had to try the menu after his wife praised the food there. Other lesser known but equally wealthy persons were also regulars at the Colony. A very dapper New York state senator by the name of James J. Walker also frequented the restaurant when he was down from Albany. When he became the mayor of New York, he dined there more frequently. Everyone who enjoyed a meal at the Colony invariably spoke about it to their friends. By the mid–1920s, the main dining room was filled to capacity every night.

The Colony was just the sort of restaurant Maury Paul, known as "Cholly Knickerbocker," would enjoy dining in—and he did often. After the first several meals there, he reported one of those visits in his newspaper column in 1924. Paul used his own unique literary dialect in his column and he described the Colony like this: "There is something so frightfully 'inty' about The Colony. Unless you are unfortunate and are seated in the 'dog house.'"[3] "Inty" was "Cholly Knickerbocker"-speak for intimate and "dog house" referred to being seated in the rear of the dining room. Paul always insisted on a table near the entrance, in the front of the dining room, so he could easily see who entered and so those customers could see *him*. For Paul, it was always a working lunch or dinner; he was there to get information to be used in his column. "The all-knowing managers of the place," Paul wrote in his column in 1925, "have no desire to broadcast the illustrious names of the celebrities who crowd their dining salon to the doors. Truth to tell, they do everything in their power to keep the masses from knowing about the classes they cater to."[4]

What effect did Prohibition have on the operation of the Colony? Other than being very secretive about the liquor store on the premises, the establishment

Newspaper columnists Lucius Beebe (left) and Maury Paul, who wrote as "Cholly Knickerbocker," were among the arbiters of Café Society. It was Paul who first coined the descriptive phrase to define the transition from Fifth Avenue Society to the new creative class of Café Society that now frequented nightclubs and the finest New York restaurants. Here, Beebe and Paul are shown at The Colony (Jerome Zerbe, by permission).

served drinks with no fear of surprise raids. They had the usual barriers to entry to slow the progress of the agents, and the liquor itself was kept in the elevator, which they had access to within the restaurant. Marco Battem, the chief barman, would send the elevator to the top floor of the building, and by then, all drinks had been removed by the waiters from the tables with well-rehearsed ease and the contents dumped down the drain.

However, if it was suspected the two men asking to be seated were agents—and they could not drop in for a meal very often due to the expense— the drinks were served to customers in demitasse cups. In one case, Cavallero was called over to a table where he knew two federal agents were surveying the surrounding customers. One of the agents him what was being served in those cups at the table next to them.

"Brandy," Cavallero replied with a perfectly straight face and just the right tone, "but not the horrible stuff you are used to confiscating."[5] The agents were overwhelmed with his frankness, charm and elegant manner, and with a few drinks themselves and a wonderful meal on the house, they promised there wouldn't be any problem then or in the future.

In 1926, the entrance to the restaurant was changed from 667 Madison Avenue to around the corner on Sixty-First Street. Vacant adjoining offices were acquired and remodeled in the nondescript but tasteful Colony style. The Colony was one of the first restaurants in New York to install air conditioning; this was a considerable expense but an excellent investment in the comfort to the customers and staff of the restaurant as well. The reputation of the Colony had spread to Europe and it was not rare for heads of state, as well as British dukes, earls and other titled men and women, to dine at what was becoming one of the most famous restaurants in the world.

One of the notable qualities which contributed to the Colony's reputation was the ability to know the likes, preferences and dislikes of each regular customer. Cavellero and Cerutti did not commit all this to memory, but there was a wall in the kitchen with carefully mounted index cards, one for each regular customer.

During the boom times of the late 1920s, the restaurant was on a very sound financial footing, and by 1928, the Colony was clearing over half a million dollars a year. Alfred Hartmann had retired as primary chef in 1927, and selling his interest in the business to the other two partners, he took his considerable profits and moved back to France. His assistant chef of several years, Edmond Berger, took over as lead chef and the remarkable menu of the Colony continued without a perceptible interruption. The stock market crash in the fall of 1929 left Cavellero and Cerutti wondering how that might affect their customers, and thus, the Colony. While the fortunes of its regular customers were in many cases affected, the loyal among them kept on coming. Sometimes, however, they did not have enough money to pay, which was only disclosed at the end of the meal. Cavellero and Cerutti were always the height of tact, understanding and compassion, and they simply put these bills on a tab. Sometimes it was years before these bills, run up during the early 1930s, were finally settled. This was another aspect of the Colony that reinforced its reputation.

Aside from all the notables who dined at The Colony, it was also frequented by the aforementioned Maury Paul and Lucius Beebe, the columnist with the *New York Herald Tribune*. Having these two avidly-read newspapermen eating at the restaurant guaranteed its frequent mention in their columns, and readers of those columns numbered in the tens of thousands. While the Great Depression wreaked its havoc on the national and New York City economy, the Colony Restaurant continued to operate very successfully and profitably. As New York Society merged into Café Society, a new generation made "See you at the Colony" their salutation to friends. Cerutti had come up with a proverb of wisdom from his years in the business: "Two waiters starting in business together can do nothing, but two waiters and a chef can make a fortune."[6]

The Plaza

New York grand hotels were often the meeting place of the city's society members during the country's Gilded Age, and then Café Society during the late 1920s and the 1930s. One of Manhattan's premier hotels was then, and remains, the Plaza. As with all great things, it was the product of bold vision backed by investors to bring about its realization. There were two generations of this hotel. The first was built on the corner of Fifth Avenue between 58th and 59th Streets, with the latter overlooking land that would become Central Park. James R. Phyfe and James Campbell purchased that prime piece of real estate and the two veteran hotel builders set about raising the needed money to build the finest hotel America had ever seen. With nearly half a million dollars of their own funds and over three-quarters of a million dollars borrowed from the New York Life Insurance Company, they began their construction. They ran out of funds, however, because estimates of the hotel's construction were woefully inadequate. The two men were foreclosed on and the venerable insurance company proceeded to recoup its investment by completing its construction and opening the Plaza in 1890.

Only fifteen years would go by before other, richer men, with even larger vision, would decide a completely new hotel needed to be built on the same location. These men were Ben Beinecke, Harry Black and John Gates—all men with considerable means and who had made fortunes directly from or related to the hotel business and in high-stakes finance. There was a fourth, crucial individual who would prove a cornerstone of the future hotel's success. He was Frederick Steery, one of the country's finest hotel managers, known for his discernment in catering to a wealthy clientele. With stringent cost estimates and the additional financial backing, the original hotel was demolished in 1905, the site cleared, and an extensive, stronger foundation was built for what would become the eighteen-story French Renaissance-inspired hotel. It was designed by one of the country's noted hotel architects, Henry J. Hardenbergh.

8. The Colony, the Plaza, the Rainbow Room and the Waldorf

The new Plaza Hotel was to be the most luxurious hotel in the United States, a true reflection of the Gilded Age in which it was conceived. It was designed with 800 rooms and 500 baths. The ballroom, one of the largest of any hotel in the United States, would be finished in white with gold trim and beautifully illuminated with electrical chandeliers. There would be ten elevators to whisk its elite clientele to and from their respective floors. The interiors were the epitome of elegance. Beinecke, Steery and Hardenbergh traveled to Europe to shop for furnishings, placed a $100,000 order for Irish linen from William Lidell of Belfast, ordered monogrammed crystal from Baccarat, and purchased tapestries and 18th century furniture while traveling around France. The George A. Fuller company built the hotel on a tightly controlled, methodical schedule; it was finished in two years, right on schedule, but the reported cost of twelve million dollars was doubted by many. Months before its scheduled opening in October 1907, many of America's wealthiest men—and a few women—were reserving the permanent suites. In fact, the Plaza was designed with them in mind, as ninety percent of the rooms were being secured by them as residences; only ten percent of the rooms were for transient guests.[7]

The news of the hotel's pending opening occupied the newspapers for weeks in advance. Opening day was scheduled for October 1, 1907. Thousands of curious onlookers lined Fifth Avenue and 59th Street, which formed the southern end of Central Park. The first to arrive was Alfred G. Vanderbilt, son of Cornelius Vanderbilt, later joined by his wife, and their entry in the hotel's register was the very first. Mr. and Mrs. George Jay Gould also signed in. John Wanamaker came from Philadelphia to secure his suite. Benjamin Duke, the tobacco multimillionaire, arrived and made the Plaza his home for many years until he built his famous mansion on Fifth Avenue designed by architect Horace Trumbauer. No Astors were present because they had hotels of their own—the Waldorf-Astoria being just one of them. All the principal backers of the Plaza naturally had their own suites there as well. Many of the wealthy who pulled up to the main entrance of the hotel were unknown to many of the onlookers, but they were invariably captains of industry or partners in banking and law firms. More than a few were retired wealthy and did not want to be bothered with the maintenance of a large mansion in the city.

The Plaza would see two financial panics and subsequent depressions: 1908 and 1929. The second was the more severe, and the Great Depression severely affected the Plaza. Prohibition had its effect on the hotel as well. The Oak Bar stopped serving drinks and was converted into an E.F. Hutton brokerage office. The elegant Rose Room also underwent change and became a showroom for Studebaker automobiles. However, the Plaza Grill remained a favored gathering spot throughout the dry era; many well-attended tea dances took place there, and continued when Prohibition was repealed. It was also discovered by Café Society during the early 1930s, but the hotel fell on hard times during that decade nevertheless. Hotel staff was greatly curtailed and those remaining often had to wait weeks for their pay. Many of the large, empty permanent residence suites were subdivided and made transient suites for temporary guests. A sign of the times was that the transient guests had to carry their own luggage or use carts. Studebaker was forced to close its showroom on the ground floor.

The repeal of Prohibition in 1933 gave the hotel management ideas of how to revive the cash flow to stem the losses it had experienced since 1929. The hotel's operating manager, Henry Rost, immediately reopened the Oak Lounge bar. He advertised the reopening in *The New Yorker* and in the city's newspapers, and Manhattanites responded. The Rose Room was still dormant, and Rost realized it could be redesigned as an elegant dining room and gathering place like numerous others in Manhattan. He contracted with Joseph Urban, a noted Broadway stage set designer, to give the room an exotic flair. Urban did not disappoint, and he produced a room with design influences from Persia with murals on the walls depicting evocative themes. All new furnishings, fabrics and drapes to complement the murals resulted in the Persian Room. To make the opening a true event, Rost made it into a charity event to benefit the New York Infirmary for Women and Children, since charity events like this brought out New York's upper crust like no other. And no grand opening could go unnoticed by *New York Herald Tribune* columnist Lucius Beebe, who never missed an opportunity to enjoy a free wonderfully prepared meal and superb drinks.

With the opening of the Persian Room, many New Yorkers with a little extra cash could enjoy the ambiance of the elegant Plaza Hotel without the expense of actually staying there. This new gathering place naturally had an orchestra, conducted by Emil Coleman, who was nearly as popular as Paul Whiteman. Among the entertainers were Tony and Renee Demarco as featured dancers. Their ballroom dancing was a sensation, and helped to usher in a new era of elegant dancing that put the frenetic dances of the 1920s to rest, evoking the era of Vernon and Irene Castle and Fred and Adele Astaire. The Demarcos did something unprecedented: as they danced near the tables with guests and customers, they casually carried on brief conversations with them, which thrilled and surprised those attending. Such an unforgettable event helped to bring them back again.

In the fall of 1934, Rost signed pianist and orchestra leader Eddy Duchin, who had gained fame performing at the Central Park Casino. Duchin's live radio program and popular recordings added to his draw in performing at the Persian Room. He often had comely and talented female singers to accompany him. By the end of 1934, the Persian Room was recording gross receipts of nearly $25,000 a week.[8] Duchin married Marjorie Oelrichs, of the socially prominent Newport, Rhode Island, Oelrichs, later that year. He had met her while both were performing at the Casino. In 1935, the Persian Room welcomed the Duchins as a performing act, and guests enjoyed listening to Mrs. Duchin sing to Mr. Duchin's smooth piano playing. The success of this new venue at the Plaza Hotel was almost immediate. The success continued throughout the 1930s and helped boost the hotel's bottom line, and helped to bring in staying guests as well.

The Rainbow Room

For over half a century, the Rainbow Room was one of the most elegant dining establishments in Manhattan, situated as it was on the sixty-fifth floor of what was for several decades the RCA Building. The creation of Rockefeller Center and the cast of characters involved with its financing, design and marketing made for the most improbable business model of the greatest building project ever seen in New York City. Before there would ever be a Rainbow Room, there had to be the building complex centerpiece, the home of David Sarnoff's Radio Corporation of America.

The Rockefeller Center complex was initially conceived during the latter roaring twenties as a project to greatly expand the Metropolitan Opera facilities. The man behind those efforts was a financier and patron of the arts, Otto Khan. He was also chairman of the MET, as it was affectionately known. The location for the new performance center was on land owned by Columbia University. Kahn would spend several years trying to get both the financing and the cooperation of Columbia in efforts to build a new opera facility, but it was not to happen in his lifetime. During the course of this initial project, John Davidson Rockefeller, Jr., would play a pivotal role, and, in fact, would ultimately become the controlling factor in the creation of the multi-block complex that would eventually be built. That complex would cover land from Fifth Avenue to Sixth Avenue and from 48th Street to 52nd Street. In January 1929, the principals signed the lease paperwork agreed to by Columbia University and the Rockefeller interests. The total sum to be paid to Columbia each year henceforth would be $3.6 million annually.[9]

"Junior," as he was referred to by his business associates by permission, had his business office at 26 Broadway. It was here he controlled all his financial and real estate dealings. With the collapse of the New York Stock Market in October and November of 1929, Rockefeller was now faced with abandoning the massive building project, or to underwrite the cost of the entire design and construction project himself. He chose the latter course, and it remains a lasting legacy to his resolve.

The competition for the selection of architects to design the buildings was among the most heated ever witnessed by the architectural profession in Manhattan, or any major city, for that matter. In the end, the firms and individual architects selected were either unknown or of lesser fame than the elites it was assumed would be chosen. To the surprise of practically everyone but the selection committee, the relatively new firm of Andrew Reinhard and Henry Hofmeister was selected to coordinate the massive design project. A consortium of three other lead architects were selected to contribute to the project: Raymond M. Hood, Harvey Corbett and Wally Harrison. These architects and the army of designers and draftsmen were the fortunate ones. Apart from Rockefeller Center, there was virtually no new commercial construction going on in Manhattan or the surrounding boroughs. The vast majority of architects were unemployed, many never recovered, and countless architectural offices closed permanently.

The process of buying out the smaller leases of businesses and individuals on the land began after the agreement between Columbia and Rockefeller was signed. It would take two years, roughly, to complete. In July 1931, the clearing of these buildings began. While the Chrysler and the Empire State buildings were indeed large construction projects, the Rockefeller Center complex dwarfed them both. The Depression had worsened by the time construction had begun, and this last and biggest project provided desperately needed work for tens of thousands of workers, not only in New York City but in states around the country that provided the iron ore to make the steel that went into the beams and girders, the quarries that provided the limestone from Indiana, granite from Maine, marble and other stone materials, the countless miles of copper wiring for electricity, the thousands of gallons of paint needed, and so on. Work on the complex went on for the entire decade, and it meant not only steady work for the men, but survival for their families.

Radio City Music Hall, with its fabulous Art Deco interior design, was the first portion to open, right after Christmas of 1932. The large performance stage overwhelmed the individual performing acts at first. In January 1933

8. The Colony, the Plaza, the Rainbow Room and the Waldorf   159

this was changed to large group stage performances, along with the latest feature film—a format that was kept for decades. Radio City Music Hall became the home of the leggy Rockettes.

The seventy-story RCA Building was the centerpiece of the entire complex, being the tallest of all the structures. The architects had set aside the sixty-fifth floor to hold a lavish restaurant and nightclub given the name the Rainbow Room. Here too, Art Deco reigned beautifully supreme. Its interior design was done by Elena Bachman Schmidt and Vincente Minnelli. It opened in October 1934. In terms of exclusivity and quality of service, El Morocco would have nothing on the Rainbow Room. Dining here would be expensive, and worth it. Now, Manhattan would have a new exclusive meeting place for New York Society itself, and it would have something the Stork Club, El Morocco and 21 could never have—a magnificent and breathtaking view of New York City at night. The windows looking out on the dazzling city lights stretched from the floor all the way to the ceiling and the tables situated next to the windows gave the diners the sensation they were floating in the air above the city. There was something else the Rainbow Room had that El Morocco, for example, did not have, and that was *room*. The tables and their chairs were generously spaced; there was never a case of crowding.

From "This New York," by Lucius Beebe, the *New York Herald Tribune*, January 1935:

> The Rainbow Room at Radio City is really the darnedest place. This department took its life in its hand (being terrified of high places) and went up those sixty-five floors after shutting its eyes and holding Margot Larsen firmly by the hand recently to hear Beatrice Lillie's new repertoire of midnight songs. In a state of exemplary sobriety we all sat down after bowing to the Sigourney Thayers at the next table and, on looking up ten minutes later, found the glittering Mrs. Charles A. Cartwright simply socked out in a diamond necklace for a neighbor. The next time we turned around there was Baron George Wrangle and Mrs. Tiffany Saportas in the same place, and a minute later the Grand Duchess Marie popped up in the identical position. It was all too confusing until we found that the ringside row of tables is on a revolving stage and you can bow casually to your friends as they pass before you without leaving your chair.

The management of the Rainbow Room, since this was in fact in Rockefeller Center, worked to emphasize its exclusivity. It was often preferred as a place for dining and elegant dancing over the flashier and noisier clubs by such legendary family names like the Astors, Warburgs, Whitneys and the Vanderbilts, among others. Dress for the men was *de rigueur* white tie and cutaway black tuxedo and only the most elegant evening dresses for the women. However, publicity was the lifeblood of practically any elegant establishment, and when Jerome Zerbe made inquiries about photographing New York's wealthiest dining at the Rainbow Room, and seeing to it those photos with suitable captions made it into the appropriate papers and magazines, it seemed a brilliant idea—and it was. Even Society enjoyed reading about themselves, and the women liked it even more, finding their photographs wearing the latest Worth gown and Tiffany jewels to be very gratifying.

The Rainbow Room was not merely for dining and dancing—it was most definitely entertainment as well. These truly were variety acts that spanned the gamut of the performing arts. Stage actress Beatrice Lillie would perform monologues and the occasional song, and would be followed by a piano soloist, then the latest dancing couple (always a good draw) and a magician performing acts of mystifying sleight of hand. The sequence of entertainers might run for a week or two, and then it would be changed. No act was too improbable. The Rainbow Room even had ping-pong champion Ruth Aarons welcome any challengers, who could win a magnum of champagne if she lost; occasionally she did.

As a means of increasing the establishment's cash flow, on the west end of the sixty-fifth floor was opened the Rainbow Grill. Ads in *The New Yorker* announced the "New Informal Rainbow Grill," which opened June 7, 1935. The Rainbow Grill was more accessible than the Rainbow Room, and one did not need to wear white tie to be admitted. One could enjoy cocktails, with no cover charge, followed by dinner for as little as $2. The Grill also had a dinner entertainment format, with opportunity for dancing to the music of Val Olman and his musical ensemble. The view from the windows of the Rainbow Grill were no less spectacular than that of the Rainbow Room.

The Waldorf Astoria Starlight Roof

William Waldorf Astor was the man behind the grand hotel that would rise during the early 1890s in the midst of America's Gilded Age. It was built on the corner of Fifth Avenue and 34th Street and opened on March 14, 1893. The general manager of the Waldorf was George C. Boldt, and he was largely responsible for seeing to it, as the hotel was being furnished, that nothing but the finest furniture, paintings, carpets and drapes were selected for this

8. The Colony, the Plaza, the Rainbow Room and the Waldorf

new hotel. The service personnel were carefully selected, and among the most notable was a gentleman named Oscar Tschirky. He became known over the subsequent decades simply as Oscar of the Waldorf.

There seemed to be a great deal of intra-family rivalry and spite among the Astors at the time; that was, after all, one of the reasons the Waldorf was constructed in the first place. When John Jacob Astor got it in his head he too must build a hotel, he chose to have it built next to his cousin's thirteen-story Waldorf Hotel. Naturally, it had to be taller, and it was by four stories. When George Boult learned of the new hotel and the competition it would pose for the Waldorf, he began a diplomatic mission, so to speak, with John Astor. By the time the Astoria Hotel opened in 1897, Mr. Boult was successfully operating two hotels with plans to merge them physically and in name. The physical bridge was a new corridor between the two hotels which subsequently became known as "Peacock Alley," as the finely dressed guests promenaded from one hotel to the next. In time, the separate buildings became known as the singular Waldorf-Astoria.

For more than thirty years, the Waldorf-Astoria catered to the upper and upper-middle classes. However, the endless tale of New York City, architecturally speaking, is change and the ownership of the hyphenated hotel shifted to another wealthy family, the Du Ponts. At a significant profit, the owners agreed to sell the site on which the hotel stood to make way for the Empire State Building. A new Waldorf-Astoria Hotel was constructed on Park Avenue between 49th and 50th Streets, and it opened in 1931. Like many New York hotels during the Great Depression, the new hotel was struggling to secure guests and permanent residents, and to keep the signature dining room, the Starlight Roof, as least breaking even.

Henry Sell, editor of *Harper's Bazaar*, also had a small advertising agency which was kept busy with clients relying on him to drive paying customers to their businesses. Sell was also doing publicity for a number of clients, one of whom was the Waldorf-Astoria Hotel. Sell had helped Gloria Braggiotti land a column, "Madame Fluttlerby," in one of the city's newspapers, and he felt she might just be the perfect person for a publicity campaign for the upper-crust hotel in desperate need of more customers.

"Henry was doing publicity for the Castle Harbor Hotel in Bermuda and the Waldorf-Astoria in New York," Braggiotti recalled in an interview.

> We thought of this publicity stunt to have auditions with society girls to sing in the Starlight Roof of the Waldorf. My brother, Mario Braggiotti, was a pianist and he had so many girlfriends he used to keep a book full of names and addresses. I used to look through his book and call up all these girls and ask

them to come and audition. If she was really good enough to sing, she would sing one chorus with the orchestra. Guy Lombardo's orchestra alternated with Xavier Cugat. Imagine! That girl was able to invite all her friends to sit at the table. They didn't have to pay for the food, only the drinks. They were all written up in the columns, along with a photo of them auditioning and later singing. The Waldorf took a very dim view of the thing but once it got going, they were thrilled because we got all these people to come who never would have dreamed of going up there. It became a big spot. I always posed with the girls as though I was singing, but I didn't really. At the end we all sang together. There were about eight of us. We called ourselves "The Singing Debutantes." We really had a wonderful time.[10]

It was through these creative publicity efforts for the Starlight Roof and other dining and entertaining venues that these establishments were able to keep operating even during the economic hardships of the 1930s. In fact, the very atmosphere and sumptuous food with their elegantly dressed customers belied the everyday life experienced by so many other New Yorkers. It was just an example of the curious counterpoint of Café Society with many of less fortunate in Manhattan.

Chapter 9

Jack and Charlie's 21 Club

During Prohibition, the city of New York spawned thousands of speakeasies. Certainly, the forces behind the dry movement had little inkling the law would produce precisely the opposite effect intended. The legislation that provided enforcement of the 18th Amendment also resulted, in many cases, in the corruption of the enforcement officers, whether they be local police officers, municipal enforcement agents, or even bureaucrats from Washington. The number of speakeasies in Manhattan was overwhelming; they could not all be investigated and closed down. Nevertheless, some speakeasies were blessed, as it were, with a combination of advantages that allowed them to flourish, survive Prohibition and even prosper during the Great Depression as legitimate establishments that went on to become legendary. Among those legendary establishments that were frequented by Café Society was Jack and Charlie's 21 Club, or simply 21 for short.

Jack Kriendler's parents arrived in New York from Poland in 1896, passed through the doors of Ellis Island, and then found their first American home in the Lower East Side. Kieve Kriendler went to work in the Brooklyn Navy Yard, and his wife Sadie raised an ever-growing brood of children. Four daughters and four sons were born to the Kriendlers. The Kriendler children all attended the public schools in the city. Being from a poor family, the sons in particular knew they would have to somehow work on the side if they wanted to attend and pay for college. Jack Kriendler was accepted into Fordham University and he attended classes there with a cousin, Charlie Burns. Another relative ran a saloon in the Jewish ghetto of lower Manhattan. Jack's Uncle Sam prospered running that saloon, and this impressed him. It seemed even then Jack Kriendler absorbed the lessons of that well-run saloon in speaking with his uncle. What Jack discovered was that Sam was instrumental in the customers' coming back to the establishment again and again. He observed how his uncle dressed in suits, had superb manners and a ready smile, and knew many of the frequent customers by their first names. He served some of the best-prepared food in the Lower East Side and drinks were served with the some of the best liquor available. When Prohibition became the law of the land, his uncle had to become creative, as most saloon keepers did. Their establishments became speakeasies.

While Jack Kriendler and Charlie Burns had plans to pursue traditional careers after graduating from Fordham University, the rise of Prohibition and the burgeoning speakeasy culture got Jack thinking. He had learned of a business a family friend by the name of Eddie Irving had purchased—a tea room, as it was referred to in those days—in Greenwich Village near New York University. Jack saw the possibilities of joining that business and helping to meet the prevailing market demand for libations which heretofore had been perfectly legal. Jack spoke with relatives and raised the cash to become a partner with Mr. Irving, who listened intently to Jack's description of what the business could truly become. In 1922, Jack Kriendler with his partner opened the Red Head. No tea was served in those cups; it was clandestine liquor mixed however the customers wanted. The place became a hangout of the NYU students and even the young women began to frequent the place with their boyfriends—and without.

Greenwich Village had become a bohemian enclave, and writers, artists, and musicians often stopped by the Red Head for drinks and camaraderie. Even then, Jack Kriendler knew the importance of music to add to the place's atmosphere, and he would have a small group to play music of the day. As business grew during 1922 and into 1923, his cousin Charlie Burns decided he liked the idea of joining Jack in running the business as an accountant and other business-related duties. Eventually, Eddie Irving was bought out and moved to Wall Street to be an investment broker. The liquor was obtained through trusted family members, and Jack's uncle, Sam Brenner, was a primary source. He took great delight in seeing his young charge do so well running the Red Head and employing the winning business practices he had told the young Jack. Nepotism was big with the Kriendlers, and Jack brought in his brothers Peter, Mac and Bob to perform various tasks there.

Prohibition had bred a criminal network in Manhattan and it was only a matter of time before Jack and Charlie were paid a visit by the local thugs who wanted to cut into their business for a percentage in order to keep operating unmolested. The first time the gangsters dropped into the Red Head and let their demands be known, Jack and Charlie firmly but smugly told them they were not interested in taking on any new partners. After a second visit produced the same noncommittal response, the word went out that a message needed to be given the naive club owners. As the two men were walking home one night, they were attacked by several members of the Hudson Dusters. The Kriendlers were almost always on the alert for this possibility, and they gave as good as they got. They survived with some cuts and bruises and put the gang members to flight.

One night Charlie Burns encountered a customer—a local fireman—who went from uncooperative to dangerous. After an argument with Charlie, the man pulled out a straight razor and succeeded in slashing Charlie several times about the face and neck, though miraculously his jugular veins were not cut. Jack took Charlie to a nearby hospital where he was stitched up. The following day, with bandages covering Charlie's numerous wounds, the two club owners visited the Charles Street police station. Some of the officers there often stopped into the Red Head for a good Polish meal and refreshment. After the story of the attack was related, Jack and Charlie were assured that it would never happen again, and it didn't.

"Sure, you had to be brave to run a speak," Charlie explained years later, "but give it up because of a corrupt official? No ... the fireman angered us more than anything else. We realized that if we wanted to stay in the business and in one piece, we had to get ourselves some protection."[1]

The mutual understanding that existed between Jack and Charlie and the local police department, aided by timely gifts of cash, thoughtful presents and the occasional meal on the house, permitted the Red Head to operate and thrive. There were unwritten rules, however; the Red Head could not stay open beyond 1:00 a.m. and they had to have an open door policy of serving anyone who walked in. Jack Kriendler bristled at these demands, and he began to look around for another possible location where these requirements could be waived.

While police presence was welcomed in and around the Red Head, there were Prohibition enforcement officers who truly took their job seriously. Two men became famous during the 1920s in New York City, and they were Isadore "Izzy" Einstein and Moe Smith. Their fame stemmed from their incredible array of disguises they created to blend in and look like anything but enforcement agents. These two agents became celebrities in their own right and were often the subject of newspaper columnists who wrote about the agents' latest bust. And while they took down many a speakeasy, they never took down the Red Head. Izzy and Moe came from the same Lower East Side neighborhood as Jack and Charlie and were known to them. In fact, the two agents often stopped in at the Red Head and enjoyed the atmosphere and food, but not the available liquor.

Jack Kriendler did not want their hours of operation limited to the hours prior to 1:00 a.m. and he wanted the freedom to decide who should and should not enter through his front door. After some careful inquiries, Kriendler found a suitable new place in 1925 in a cellar on the corner of Washington Place and Sixth Avenue in the Village. This place too was basic in its furnishings, but Jack and Charlie worked to make it comfortable and a desirable place for patrons to frequent. They called it the Fronton, and soon the word got around and the notables started dropping in. Kriendler was also dressed smartly, as was everyone who worked there; service was excellent, and it went without saying the liquor was of the highest quality. Newspaper publisher Herbert B. Swope often dropped in, Edna St. Vincent Millay was a patron who recommended it to her friends, and even Mayor Jimmy Walker was a regular from his earlier days at the Red Head. Kriendler hired a skilled chef who helped to put the Fronton on the lower Manhattan map.

Jack and Charlie did their part to contribute to the Roaring Twenties. Instead of the roar of machine guns, the Fronton provided entertainment that left its customers roaring for more. The new place was a complete package: food, drink and entertainment. Young, attractive women were hired to act as hostesses and provide dancing to the hits of the day. In addition, most nights would find a torch singer with the theatrical name Flame Moore singing to piano tunes played by Al Segal, who was a powerful draw all by himself.

For the first time, Jack and Charlie began to selectively choose who could enter the Fronton and who would be turned away. The two speakeasy owners wanted their clientele to go uptown, in a manner of speaking. They wanted customers who could and would pay the premium for entering the Fronton. Many evenings, the place didn't become active until ten or eleven at night, and would operate into the early morning hours until the last customer walked out the door. The food offered at the Fronton was drawing accolades from customers and magazine and newspaper columnists, and this was attributed to a skilled Italian chef. In addition, Jack and Charlie decided to build an impressive wine list with the best imported French and German wines available.

While the décor, food and drinks were excellent for the Village, the below-street-level location was not ideal. Three events forced the fate of the Fronton. The first was a flooding episode, and once that was handled and the place dried out and redecorated, the second sign was a fire which no one could seem to explain. The third event was a condemnation notice in 1926 from the city of Manhattan saying all businesses and residences had to vacate to make way for a new subway station. Jack and Charlie had to move and expand again, and they chose to move to mid-town.

They found a place available at 42 West 49th street. It took several weeks to outfit the place the way they knew it needed to be, and then the Puncheon Grotto was open for business. This was closer to the members of the Algonquin Round Table, and one of its charter members, Robert Benchley, spread the word of the new speakeasy at No. 42. Soon, Alexander Woollcott, Dorothy Parker, Franklin P. Adams, George S. Kaufman, and Donald Ogden Stewart, among others, were toasting one another at the Puncheon, as Jack and Charlie preferred to call it. Jack's brother Peter struck up a friendship with Robert Benchley and he found, as people often did, that simply being around Benchley and listening to whatever he had to say made him feel happy. Benchley had that effect on people. He was the polar opposite of Woollcott, who always had some caustic remark to fling at some poor unfortunate. All the literary lights of the Round Table were welcomed at the Puncheon, but the proprietors continued their strict rules of entry to ensure only Manhattan's noted and accomplished passed through, first, an ornate iron gate, then its closely guarded door. During the later 1920s, this became one of the most exclusive speakeasies in Manhattan.

Jack and Charlie had indeed been fortunate in dodging the dark forces that had succeeded in closing down countless other speakeasies in the city, but their good fortune ran out when they opened on 49th Street. The assistant attorney general in charge of Prohibition enforcement in Washington, Mabel Walker Willenbrandt, finally got wind of Jack and Charlie and their illicit establishment in New York City, and she personally dispatched federal agents to shut the place down. The raid was a closely guarded secret and Jack and Charlie suspected nothing until the federal agents forced their way in. They found liquor in abundance and on every table. All the liquor, which was substantial, was seized. The two men managed to get by with striking a plea agreement with the municipal prosecutor, and they paid a necessary fine. The Puncheon stayed open.

With their success operating their previous establishments, the two businessmen could afford to hire the best chef they could lure away, and they hired Henri Geib, who had been chef to Germany's Kaiser Wilhelm II. The menu was revamped to include many of Geib's finest recipes and dishes. In addition to the growing wine list and well-known hard liquor, a variety of champagne and cognac labels were also now available. Compared to other establishments in mid–Manhattan, the Puncheon was expensive. That was by necessity and by design. The prices reflected the quality of the food and drinks served there, and it also acted as a barrier to some of the less desirable customers. Jack Kriendler and Charles Burns *wanted* their place to have the reputation of being expensive, which added to its exclusivity.

The two establishment owners had excellent contacts in the city for obtaining whatever they needed that came in a bottle. There was no need for them to get their needed liquor, wine, and other contraband themselves. There were bootleggers who were quite skilled in this area and they welcomed the business with the Puncheon Grotto. One of those bootleggers revealed how the transportation of liquor to the business took place. "Jack and Charlie had fellows who worked the docks ... and they took dozens of cases of liquor and wines at a time off the steamships with the cooperation of the crews," the bootlegger revealed. "One of the unusual booties I knew who supplied the Puncheon ... took small lots of bottles off steamers by hiding them in his overcoat, a big thing that swept down to the ground and had rows and rows of pockets inside. He would walk off a boat loaded with booze and go straight to No. 42 and into the coatroom, where he unloaded his pockets, then go back to the ships for more, making many trips across town each day."[2]

The Puncheon's fame for fine food and drink spread and other desirables started making No. 42 a favored gathering place. Author H.L. Mencken, *Vanity Fair* publisher Frank Crowninshield, Will Rogers, Ernest Hemingway and F. Scott Fitzgerald added to the Puncheon's elite reputation. It was the subject of a profile, with suitable vague location description, in *The New Yorker* as part of the magazine's ongoing series on speakeasies. Lucius Beebe joined the staff of the *New York Herald Tribune*, and wasted no time in adding the Puncheon to his short list of favorite speakeasies. However, several events occurred during 1929 that would cause them to pull up stakes yet again. They received a notice to vacate because the entire block and a whole lot more was going to become the future home of what would be called Rockefeller Center. They had six months to find other surroundings. In October of that year, the stock market collapsed and Jack and Charlie saw a significant number of their patrons' finances severely affected. Peter Kriendler did not record how his brother Jack and partner Charlie were themselves affected by the collapse of the stock market in his book on the history of the 21 Club, but apparently the finances remained sound enough that Jack and Charlie moved forward with their plans to open a new place at another location.

As before, the crucial aspect of running a speakeasy was a benevolent lack of interest on the part of the prohibition enforcement agents. Through their contacts, Jack and Charlie learned of a five-story brownstone available for sale at 21 West 52nd Street. The two speakeasy owners had amassed a significant fortune in the previous seven years and they had the cash to pay the $130,000 asking price. Once the deed was in their hands, they could pretty much do what they wanted with the building's interior. This time, the two men vowed, there would be no cause or reason to move again.

When Robert Benchley learned that the Puncheon Grotto would have to close, he came up with a unique idea. He suggested to Jack and Charlie of having a grand closing of the Puncheon to which they would invite all their regular patrons. This closing, however, would be quite different. Since the property was destined for eventual destruction, Benchley suggested, why not let the patrons have their hand at dismantling the interior appointments to help things along? Jack and Charlie immediately liked the idea and sent the word out, giving the time and date.

At the appointed time, the invited patrons began showing up at No. 42 West 49th Street. As they stepped inside, they were informed they had their choice of destructive implements: ax, crowbar, sledgehammer—whatever struck their fancy. John H. Whitney grabbed his weapon of choice and selected the large plate glass mirror against the wall behind the bar. He closed his eyes, swung mightily, and the mirror was shattered into a hundred shards. Joseph Sheffield wreaked destruction upon the principal chandelier in the room. William H. Vanderbilt did his share of dismantling. Beatrice Lillie made for the ladies' room to see what could be removed or somehow made inoperable. A group of men counted among Manhattan's upper crust chose to destroy the steps leading to the second floor. Robert Benchley made good use of his ax. A mounted policeman sauntering by stopped his horse to investigate the sounds of shattering glass and splintering wood. Jack and Charlie invited him in—on his horse—to reach some otherwise out-of-reach wall fixtures, and the officer was happy to oblige.

Years later, Lucius Beebe, who was present for the demolition party, wrote: "It is improbable that so much destruction was ever accomplished by so blue-blooded a wrecking crew as that which closed one era of Jack & Charlie's and inaugurated another."[3]

With substantial funds to outfit the new drinking and eating establishment, the men hired Frank A. Buchanan, an architectural engineer who had a reputation for successful hotel and club commissions. Among his most famous clients were the West Palm Beach Hotel and the Sleepy Hollow Country Club in Westchester County. Buchanan's design was unremarkable and in every way predictable in that it was wonderfully elegant; it was produced with Jack and Charlie's input, and the resulting décor was exactly what the business partners wanted. They initially failed to take the extraordinary steps to safeguard their liquor supply, believing falsely that they would be immune to any kind of raid in their new location. They were mistaken. After their first raid at 21, which nearly resulted in their spending time in prison, Jack and Charlie agreed they had also had their last raid. They called up Buchanan and informed him they needed his services again.

Now, extraordinary features would be designed in to store, hide and make inaccessible to any municipal or federal enforcement agent the abundant liquor and wine onsite. Buchanan worked with the proprietors to design and have built clandestine storage facilities throughout the place that were completely undetectable. First, electrical pushbuttons were located at several inside locations near the entrance, which could be pressed to alert the owners agents were outside the door. Various closets were converted to conceal clever storage areas behind each, and there was no way to detect that the back of the closet could pivot to reveal the liquor stored there. However, the *pièce de résistance* was a storage vault downstairs constructed behind a foundation wall that was hinged like some massive bank vault and was built with such precision, the line that separated the door from the wall could not be found. The opening mechanism could only be triggered to open by inserting a thin rod in a small hole near the floor that looked like numerous other small holes in the wall. This door had a special locking mechanism that ensured no one would get access to this secret liquor supply room except Jack, Charlie or one of their trusted aides.

Jack and Charlie's 21 became a prime mid-Manhattan locale for the city's elite to eat and drink—and carry on illicit romantic relationships. The upper floors of the building were private rooms for Jack and Charlie—or some very special clients when the need arose. Ernest Hemingway enjoyed the food and drink at 21, but one evening during December 1931 he discovered something that was not on the famous menu. He struck up a conversation with a beautiful young Italian woman who captivated Hemingway in ways he wanted to fulfill. She was positively the most beautiful woman he had ever met. She was not accompanied by any man, so he pressed his advantage after the place had closed. They ended up in the kitchen making love, and their passion continued on and off for several hours. Hemingway offered to take her home but she insisted she would take a cab. The following day, unable to get the woman out of his mind, Hemingway shared his amorous encounter with Jack, who became alarmed when he learned the identity of the woman. Hemingway was informed the beauty in question was the mistress of crime boss Legs Diamond, and if word got back to him about the affair, Hemingway was as good as dead. As it turned out, a week before Christmas two hit men waited patiently for the criminal to be fast asleep in a seedy hotel in Albany, New York, and killed him in a classic gangland hit.

9. Jack and Charlie's 21 Club

Maury Paul, singer Libby Holman, author Paul Chavchavadze, columnist Gloria Braggiotti and Lucius Beebe enjoy each other's company. Café Society was a cultural fascination with millions of readers around the United States during the Great Depression, as Café Society itself deftly skirted the economic debacle (Jerome Zerbe, by permission).

As recorded earlier in this book, Mayor Jimmy Walker had a thing for singer Betty Compton, and the couple spent numerous evenings at 21 in the private meeting rooms of the august establishment. Jack and Charlie only made these special accommodations for a select few, not wanting their place to become known for more than very fine food and drink. When other customers asked for such favors, they were directed to try any one of the nearby hotels.

One day in June of 1932, there was another raid on 21 that put to the test the extensive measures taken to protect and preserve all liquor kept on the premises. When Jimmie Coslove, the first line of defense for 21, looked through the small peephole in the entrance door, he saw several men standing there he did not recognize. He suspected a raid was imminent. He immediately informed Jack of who was at the door, and Jack announced to the assembled customers there was about to be a raid. He advised them to finish their drinks, but not to be alarmed. The tables were swept of their glasses; somewhere a button was pushed, the shelf holding the immediate supply of liquor for the guests pivoted, and the bottles disappeared down a chute. Then the agents with their search warrant were allowed to enter the restaurant. For hours they combed the entire place and found not a single bottle of liquor and failed to detect any place of storage.

Prohibition Is Repealed

In November of 1932, Franklin D. Roosevelt won the presidential election over the incumbent, Herbert Hoover. Roosevelt had campaigned on, among other things, overturning the failed Eighteenth Amendment. For nearly 13 years, the amendment and the laws that gave it teeth had been in force and had failed terribly to accomplish its intent. In addition, it had served at the basis for the growth of organized crime to traffic in all forms of alcoholic beverages. Finally, prohibition laws were without question the most disregarded laws by Americans in the country's history. It would take a new amendment to repeal the Eighteenth Amendment. By that time, two other amendments to the Constitution had been ratified, so it fell to the Twenty-First Amendment to accomplish this. The House and then the Senate passed it, and in February 1933 it was sent to the individual states for ratification. Be December of that year, the Twenty-First Amendment was ratified. It was a new era for establishments, and 21 could now operate without the specter of Prohibition.

However, many of the speakeasies that came into being as a result of Prohibition now had to compete with one another for legitimate business. It was now a buyers' market and many of those buyers were free to go wherever they wanted or even keep liquor in their own homes. For many speakeasies, now legit drinking places, the customers simply disappeared. Jack and Charlie continued to operate 21 as if nothing had happened because it was primarily a restaurant—which just so happened to also serve drinks. The peephole in the front door of 21 became inoperative, and the only change to the décor of the place was the liquor license on prominent display for all to see.

Nevertheless, repeal of the Eighteenth Amendment suddenly resulted in a host of new establishments opening up in midtown Manhattan, and formerly clandestine establishments now gladly opened their doors to customers who no longer had to skulk from place to place but could freely go where they wanted. In other words, now 21 had serious competition, and Jack and Charlie watched the number of customers slowly dwindle. Advertisements were placed in New York newspapers and magazines inviting readers to dine at 21, and still the number of customers continued to fall. Of course, the continuing economic depression was also having a powerful effect in keeping away customers who now had less money to spend on the expensive menu items.

The two owners of 21 had to come up with a plan for other revenue, and the repeal of Prohibition provided just the means. They chose to become the exclusive importer of several liquor brands that were frequently requested there and often available nowhere else in New York. They got exclusive rights to import and distribute Ballantine's Scotch Whiskey and several other select liquors. They established a new business, 21 Brands, to do this. For legal reasons, their formal business partnership had to be terminated so Jack could be sole proprietor of 21 and Charlie would be head of 21 Brands. Naturally, Charlie now needed salesmen to get the product out there and sell as if their business depended on it—which it did. Among the new hires was a very dapper young British fellow by the name of David Niven. Unfortunately, selling liquor was not Niven's forte. In addition to that, he had to deal with some rather hardboiled types—former bootleggers—and his soft manner had no effect on them, accent or no accent. Charlie would remember David Niven as his worst salesman many years after he had become a famous actor. 21 Brands became a significant distributor during the Depression years of the 1930s and added significantly to the fortunes of both Jack and Charlie.

Business was once again booming for 21 by late 1935, so much so that they had to expand. The property next door at No. 19 was purchased, and was remodeled to continue the ambiance of 21. In fact, Jack and Charlie's 21 was an economic oasis in a city still feeling the effects of the lingering Depression. There were other outward signs of architectural prosperity visible by simply walking down the street. There were the Chrysler and the Empire State Buildings, and now the striking Rockefeller Center with the Rainbow Room on the 65th floor, which served sumptuous dinners overlooking glittering Manhattan. Whether it was dining at 21, the Rainbow Room, or one of a dozen other exclusive restaurants and nightclubs, the very luxurious atmosphere made one feel privileged and wealthy. This was all carefully cultivated and maintained and was in stark contrast to those businesses still struggling, let alone the businesses that had vanished in one of the worst economic depressions in the history of America.

A key ingredient in this cultivated air of exclusivity was Jack Kriendler himself. Charlie Burns could not be an active partner and remained behind the scenes as he devoted himself to 21 Brands. Like the great proprietor that he was, Kriendler met and greeted his customers, and the regulars were always addressed by their first names. He made it a point to ask how the patrons themselves were doing and their families, and this made them feel especially welcomed and special. Apart from this, Kriendler himself was always impeccably dressed in suits custom-tailored by the famed Spitz clothiers of Manhattan. His shirts were custom-tailored as well. Charlie Burns also had his suits made by Spitz. Their personalities were decidedly different, but obviously complementary. The two men had learned long ago how to work well together; they respected each other and agreed on practically everything. The customers and regular patrons sensed this compatible quality between the men, and this added to the pleasant ambiance of 21.

Kriendler had prospered 21 by employing a suite of executive skills, savvy business acumen, discipline and a dose of common sense. Over the decade of operating his various places, he had become wealthy, and this allowed him to indulge in spending that was at odds with many others who were so adversely affected by the Great Depression. He had longed to have his own place on Long Island, and he found a 20-acre property with a home near Hampton Bays overlooking the Sound. On Fridays, Kriendler would leave the operation of 21 to his brothers, and he would head out to his Long Island place in his Cadillac drophead coupé for the weekend. However, ever the host, he usually planned to also entertain friends and regular customers of 21 at this retreat. The drinks and meals there were naturally first-class, and he had a small staff there to see everything went smoothly. A typical meal would begin with caviar as an appetizer, with oysters and lobsters directly from the waters of the Sound, steak and potatoes and vegetables grown in his own garden. He varied this as his mood dictated.

The continuing popularity of 21 can also be attributed to its prime location. Fifty-Second Street just off Fifth Avenue in Manhattan had become known as "Swing Street." During the Great Depression, despite the economy, the mix of clubs and restaurants along the street was eclectic. Most of the establishments not only kept their doors open, they continued to operate profitably. Starting at Fifth Avenue on the north side of the street and walking toward Sixth Avenue, one passed Ella Barbour, Town Casino, Jack and Charlie's 21, Leon & Eddie's, Café Maria, Packard's, Chalet Suisse, and finally Tony's. Businesses other than those serving food, drinks or entertainment occupied the rest of the addresses to Sixth Avenue. Then, crossing the street and heading back to Fifth Avenue there were the Onyx Club, Chez Lina, Caliente, Lout Richman's Dizzy Club, the Clover Club, Mammy's Chicken Koop, Reilly's Tavern, du Pierrot, Maison Jacques, Rey et Pierre, Covent Garden, the Yacht Club, Billy Reed's Club Rhumba, Club 18, the Gangplank, and La Petite Suisse, with the landmark Vanderbilt mansion on the corner.[4] Across Fifth Avenue, at 3 East Fifty-Second Street, was the famed Stork Club run by Sherman Billingsley.

A restaurant of the established caliber of customers attracted the most famous names of the era. One evening, actress Arline Judge Ruggles looked around the restaurant and saw so many Hollywood stars, she wrote them down for posterity. They included Joan Bennett, Cary Grant, Katharine Hepburn, Tallulah Bankhead, Edward G. Robinson, Norma Shearer, Delores Del Rio, Charles Laughton, Leslie Howard, Irene Dunne, Clark Gable, Lupe Velez and Betty Furness.[5]

Jack and Charlie's 21 had competed with the finest restaurants in Manhattan, and its excellent cuisine was the draw not only for the greatest Hollywood stars when in New York, it was also the frequent dining destination for many members of Café Society. If they frequented El Morocco, the Stork Club and the Colony, 21 was also on their A-list. In fact, 21 would become an American institution. As the decade rolled on into the 1940s and beyond, 21 holds the unique distinction of continuous operation to the present.

CHAPTER 10

The Stork Club

Prohibition was the crucible for speakeasies in the 1920s. There were thousands operating in Manhattan and the surrounding boroughs. Had prohibition laws not been passed, there would not have been the market demand for forbidden drink. As recorded earlier in this volume, the nationwide law passed by Congress had its impetus in the majority of states which had first passed their own liquor prohibition laws. Among the Manhattan speakeasies that eventually became legendary among Café Society was the Stork Club. The irony is that is club had its roots in Oklahoma.

John Sherman Billingsley, born in 1896, was the last of the seven children of Robert and Emily Billingsley in Enid, Oklahoma, north of Oklahoma City. Sherman's brother Logan was often in trouble with the law, something all the brothers would experience over the next several years. One of the brothers, Robert, Jr., contracted influenza and died in 1906. The family moved to Oklahoma City and Sherman attended the schools there. In his free time he delivered newspapers, mowed lawns, got a job in a candy factory—the jobs were many and varied for a boy not yet sixteen.

Along with his older brother Fred, Sherman opened a pharmacy in 1912, and it was then the die was cast. Pharmacies became a major conduit for liquor when prohibition laws began to be passed in the United States. This was achieved by acquiring a "medicinal" liquor license. Strict quantities were proscribed by law, but every so-called pharmacist knew the loopholes to secure the desired quantities. The cases of liquor were stored at a nearby location, but only a few bottles were kept at the pharmacy in the event of inspections to prevent confiscation. Many clever ways were devised to sell the liquor outside of business hours.

Rumrunning was a common term to describe the purchase and transport of that distilled product, but it really applied to all forms of liquor purchased and transported illegally. Fred, Ora, Sherman and Logan learned the tricks of the trade running booze between Oklahoma and Texas. The Billingsley brothers had liquor operations as far away as Seattle, Washington. With prohibition laws in place, it was not difficult to run afoul of the law; Sherman himself was occasionally charged, but managed to get out of jail time by having a good attorney. The brothers might have called themselves the Billingsley Gang with the reputation they had acquired, but gunplay was never their modus operandi.

As individual states went dry, the Billingsleys tried to expand their business empire to northern states near dry states, including Michigan. They operated several businesses in Detroit, but the brothers became targets of opportunity for law enforcement. In 1919, Ora was sentenced to two years and six months and Sherman fifteen months in Leavenworth Prison in Kansas. Billingsley was just one of many thousands of Americans who were criminally charged with selling something that had been legal since the founding of the country. Upon his release, Sherman, along with his wife, decided to travel to New York City, where they arrived in May 1920. This was a turning point in the life of Sherman Billingsley, then twenty-four years old, and the path that led to the eventual establishment of the Stork Club.

From his successful experience, Billingsley knew a pharmacy would make an ideal front to begin his liquor business. Instead of setting up in Manhattan, initially he decided on the Bronx. He found the Morris Heights Pharmacy was for sale for $5,000. He borrowed the funds from his brother Logan, who already had a thriving real estate business in the Bronx. Together they found a comfortable home for their mother to live in there as well. Billingsley made certain to introduce himself to the Morris Heights neighborhood police, especially Captain James Brody, who was very agreeable to receiving any necessary medicinal supplies. The meeting went well.

Although married, the undeniably handsome Billingsley had a fondness for Ziegfeld showgirls and other lovely ladies of the theater. Manhattan and the surrounding boroughs provided many clubs for him to visit and find how they conducted their liquor business and to surveying the number of stunning women these places also attracted. He particularly had an eye for high-profile ladies such as Marilyn Miller, Helen Morgan, Hazel Donnelly and Ann Pennington, among others. Billingsley was a charmer, and persistent. In practically every case, the woman of his desire would eventually consent to go out with him. In 1925, Billingsley divorced his wife Dee Dee and married the woman of his greatest desire, Hazel Donnelly. The following year the couple had their first daughter, Jacqueline.

Prohibition also resulted in expanding the power of existing criminal elements that exploited the law to control the flow of liquor and the establishments which sold it. In many cases these criminals already had control of the service unions within established restaurants. When a new establishment opened up, the unsuspecting proprietor would invariably be paid a visit by the local thugs who would inform him that he had partners, and they expected a percentage of the profits. Those who refused to go along found life became very difficult. Billingsley clearly knew how such criminal gangs operated, but his bootlegging operations in other parts of the country were conducted with a fair degree of autonomy. In New York, he would learn the harsh realities of illegal booze. Prohibition would come to be identified as the Noble Experiment, but the stupidity of the law was readily confirmed when even elderly women could be arrested and sent to jail for possession. By 1925, one in ten New Yorkers had criminal records as a result of Prohibition.[1] Historians have marveled that such a draconian law could remain on the books for as long as it did.

Brother Logan was doing quite well in his real estate business, so Billingsley acquired a real estate license. He established the Billingsley Real Estate Company and his business grew rapidly. His timing may have been inadvertent but it was nevertheless perfect. With the continued influx of European immigrants into the Bronx, Billingsley was buying, selling and renting properties to these working-class people. He was a shrewd realtor, usually making deals with other people's money, not his own.

The Stork Club Is Born

In 1929, months before the stock market crash, Billingsley was visited by John Patten and Carl Henninger. He had met the two men previously in Oklahoma in a gambling house. Patten and Henninger were interested in opening a restaurant in New York City and wanted Billingsley's help in finding a suitable property. He located an available building at 132 West Fifty-Eighth Street. Billingsley negotiated a twenty-one-year lease with the property owner under the agreement that the townhouse would be converted for business use. When Patten and Henninger came in to sign the paperwork, they had a surprise for Billingsley. They wanted him to become a partner in the business, and they were insistent. What they wanted, in fact, was to have Billingsley set up and run the restaurant.

To Billingsley, this actually seemed like a good idea because he had his supplies of liquor, and he knew many upscale restaurants were doing quite well and their owners were becoming quite wealthy. He could get others to do the high-risk liquor transactions, while he was comfortably running a restaurant club. The more he thought about it the better he liked the idea and he went in with Patten and Henninger. But what to name the club? Billingsley settled on the Stork Club, and in the decades after it first opened its doors, an adequate explanation of the selection of the long-legged bird as the inspiration for the name was never definitively established.

When the club opened, it had the distinction of displaying one of the few canopies leading to the entry door. Most speakeasy owners wanted to remain obscure. The canopy made the Stork Club easy to find. Patrons had their choice of ground level, second or third floors. Billingsley had musicians to provide entertainment on every floor. He hired the best chefs he could find, and this established a trend that built the Stork's reputation. However,

Among the finest eating and drinking establishments frequented by Café Society was the Stork Club, operated by Sherman Billingsley. He is shown here, with Coca-Cola in hand, sharing a table at "the Stork" with Lucius Beebe, enjoying Russian caviar and Bollinger Champagne (courtesy Stork Club Enterprises LLC).

when it came to food preparation and serving, Billingsley was in new territory. He was nevertheless discriminating; he wanted his place to attract a higher level of clientele. He turned away known prostitutes, gamblers and those he simply did not like the looks of. He welcomed the noteworthy, the achievers, the famous—in short, he threw open the door to Café Society.

Billingsley was a relentless promoter of his club. He not only used typical means of making New Yorkers aware of the club, he devised clever ways to passively promote the Stork Club. When customers left their coats with the coat-check girl, he had her place matchbooks with the iconic stork on the cover in the coat pockets—whether the customers smoked or not. He made an indelible impression with any New York cab driver who picked him up; he always tipped in silver dollars. The cabbie enjoyed telling every fare he picked up that the owner of the Stork Club was such a classy guy, he tipped with silver dollars. Billingsley gave upwards of $100,000 in gifts to his favorite patrons. These gifts included Sortilege perfume, Moët & Chandon champagne, silk ties for the men and silk stockings (highly coveted during World War II) for the ladies, and many forms of jewelry.

Patton and Henninger were uninvolved in the club and did not take an active interest in it. Billingsley rarely saw his partners. The first several years of running the Stork Club were a struggle. Billingsley, he recalled years later, received a "blessed event" when club owner Texas Guinan told columnist Walter Winchell to visit the Stork Club and to give the club a write-up in his column. Guinan introduced Winchell to Billingsley in September 1930, and after thoroughly enjoying the food and ambiance, he gave the club the highest accolade Billingsley could hope for. The famous journalist wrote, "The New Yorkiest spot in New York is the Stork Club on West 58th Street which entices the well knowns from all divisions nightly."[2] The Stork Club became Winchell's frequent evening hangout in order to gather information he needed for his column. The onset of the Great Depression forced the club to operate in the red. Billingsley was not above asking his regular customers for names and even business cards of their friends and business associates to contact.

It was during this period Billingsley learned the truth of who the real partners were in the ownership of his club. They were three of the most notorious criminals in New York City. The men were William "Big Bill" Dwyer, George "Frenchy" De Mange, and Owney Madden. They all paid Billingsley a visit at the Stork Club one day. They came in and they did the talking. If Billingsley had any doubt who his real partners were before, he had absolutely no doubt after they left. He was so unnerved by their visit, he had to go for a walk, puffing on a cigar to mull over the reality. The three men actually controlled numerous nightclubs in the city. These included the Five O'Clock, the Park Avenue Club, the Napoleon Club, Texas Guinan's Club and numerous others. The gangsters were so impressed with Billingsley's club management they called on him to run their other clubs as well. Billingsley had to delegate, as he could not be in half a dozen clubs at once, but he did spend a lot of time on the phone and frequently visited them to make sure they were operating up to his standards.

The Stork Club was one of the highest profile clubs in Manhattan, so it naturally drew the attention of other criminals wanting control. The notorious Jack "Legs" Diamond also paid Billingsley a visit one day. It merely took the persuasive powers of Dwyer, Madden and De Mange to send Diamond looking for another prospective club to control. Billingsley was actually kidnapped by Vincent "Mad Dog" Coll and held for ransom. His wife and the employees at the Stork Club did not know where he was for two days. When he finally escaped, he had to jump out of a moving automobile, but at least he was alive. His kidnappers were arrested but were back on the street in short order.

On a night in December 1931 before Christmas, a vicious raid by Prohibition agents took place at the Stork Club. After the employees were hauled off to jail and the customers had fled, the agents—both local and federal—then proceeded to dismantle the place. All liquor was confiscated, and then the destruction of the Stork Club began. Billingsley got on the phone and called his lawyer in a panic, but to no avail. In a matter of hours, the Stork Club was out of business. He was unsure of the fate of the other clubs he was running, but his premier club, at least in its present location, would never serve another drink or hear the sound of jazz music.

Billingsley ultimately succeeded in regaining complete control of the Stork Club from Dwyer, De Mange and Madden and survived both personally and professionally.

It was a month later before he located a new building, a five-story townhouse, at 53 East Fifty-First Street near Park Avenue. This place also had to be converted in order to permit the preparation of food, and yes, the serving of liquor, as well as sufficient bathroom facilities and other amenities Billingsley wanted for his customers. In particular, he had acquired a twenty-foot square bar made of walnut. It took some weeks to get it ready, but the new Stork Club opened to much fanfare and the patrons came back.

Billingsley's troubles with law enforcement were not behind him. On an evening in August 1932, plainclothes detectives managed to get into the club, and as a musical number ended, one of the detectives moved to the microphone and informed all the guests the place was under control of the police for violations of the federal law. Customers just laughed, thinking it was a prank. When they started seeing employees of the Stork Club being arrested and being taken away to awaiting police cars, the place started to empty quickly. Billingsley was livid. He knew the tide had turned regarding Prohibition and there were strong advocates in Washington and across the United States working for repeal of the Eighteenth Amendment. It would be more than a year before that day came. However, this raid was far more benign and there was no destruction of his property.

The Stork Spreads Its Wings

Billingsley and every other speakeasy, restaurant and night club owner watched the progress in Washington on the repeal of the ill-conceived amendment that banned liquor in all its forms. The road to hell is paved with good intentions, and the Eighteenth Amendment proved disastrous for Americans and America. By the time the Twenty-First Amendment was ratified, the toll on the country over the previous thirteen years was appalling. There was shocking loss of life, with ninety-two federal agents and seventy-eight civilians killed. Over half a million citizens were criminalized and fines totaled more than $80 million. The destruction and seizure of property rose to $200 million.[3] On December 5, 1933, just after 5:30 p.m. in New York, liquor once again became legal. However, it took one year for the Stork Club to receive its state license to serve liquor.

Once again, Billingsley felt the need for a new and larger place. It took him months to find a suitable building. The issuance of the liquor license coincided with the relocation of the Stork Club to 3 East Fifty-Third Street just off Fifth Avenue. For the remainder of the 1930s, Billingsley battled with mob-controlled unions; he found a way around this temporarily by paying higher than union-mandated wages. The Stork Club was certainly not the only one to have this issue to deal with, but Billingsley was clever in how he dealt with it.

Among the noteworthy appeals of the club were the ingenious novelty parties and gifts awarded or randomly handed out. One of these customer-pleasing activities included a Balloon Party with a certain number of inflated balloons holding a one-hundred dollar bill. Even in the midst of the Depression, the Stork Club succeeded in pulling in one million dollars a year. Billingsley had management staff to keep the place running smoothly, but the Stork Club was his life from the time he awoke at midday until 4:00 a.m. the following morning.

The expenses of running the Stork Club were in keeping with its clientele, atmosphere, entertainment and cuisine. The orchestras which entertained there commanded $6,000 a month. Fresh flowers practically everywhere added to the elegance of the club and cost nearly a thousand dollars a month. The staff were among the highest-paid in New York because Billingsley wanted and demanded his people to be impeccably dressed with service to match to wait on his customers. It was all part of the Stork Club ambiance.

Broadway stars loved to visit the club after their evening performances. It also became the haunt of some of the biggest names in literature and music. The Stork Club was a mecca for New York's elite, a veritable "Who's Who" not only of Manhattan but pulling the famous and accomplished from as far away as Hollywood, California. Although Billingsley had his own methods for getting the word out, he always welcomed newspaper journalists, of whom Winchell was the first. Maury "Cholly Knickerbocker" Paul could be counted on to recall who he had seen there, and with whom they had been seen. The Stork Club was among Lucius Beebe's favorite nightspots, and it provided him a rich source of material to mention in his newspaper column, "This New York." Beebe witnessed Café Society in its heyday at places like the Stork Club and he attributed the club's success to several factors, but above all to Billingsley's discernment and clever promotion. "Billingsley's sense of social and promotional values hardly ever makes a mistake," Beebe wrote in one of his books published in 1943. "He distributes free orchids and other costly corsages, magnums of champagne, Cartier clips and match-boxes, dollar cigars and other glittering largesse to customers who will most appreciate it and will talk about it most afterward."[4]

Over the years, Billingsley had developed an array of hand signals for his staff regarding the guests at nearby preferred tables. When he sat at a table with guests and he placed his hand on his necktie, it meant "No check for this table." When he pointed his index finger toward the table it meant "Bring a round of drinks." When his palm faced upward, champagne would soon be served at the table. If he rubbed his nose, it meant "Not important people" or worse, "Their check is no good"—in which case the demand was made for cash to pay the bill. The worst signal for any guest was when fingers of both hands were interlocked and one thumb was lifted; that meant, "Get them out and don't let them in again."

Not only did the Stork Club prosper during the latter thirties, so did Billingsley, who was, by 1940, a wealthy man. Billingsley acquired the property west of his, and first created the Cub Room, perhaps after a suggestion by Winchell, who was once a cub reporter. Beyond this was what Billingsley called the Loners Room, something of a males-only enclave. Going up a flight of stairs led to the Blessed Events Room. Here, special catered meals could be served in privacy and relative quite away from the noisy main room at the club. Billingsley even installed a small barbershop where gentlemen could get a trim.

With the bombing of Pearl Harbor in December 1941, America entered World War II. Billingsley made it a policy to warmly welcome every serviceman and servicewoman in uniform at the Stork Club. And it was not uncommon to see actor Bob Hope with numerous lovely actresses who were part of the USO tours, before they would go over to Europe and the Pacific islands to entertain the troops. Billingsley sporadically published a club magazine, *Stork Club Talk*, issues of which were prized reading material for troops overseas. After the war, the Stork Club continued to host the rich and the famous to fine meals with legendary service and great entertainment.

The economic times of the Great Depression were long gone, and yet the mood was somehow different. The socioeconomic factors that had given rise to Café Society were no longer present, and the cachet surrounding these men and women and the places they frequented began a subtle change as well. The Stork Club, however, never deviated from its standards and continued to operate under Billingsley's management until the mid-1960s. The iconic restaurant closed its doors forever in October 1965, and its creator, Sherman Billingsley, died a year later. It had been a symbol of the finest New York had to offer, operated successfully in good times and bad, and the debonair Billingsley and the Stork Club remain a legend to this day.

CHAPTER 11

El Morocco

A main factor contributing to the new, emerging social elite of Manhattan was Prohibition, and its subsequent repeal. Beebe called Prohibition the "Great Foolishness." As a natural consequence of the 18th Amendment, the speakeasy was born. One of the most successful proprietors of speakeasies was the handsome and ebullient John Perona.

Born Eriane Giovanni Perona in Chiaverano, Italy, Perona had made his way to England by the time he was sixteen. Legend has it he signed on as a deckhand for a gleaming new oceangoing liner of the White Star Line, but on the day it was to debark, he met a winsome girl and he lost track of time. When he realized what had happened, he raced to the dock, but the RMS *Titanic* had made for Cherbourg, France, before heading for New York harbor—a destination it never reached. Financier J.P. Morgan had also booked a suite aboard the doomed liner, but canceled, and read of the tragedy in the papers with shock.

Perona spent some time in South America as a boxer and sparring partner, but later followed his dreams of success and fortune to New York. His first job was at the Knickerbocker Grill, and he was a fast learner. Perona had a sharp business mind and carefully absorbed the method of operating a liquor and food establishment, even though liquor became illegal with the advent of Prohibition. Others were opening speakeasies and running them with success. Perona opened his first restaurant and speakeasy, the Surf Club, at 232 West Forty-Ninth Street. With his handsome looks, sharply tailored suits, welcoming smile and wonderful manner, Perona soon had a dedicated clientele. He worked to acquire the best liquor he could buy, knowing his customers would discern the quality. His reputation for doing so spread quickly and he had no lack of customers. He operated the Surf Club for a period of time, but eventually it must have been closed down by Prohibition agents, because he eventually found another more discreet location and opened a new speakeasy, the Bath Club.

Perona was following the same procedure of most other padlocked speakeasies: the owner would not battle to reopen the previous establishment; he would simply relocate, adopt a new name and resume business. Perona used the same successful formula at the Bath Club at 39 West Forty-Ninth Street. He refined the furniture and décor and worked to establish a degree of exclusivity which proved to be a drawing card for a number of upscale clubs. Directly across the street from Perona's Bath Club at No. 42 was Jack Kriendler's and Charlie Burns's Puncheon Grotto.[1] In fact the entire block on both sides of the street had numerous speakeasies, but Perona's Bath Club, along with the Puncheon, were among two of the most desirable establishments serving liquor on West 49th Street. Eventually, Jack and Charlie moved their business to the immortal address No. 21 West Fifty-Second Street.

Perona operated the Bath Club for a period of time, but desired to have an even better location in midtown Manhattan. He made inquiries and learned of an available location at 154 East Fifty-Fourth Street. Perona decided to heighten the place's exclusivity by adding an exotic dash in the new name: El Morocco. He began renovations at the location on Fifty-Fourth Street in 1932, as the economic depression was reaching its nadir, so it is difficult to surmise if Perona sensed the pending repeal of Prohibition that would prove a boon to his new *grand lux* club. Nevertheless, his timing was propitious. Perona opened El Morocco in the waning days of Prohibition, still paying off whomever he had to in order to keep the liquor flowing smoothly for his eager customers. Perona indeed went upscale with his latest club, which would become one of the most famous in Manhattan, and some argued, the epicenter of Café Society.

While El Morocco operated successfully even during the closing days of Prohibition, its repeal allowed Perona to operate without the costs formerly related to keeping it running with the laws in place. More important, the customers could arrive openly and enjoy drinks served legally. Those who entered El Morocco immediately sensed the atmosphere was different—and very exclusive. Virtually all the men wore evening tuxes, and the ladies were dressed in the most elegant evening gowns. Among the first to sample that atmosphere, and a former customer of the Bath Club, was Lucius Beebe, who arrived in correct evening attire, even to the polished sheen of his top hat. Beebe wrote his first observations later and stated El Morocco was "decorated in deep blue and white (zebra stripe seating upholstery), with palm trees of gold leaf along the walls and tiny stars winking on and off in the azure ceiling."[2]

11. El Morocco

However, the impression of El Morocco began before one even set foot inside. The limousines, and the occasional cab, pulled up to No. 154, and the expectant patrons stepped onto the curb and stepped underneath the canopy that led to the front doors. There, two liveried doormen had the sole function of opening the doors to allow entrance. While the guests may have entered El Morocco, they were not yet *in*. Guests were met by one or two stone-faced men whose job was to escort accepted guests to an assigned table, but first they had to get past the glacial stare of the maître d', Carino. He wielded immense power, given him by Perona, for Carino determined who could have a table at El Morocco and who could not. The ladies would smile at him, hoping for some bit of influence on Carino's decision, and then would nervously turn away as they waited. If the man who greeted Carino was known to him, there was a suitable pause to determine the appropriate table for the guests, then he nodded and they were swept into the glittering enclave with the music drawing them to their reward. However, those unknown to Carino were invariably greeted with the words there were no tables available, and the humiliated guests had to leave and make other arrangements.

Carino's means of natural selection was an essential element of El Morocco's exclusivity. Only those with "names that made news," as Beebe often wrote in his column, were welcomed and often personally greeted by Perona as they entered. They came to see and be seen, and it was the height of 1930s social strata in New York City to sit amongst these glittering elite. Two bands alternated playing music throughout the night and into the early morning. The small dance floor with its swaying patrons would slowly give way to more tables for guests, until no one could dance at all. Nevertheless, the music played on and so did the conversations.

Before El Morocco reached capacity, however, dancing was very much part of the scene. This was done not only to enjoy dancing with one's partner, but to see who else was at the club that night, and to be seen by them. Those seated at the perimeter of the dance floor casually studied those swaying to the music, and vice versa. Playwright Moss Hart deftly moved Tallulah Bankhead around the floor. Stage star Hope Williams was entwined with Whiney Bolton, managing editor of the *Morning Telegraph*. Modernist painter Emlen Etting embraced his future wife Gloria Braggiotti. Van Vorhees, the voice of *The March of Time*, was dancing with Mrs. Harrison Williams.

Among the regulars seated at the tables was Maury Paul, who was none other than "Cholly Knickerbocker," and he was there not simply to enjoy the company of his peers, but he was working. There was much information to gather for his column and he could do it most effectively from his reserved table near the front of the room so he could observe who entered and with whom. Beebe would occasionally sit with Paul, but their interest in each other was strictly professional. Beebe would often get a table of his own and be joined at various times by Mary Anita Loos, photographer Howard Cagle, Marion Tiffany Saportas, George and Valentina Schlee, elegant man-about-town Joseph J. O'Donohue IV, Gloria Braggiotti when she wasn't with Emlen Etting, Beatrice Lillie, singer Libby Holman, and Reginald Gardner. Today, most of these names would not draw much recognition, but in Café Society in the 1930s, these were names indeed.

Café society at El Morocco did not exist in a vacuum. Notoriety meant publicity, and this publicity was to everyone's mutual advantage. This explained the importance of having some occupation, meritorious achievement, distinction or even a notorious weakness. It provided a convenient handle for columnists to report. Gossip scribes had been around long before the thirties, but during America's Depression, they were the crucial ingredient to the circumambience that produced Café Society. There were roughly half a dozen at the top during this time among New York's newspapers, and many copycats. Perhaps Paul and Beebe got along so well at El Morocco because each respected the other's territory. Paul had been writing about the goings-on in Manhattan nearly a decade before Beebe arrived in the city, but each had his own distinctive style of reporting and they did not cramp one another.

There was one more element that made El Morocco the legend it quickly became in the 1930s, and that was photographer Jerome Zerbe. How he ended up in New York City snapping photos of Manhattan's nightclub elite and thereby establishing a photographic genre is a fascinating story. He was born in Euclid, Ohio, in 1904, the second of two children to Jerome and Susan Zerbe. The Zerbe family tree included the names Widener, Ring and Rittenhouse. The Zerbes were prominent in Cleveland, and when he grew up and attended high school, he was chauffeured to school. The family's wealth came from Zerbe Sr.'s position as president of the Ohio and Pennsylvania Coal Company.

After attending a suitable prep school where he displayed a distinctive artistic streak, Zerbe applied to and was accepted to Yale. He entered in the fall of 1924. He lived in style while attending Yale, with an apartment overlooking Harkness Quadrangle. It had a completely stocked wet bar and his apartment was the scene of many a party over the next four years. Zerbe did not forget what he was there for, and he graduated in 1928 with a bachelor of arts degree. He convinced his father that he could support himself from portraits of the film stars in Hollywood. Using letters of introduction, he

11. El Morocco 189

Lucius Beebe, photographer Jerome Zerbe, Mary Anita Loos and two friends photographed against the unmistakable zebra stripe upholstery of El Morocco. Zerbe set up his Speed Graphic camera on a tripod, joined the group, and had someone take the photograph. At far left, one visitor does not want to be identified (Jerome Zerbe, by permission).

was soon rubbing shoulders with the stars of the silver screen, and succeeded in landing sketch portrait commissions from Cecil B. De Mille, Norma Shirer and Basil Rathbone, among others. He ended up making friends of Gary Cooper, Cary Grant, Randolph Scott, Paulette Goddard and Marion Davies.[3] Despite this intoxicating environment, he chose to leave Hollywood for some time in Paris in 1929. Zerbe Sr., was not so sure his son could survive in Paris, which had thousands of artists, many of them far more skilled than his son, so he provided Jerome a monthly stipend of $300 to supplement whatever he might actually earn. Once there, he enrolled in the Académie Julian. Zerbe saw himself as a portrait painter in the school of John Singer Sargent.

In typical fashion, Zerbe was soon mingling with the Paris arts crowd and Parisian society itself. He had an innate ability to seek out and attract such people. It was while he was in Paris he took up the camera to take photo portraits of those he met, and the die was cast. He began to arrange scrapbooks of his photos, something he would do all during his years in New York. His idyllic days in Paris came to an end when his father called him home to Cleveland if for no other reason than to take up some serious work. Through some contacts, he joined in the launch of a new Cleveland-oriented style magazine called *Parade*. Zerbe floated the idea with editor Windsor French to start including portraits Cleveland society ladies. These weren't formal portraits, but Zerbe had them pose casually, naturally. He also photographed them in various outdoor venues playing tennis, or some other sporting activity. This certainly was different in society photography, and the magazine and Zerbe's unique photography soon came to the attention of Harry Bull of *Town & Country* magazine. Bull made Zerbe a contributing photographer about the time *Parade* folded around 1932. He was still living in Cleveland, but was busy traveling and doing photography work for Bull. A heated argument with his mother that seemed to have no resolution forced him to look east. He inquired with Harry Bull about joining the staff of *Town & Country*, Bull offered him $150 a month, and Zerbe accepted. He left for New York in 1933. He was 29 years old.

Zerbe found an apartment on East 56th Street. The first order of business was finding a suitable speakeasy, and it didn't take him long.

"I came to New York in 1933, just before the repeal of Prohibition," Zerbe told this author in an interview in 1981 at his Sutton Place apartment. "There was one speakeasy for men only run by Jimmy Kirkland in his apartment. I was told about it and I called up. Jimmy said, 'Of course, Mr. Zerbe, I know who you are. Come on up.' Jimmy paid off, I'm sure, because there was no pressure from the police. You could sit and talk and laugh. It was very smart and very chic. I went up and there was this great tall guy—Lucius Beebe. We immediately got in a very animated conversation. And that was the beginning of our friendship."[4]

Beebe gladly showed Zerbe the ropes in terms of getting around Manhattan and into the best clubs. That was play, but Zerbe had a job to do and reported to Harry Bull at *Town & Country*. After meeting with Bull to discuss assignments, it became clear he would have a lot of time on his hands. He spent the remainder of 1933 using his Graflex Speed Graphic camera on assignments for the magazine, and any jobs he could muster on the side. He soon realized he would need a more substantial second income because it would be tough making ends meet on $150 a month plus his freelance revenue. He had a friend in Manhattan who knew John Roy, manager of the Rainbow Room atop the RCA building in Rockefeller Center that opened in 1934.

11. El Morocco

A rare photograph showing the owner of El Morocco, John Perona, second from left, with guests, including Lucius Beebe on the far right. Jerome Zerbe was photographer at El Morocco for several years, and this appears to be a publicity photograph for the club's promotion (Jerome Zerbe, by permission).

Roy was looking for a means to drum up business. The view of Manhattan at night from the 65th-floor windows of the Rainbow Room was breathtaking, the meals were superb, the musical entertainment the best—and the place was dying for customers. Like so many other restaurants and bars during the Depression, it was losing alarming sums of money.

Zerbe met with Roy and laid out his ideas. He knew he could stock the restaurant with friends and acquaintances to make it appear busy, photograph them and have the photographs appear in the papers—there were seven newspapers and three wire services as sources for his photos—and this, he believed, would make the Rainbow Room a desirable place to dine and dance for paying customers who saw the photos in the city's newspapers. Roy liked the idea and offered Zerbe $75 a week for three nights' work, and all the food and a reasonable number of drinks he could handle. Zerbe was more interested in the money, and the income he would earn was double his monthly salary from *Town & Country*. They shook hands and sealed the arrangement.

Zerbe was jubilant. He wanted to celebrate, and the evening after the interview with Roy, he dropped in at El Morocco. Carino eyed the handsome newcomer with admiration but also some doubt. Perona came over, Zerbe introduced himself, dropped the appropriate names, and he was in. In chatting with Perona, Zerbe revealed his duties designed to boost the number of customers at the Rainbow Room. Perona was vexed. He saw the marketing brilliance of the plan and wondered why he had not thought of it himself. Every club owner had lost business because of the economic depression; even 21 and the Stork Club had seen the number of customers drop off precipitously. He asked Zerbe if he would work at El Morocco on those evenings when he wasn't working at the Rainbow Room, and on those nights when he worked until closing there, he could catch a cab for El Morocco. Perona offered him the same rate, and Zerbe agreed.

After several weeks of dashing back and forth across town, Perona finally convinced the photographer to put his camera to work exclusively at El Morocco. It proved to be one of the smartest business decisions Perona ever made. Virtually no one objected to having his photograph taken by the handsome, persuasive and smiling Zerbe. The papers hungered for these photos to illustrate the columns, and in practically every photo could be seen the distinctive El Morocco zebra-striped seat cushions which had been designed by decorator Vernon McFarlane for Perona. Zerbe effectively launched a new career for himself. He worked at El Morocco from nine in the evening to sometimes five in the morning. When he had gathered all the photos he felt he needed for the evening, he took the sealed film negatives to a processing lab for developing and had prints made of each one. From these, he selected the best and most flattering photos to get to select newspapers. And "Photo by Jerome Zerbe" that followed the captions started to build his reputation.

"Jerome was so funny and amusing," remembered Gloria Braggiotti, who later married artist Emlen Etting. "Going around with that big Speed Graphic, he was ruthless. He had a wonderful way of pushing you around, and such charm that he could make anybody pose for him."[5]

Zerbe wasn't the first to photograph New York's rich, famous or otherwise notable. Izzy Kaplan at the *Daily Mirror* had been doing that for years. Zerbe, however, had a different sense of style, composition and consideration. He was also more refined and typically better dressed than Kaplan. Zerbe more or less invented nightclub photography as a niche; Kaplan was a photographer at large, day or night. Other imitators naturally followed suit, among them Marty Black of the *New York American*, and Tony Sarno of the

International News. None could match Zerbe's combination of panache, photographic style and friendly manner.

In a matter of months, Zerbe had amassed a considerable library of negatives and prints. Probably at the urging of Harry Bull, Zerbe agreed to put together a collection of the photos he had taken on assignment for *Town & Country* at El Morocco and various other bars and restaurants in Manhattan, as well as for the *New York American*, the *New York Evening Journal, Stage, The Spur, White Rock*, and other photos he had taken for various assignments in Miami Beach, Palm Beach, Pittsburgh, Detroit, Cleveland, Nantucket, and other locales. *People on Parade* was published in 1934, and it was significant in that it was the first collection of photos of Café Society published as a book. It offered a window on a very different world from that experienced by many in the Great Depression.

Not surprisingly, Lucius Beebe wrote the introduction to the book. He opened with these facts: "More than anything else, people are news. Events, catastrophes, the contriving of human intelligence, the record of a mutable world, manifestations of nature, all of them, however arresting, are secondary in interest to individuals and the trivia of their lives. That is why Jerome Zerbe's photographs are news photographs and why this book has every right to be called a document. Usually 'documents,' profound, vital 'documents,' are dull as a bottle of corked Vouvray, but *People on Parade* is a notable and happy exception."[6]

The book proved Zerbe was far from sedentary or focused only on Manhattan nightlife. It also showed Café Society at play and rest. "Laddie" Sanford—a noted polo player—was shown relaxing with his wife by the waters of Long Island Sound. Mrs. James W. Corrigan, perhaps the most prominent socialite in Cleveland—would certainly be counted among the 400 if she lived in New York, and if the 400 still existed from the days of Caroline Astor. Constance Collier merited an entire page with her portrait; she had successfully performed in *Dinner at Eight* between 1932 and 1933 and had starred in numerous films with a cinematic career that would stretch into the late 1940s. Laurence Olivier was snapped sharing a table with Richard Aldrich. The Oasis Night at El Morocco was duly recorded by Zerbe. New York socialite Mrs. Tiffany Saportas also received her own full-page portrait. Governor Paul McNutt of Indiana was pictured enjoying the sun, sea and sand in Miami Beach. Cole Porter was shown admiring a sculpture at a New York art gallery. Hollywood actress Dolores Del Rio's dazzling beauty was captured by Zerbe's Speed Graphic. Elza Maxwell, a relentless party-giver, featured prominently in Zerbe's book. Author Dashiell Hammett, looking impeccable in a double-breasted pinstripe suit, smiled for the camera. Architect Philip Johnson was shown lounging on a Mies van der Rohe furniture piece with his sister. Lucius Beebe and Maury Paul were among the people on parade. Few composers defined jazz music in the 1930s better than George Gershwin, who was photographed as well.

From "So This Is New York!" by Lucius Beebe, the *Philadelphia Inquirer*, April 1, 1934:

> Jerome Zerbe, Jr., the boy photographer, is taking New York in his stride, just as he did Cleveland a few years since. An exotic and vivid youth with a flair for distinguished camera studies and sketches, he is very much a part of the Mayfair scene, and in the lobby of the Weylin along the avenue of a sunny morning or at Westchester weekend parties he is gaily occupied snapping the youth and chivalry of the town's social parade. He even clicks cameras at persons who don't merit his attentions just so they may feel, more or less literally, in the picture. To walk into the Madison at lunch time or a smart opening night with him is to participate in what amounts to a levee. Everyone knows him and he knows everyone. Fashion arbiters and smart shops retain him to prepare advertising copy and art for them, and the coated paper periodicals of society and the stage are incomplete unless somewhere in every issue at least one camera study bears his signature. His personal photograph albums, which he shows friends at his midtown apartment, are a sort of illustrated Social Register or Debrett. His initial venture, before coming to New York, was "Parade," a magazine which achieved an immense Mid-Western success he rode amid cheers and exploding flashlights into the midst of New York's most madhouse activities. Last week he achieved the ultimate metropolitan accolade of being burlesqued in a sketch in the sophisticated revue "New Faces."

Time magazine reviewed the book and it was favorable. Brendan Gill included an excerpt from the book review in his profile of Zerbe for *The New Yorker*: "Always immaculately groomed, with impressive acquaintances among New York's bright young people, he flashlights all the swankier bars, nightclubs, balls, routs and receptions. With determination and no little skill, Photographer Zerbe has dedicated his life to recording the lives of the champagne set in its moment of abandon."[7]

Zerbe's first book was a loving portrait of Café Society, but he had another one in the works. The photographs Zerbe took nightly at El Morocco which appeared in the New York newspapers and magazines were having the desired effect, and the nightclub was running at full capacity and providing Perona with the most desirable customers to sit at its tables. Zerbe soon

11. El Morocco

hatched the idea to have a book solely devoted to the frequent friends at the nightclub, and *The El Morocco Family Album* was born. Whether it was his own idea or suggested by Perona is a moot point of history. Zerbe pored over the hundreds of photos he had taken thus far at El Morocco, and selected the most interesting, amusing and revealing portraits. His publisher, David Kemp, however, was not interested in publishing such a niche title. Zerbe could not interest any other publisher in New York either. He chose to have it privately published in a limited run in 1937.

Increasingly, El Morocco became the most visited club by Hollywood stars when visiting New York. They included Clark Gable, Gloria Swanson, Errol Flynn, Joan Blondell, Gary Cooper, Paulette Goddard—the stars who were in their ascendance would drop in at El Morocco, and they would always get a table. Carino made sure of that.

Gloria Braggiotti recalls the evenings at El Morocco as a blur. Always elegantly turned out, she was inevitably in the company of Lucius Beebe, Jerome Zerbe, Maury Paul—or all three. She was taken into their circle at El Morocco because she was accepting of their private lifestyles, and they in turn embraced her. She particularly admired Beebe, and she explained Beebe's incongruous attraction to her, and his behavior at El Morocco with Zerbe:

> He liked to be with women who had a certain glamor and chic, to be seen with an attractive woman because he was so dapper and good-looking himself. I think one of the most extraordinary things about Lucius was he had a fantastic memory and he had the most amazing vocabulary and used the most wonderful words. He had a deep voice and was kind of scary. I was thrilled that he liked me. Jerome and Lucius would be together and I was one of the few women that they could kid in front of and act like lovers. They didn't hold back in front of me. They sometimes had fights at the dinner table. Jerome would get in a tiff and leave. He was very dramatic about the whole thing. I didn't pay any attention to it, but I thought they were very amusing and I had such a good time when I was with them.[8]

Every night at El Morocco was pretty much like the night before and the night that would come after. Perona kept it interesting by adding fresh new faces to his guests, serving the finest liquor, having the best musicians playing the latest dance tunes, and allowing Lucius Beebe and Maury Paul write about those whose comings and goings at El Morocco provided such interesting reading during the Depression years of the 1930s. Years later, Zerbe reflected on the effect his photographs taken at El Morocco had on those who viewed them in the papers and read their captions and attending article, if any. Knowing the economic conditions for many people in New York and the country at large, he could not understand why there weren't protestors outside

Marion Tiffany Saportas (left) and Lucius Beebe admire Mrs. Antoinette Johnson's new gift at El Morocco. Unlike Maury Paul, Beebe enjoyed the company of ladies (Jerome Zerbe, by permission).

the elite nightclub, or worse, why he and those he photographed were not attacked by starving mobs. Zerbe likened himself to Marie Antoinette, who might any day be taken away to be executed. Instead, he recalled, he was cheered for his work. Perhaps it came down to the fact people enjoyed seeing others truly enjoying the better things in life, and that life was not drudgery and want for everyone.

As for Café Society itself, Zerbe reflected that El Morocco's success depended on the people of note of the day, those with some form of accomplishment or particular notoriety that made that man or woman uniquely interesting and someone others would enjoy being around. For the most part, it had little if anything to do with wealth. Zerbe's success during the Great Depression seemed to be one of serendipity, a wonderful string of fortuitous events where he just happened to be in the right place at the right time. However, Zerbe indeed made his own success, and became successful because he was doing what he loved to do, but also did it better than anyone else.

Eventually, Zerbe felt he needed to move on from El Morocco in 1938, but his reputation was well-established and he had no shortage of photographic commissions, remaining very busy up until the advent of World War II. He chose to enlist and he became a capable and distinguished photographer of frontline battle, and returned from the war with distinction.

The nights at El Morocco during the Depression years of the 1930s were a curious counterpoint to the workaday world of the vast majority of New Yorkers, who still enjoyed a fascination with Café Society in the pages of the city's newspapers, as Zerbe reflected years later. For many of those in this "Chromium Mist"—Beebe's descriptive term for Café Society—of luxurious living, there was only a vague awareness of the economic calamity that gripped so many others. The cost of enjoying the privilege of seeing and being seen at El Morocco rivaled that of 21 and the Stork Club. Zerbe's photography had worked its magic, and "Elmo," as the frequent attendees nicknamed it, was almost always filled to capacity until Carino did indeed have to turn everyone else away. Perhaps Marion Tiffany Saportas, one of Zerbe's favorite photo subjects, put it best:

"How anybody afforded it, I don't understand. But it was all so gay. I suppose it was a very superficial life then, really."[9]

CHAPTER 12

Café Society Fades Away

Columnist Maury Paul, as the ubiquitous "Cholly Knickerbocker," had been working relentlessly at his job for over twenty years, having first come to New York in 1919. By 1940, it had all started to take a toll on his health, compounded by his cigarette smoking he swore to give up but never did. He began suffering from bouts of depression and he often chose to stay in his apartment rather than travel to his office at the *Journal-American*. He would phone his secretarial assistant, Eve Brown, and issue orders as to what to write, what photos to run—essentially the same thing she had been doing for years. Many of the columns that appeared in "Cholly Knickerbocker" were, in fact, written by her with direction from Paul. This happened with greater frequency during 1941 and early 1942.

Brown could see that Paul was sick, and his coughing became more prevalent. By January 1942, even he realized he had to slow down, change his debilitating habits and go on the diet his doctor insisted he follow. One day that January at his office, Brown had noticed Paul was sluggish and morose. Finally he looked up from his typewriter and said he was going to go to Florida for a month-long vacation. A week later, he left Brown to run the affairs of the office and put out the column. One month turned into two, then three. He finally returned to New York in May, and Brown was shocked by his appearance. Although tanned, his complexion appeared almost grey. He was admitted to St. Luke's Hospital where the physicians ran tests on him and discovered he had cancer.[1] They immediately began radium treatments, but the damage was already done; Maury Paul was dying.

He stayed in the hospital for a month. When he finally left, he did not return to work but had a hospital bed installed in his bedroom, outfitted with an oxygen tent. Paul informed Brown he would not return to work until September. She realized then he would probably never return at all, and pondered

12. Café Society Fades Away

how much longer he really had to live. Paul received friends at his apartment, among them Clifton Webb, Dwight Fiske and Lucius Beebe. He always appeared upbeat to them, but Paul was resigned to his impending death. His devoted mother saw to his every need, and she was a great comfort to him.

In the early morning hours of July 17, 1942, Paul called out to his mother and soon she was at his bedside. She sat down and took his hand. His breathing was shallow and he had a look of resignation on his face. They spent their last few minutes together talking, but saying as few words as possible. He was in pain but he smiled at her for the last time and passed away. She wept for her only son, and an hour later, she went to the phone and called Brown, who had been expecting the call any day now. She dressed quickly and caught a cab to the Paul's apartment on East Sixty-Fourth Street. Brown made the funeral arrangements, but Paul had set everything up for his funeral service and burial.

Every New York newspaper and many other metropolitan newspapers had news of Paul's death in the late morning editions. An icon of New York Café Society was dead. The avid readers of "Cholly Knickerbocker" were shocked and saddened. His funeral service was held July 20 at St. Bartholomew's Church, half a block from the Waldorf-Astoria Hotel. Every pew in the church was filled by Society and Café Society members who came to pay their respects. The pallbearers included Dwight Fiske, William Randolph Hearst, Clifton Webb and several other friends of Paul's. Curiously, Paul was not buried in New York, but his body was interred at Woodlawn Park North Cemetery and Mausoleum in Miami, Florida.

The war had been raging in Europe for nearly three years, and America had been drawn into the war with the Japanese bombing of the Pacific fleet at Pearl Harbor, Hawaii, on December 7, 1941. Jerome Zerbe enlisted in the Navy in 1942 as a chief photographer's mate, and after saying his goodbyes to his friends in New York, he carefully packed his Speed Graphic camera and other essentials, and took a train to Hawthorne, Nevada, for basic training. After completing their training, his unit was sent to California, and while waiting to be deployed, Zerbe stayed with friends in San Francisco. Because of his specific and recognized talent, Zerbe was assigned to a photographic unit within Admiral Nimitz's headquarters based on the island of Guam.

Not long after Zerbe's arrival on Guam, Admiral Nimitz informed him he was going to be visited by Robert E. Sherwood, noted American playwright, a founding member of the Algonquin Round Table, and now a speechwriter for President Roosevelt. Zerbe and Sherwood were in fact friends, and this was great news. It was not long before Zerbe's photographic skill and easy manner moved the admiral to assign Zerbe as his personal photographer. This meant Zerbe followed Nimitz everywhere, even into pitched battles. Zerbe was on the ground recording the battles on Okinawa and Iwo Jima and was fearless in following the Marines into combat. He specifically served on two aircraft carriers: the *Hancock* and the *Essex*. He photographed everything, including crash landings; deaths of the deck crews struck by landing aircraft; burial at sea and the funeral services on the Pacific islands; the transfer of vital food, medical supplies and mail from ship to another in violent seas; the idle moments of the servicemen during the recreation time and quiet time; and USO performances. He took thousands of photographs during his three years in the Navy. His wartime photographic record was extraordinary.

Even though death could strike unexpectedly, this heightened the gift of life for every serviceman. Zerbe was blessed with friends even during his time on the islands in the Pacific. While on Guam, he was visited by Gertrude Lawrence, regulars he had photographed at El Morocco, Winthrop Rockefeller (who was stationed there), and numerous others. When American bomber crews dropped an atomic bomb on the city of Hiroshima on August 6, 1945, and another atomic bomb on Nagasaki three days later, the Japanese government moved to end hostilities. Zerbe was present to record the signing ceremony on the USS *Missouri* when Japan formally surrendered on September 2, 1945. He received a Bronze Star for his military service with a citation signed by Admiral Nimitz himself.[2]

Zerbe had wisely sublet his furnished New York apartment on East Fifty-Sixth Street and he very much looked forward to getting home. His many friends who had remained in New York were elated and relieved New York's most famous photographer was safely home. He was constantly asked what the war had been like and what he saw, but he graciously dodged these questions with the remark he was just glad he was home and it was all behind him. He simply did not want to talk about the war and the horrible scenes he had witnessed. He was grateful to be safely back in his beloved apartment, and proceeded to visit his favorite places, including El Morocco. He stopped in at the offices of *Town & Country* to resume work for the magazine, and reestablished his business contacts to get new photographic assignments.

What had Café Society been doing during the war years, and what, if anything, had changed in New York? Perhaps this could best be exemplified by the experience of Pulitzer Prize-winning journalist Carlos Romulo, who was with General Douglas MacArthur's staff on the island of Corregidor during the first months of the Pacific campaign. When Romulo returned to the United States, he made for New York. He received an invitation to a gath-

12. Café Society Fades Away

ering at the Waldorf-Astoria, and nearly experienced culture shock after witnessing the carnage on Corregidor. "I came from the battlefield into the Starlight Room of the Waldorf where men and women in evening clothes were dancing to Cugat's music," he recalled later. "Everyone was out having fun, and only the paper hats and horns were lacking to make every night a perpetual New Year's Eve."[3]

Lucius Beebe continued his weekly snapshot of high life in Manhattan uninterrupted throughout the war years. The tone of his column, "This New York," was indistinguishable from those of the 1930s. That was the way the

Gossip columnist Hedda Hopper (left) on the town with splendidly turned out Lucius Beebe and fellow editor at the *Herald Tribune*, Kay Vincent. Zerbe snapped this photograph during the early 1940s (Jerome Zerbe, by permission).

New York Herald Tribune liked it, and that was the way Beebe's readers liked it, who wanted to read about *someone* having a good time. However, Beebe did not stick his head in the proverbial sand and write as if nothing were happening in America regarding the war in Europe and in the Pacific.

In his column written exactly one year before the Japanese bombing of Pearl Harbor, Beebe acknowledged New York City was already a nest of foreign and domestic spies who operated in disguise while openly enjoying the best the city had to offer. Beebe wrote, "The night clubs and deluxe restaurants crawl with Russians, Japanese, Germans and Italians with supporting casts of bedizened dolls and pony ballets, of airplane manufacturers, brokers in gunpowder, labor needlers and lobbyists of the don't-you-think-we-had-better-talk-this-over-in-private variety."[4]

Beebe never forgot who his readership was and stuck to what he wrote about best. However, Walter Winchell relished first the rumblings of war in Europe and its eventual outbreak, then spent much of his time recording its events and happenings both in America and overseas. In fact, Winchell became very proactive during the years 1940 to 1945, almost to the neglect of who his traditional readership and radio audience was. With the bombing of Pearl Harbor on December 7, 1941, he prepared his copy for the radio broadcast that evening. In a voice charged with tension and urgency, he said, "Good evening, Mr. and Mrs. America. The American population is electrified tonight with the knowledge that every quarter of the globe will be at war tomorrow night."[5] Winchell, then forty-four years old, was actually a lieutenant commander in the U.S. Naval Reserve and tried actively to enlist, but he was rejected. He resolved to become the most vocal American journalist on the issues and events surrounding the war. He also cultivated his relationship with FBI Director J. Edgar Hoover and President Franklin Delano Roosevelt.

The charter members of the informal Algonquin Round Table had gone their separate ways before the end of the 1930s. Harold Ross had shepherded *The New Yorker* successfully through the Great Depression and circulation miraculously grew, albeit slowly. Subscriptions to the urbane, literary magazine grew from 43,403 in 1930 to 67,267 by 1935, and by 1941 the magazine had 105,105 subscribers.[6] Its advertising revenue essentially followed the general economic indicators of the decade, but rose steadily during the latter 1930s. Dorothy Parker had left the group in 1933 for Hollywood and wrote fifteen screenplays over the next five years, including *A Star Is Born*. Franklin P. Adams, who insisted throughout the 1930s and 1940s on using only his initials FPA, weathered the demise of the *New York World* when it merged with the *New York Telegram*. He went on to write for the *Herald Tribune* and later the *New York Post*. Alexander Woollcott continued to be a contributor to *The New Yorker* throughout this period, but his working relationship with Ross was strained. Robert Benchley found his true calling as an actor, and performed in films made in Hollywood and New York for Paramount Pictures. He died in 1945. George Kaufman maintained a prolific playwriting career throughout the 1930s and 1940s. Marc Connelly had received the Pulitzer Prize in 1930 for Drama for *The Green Pastures* (Kaufman received the prize in 1937). Kaufman continued writing for the stage as well as for various periodicals throughout the 1930s and 1940s.

As for the legendary haunts of Café Society during the war, the only visible change involved that of seeing uniformed officers among those at El Morocco, the Stork Club, 21 and other favored gathering places. However, the war years had an indefinable effect both on the establishments and on Café Society itself. The Chromium Mist, as Lucius Beebe had come to call it during the 1930s, had begun to slowly fade away. The cachet of Café Society seemed to have faded during the 1940s. For one thing, the latter 1940s witnessed a relaxing of the formal dress code at places like El Morocco, although the standards for food and drink and service had not been lowered. In fact, in those respects, the elite gathering places in Manhattan had changed not at all. It was the mood that had changed.

One August evening in 1947 at 21, Jack Kriendler stopped by the booth where his brother Pete was speaking with a dinner guest and said he was going upstairs for a few minutes. Pete was immediately concerned but did not say anything at the time. After several minutes he excused himself and went upstarts to Jack's personal apartment, where he found his brother writhing in pain, clutching his chest. Jack Kriendler died that evening at the age of forty-nine. The other Kriendler brothers, Pete, Mac and Bob, had already been involved in the restaurant for years, and the famed restaurant carried on with no noticeable interruption of the fine food and service the establishment was known for.

The Stork Club remained one of the favored places to go in Manhattan, and Sherman Billingsley was there every day and night to ensure the drinking and dining experience of the legendary club remained as it always had. At El Morocco, John Perona's son eventually took over the operation of the club and a younger generation of overachievers basked in the admiring glances of the lesser-known.

By 1950 even Lucius Beebe sensed it was time to leave his beloved New York and move west. He wrote an article in 1950 titled "I Saw the Elephant," a curious title which he never adequately explained, but for him it was the metaphor of seeing the handwriting on the wall, and he made plans to leave Manhattan. He resigned from the *Herald Tribune* and moved to Nevada. There, he succeeded in reviving the *Territorial Enterprise*, a newspaper Mark Twain had once written for and managed. Beebe was now able to completely indulge in his love of railroading, both steam and the emerging electric-diesel. He became a noted railroad photographer and wrote and illustrated numerous books on the subject.

Walter Winchell became involved in the anti–Communist movement and closely followed the congressional investigations that were headline news. It would ultimately prove his undoing as a journalist. A decade after his death, Maury Paul was only a distant memory among those who so fondly remembered reading his column under the byline "Cholly Knickerbocker."

New York Café Society was a fascinating counterpoint to the economic ruin of so many people in America during the 1930s. It reflected glamor, talent, elegance and above all, fun. Café Society became the object of great interest and a welcome diversion to countless magazine and newspaper readers chiefly during the Great Depression. With the advent of World War II and the postwar prosperity, American's former fascination with Café Society faded, and nothing else came along to replace it.

Chapter Notes

Chapter 1

1. Ward McAllister, *Society as I Have Found It* (New York: Cassell, 1890), 157–158.
2. Allen Churchill, *The Upper Crust: An Informal History of New York's Highest Society* (New York: Prentice-Hall, 1970), 85.
3. Eric Homberger, *Mrs. Astor's New York* (New Haven: Yale University Press, 2002), 265–274.
4. Douglas Steeples and David O. Whitten, *Democracy in Desperation: The Depression of 1893* (New York: Praeger, 1998), 47.
5. "Mrs. Astor Censures Some Society Women," *New York Times*, September 15, 1908.

Chapter 2

1. Daniel Okrent, *Last Call: The Rise and Fall of Prohibition* (New York: Scribner, 2010), 8.
2. Okrent, *Last Call*, 16.
3. Okrent, *Last Call*, 26.
4. Okrent, *Last Call*.
5. Michael A. Lerner, *Dry Manhattan: Prohibition in New York City* (Cambridge: Harvard University Press, 2007), 7–14.
6. Lerner, 46.
7. Okrent, *Last Call*, 124.
8. Lerner, 76, 96.
9. Lerner, 94.
10. Lerner, 71.
11. Lerner, 186–188.
12. Charles Baskerville, "When Nights Are Bold," *The New Yorker*, 25 April 1925.
13. Charles Baskerville, "When Nights Are Bold," *The New Yorker*, 13 June 1925.
14. Charles Baskerville, "When Nights Are Bold," *The New Yorker*, 2 May 1925.
15. Charles Baskerville, "When Nights Are Bold," *The New Yorker*, 4 July 1925.
16. Lois Long, "Tables for Two," *The New Yorker*, 12 September 1925.
17. Burton W. Peretti, *Nightclub City: Politics and Amusement in Manhattan* (Philadelphia: University of Pennsylvania Press, 2007), 11.
18. Niven Busch Jr., "Speakeasy Nights," *The New Yorker*, 28 March 1928.
19. Niven Busch Jr., "Speakeasy Nights," *The New Yorker*, 16 June 1928.
20. Okrent, *Last Call*, 254.
21. Lerner, 145.
22. Lerner, 192–193.
23. Lerner, 236.

Chapter 3

1. David Wallace, *Capital of the World: A Portrait of New York City in the Roaring Twenties* (Guilford, CT: Lyons Press, 2011), 6.
2. Geraldine Farrar, *Geraldine Farrar: The Story of an American Singer* (New York: Houghton Mifflin, 1916), 37.
3. David Wallace, 136.
4. Charles A. Lindbergh, *We* (New York: Putnam's, 1927), 62.
5. Thomas Kessner, *The Flight of the Century: Charles Lindbergh and the Rise of American Aviation* (New York: Oxford University Press, 2010), 55.
6. *Spirit of St. Louis*. Charles Lindbergh— An American Aviator. http://www.charleslindbergh.com/history/sec/. Accessed December 21, 2012.
7. Wallace, 243.
8. Glenn Stout and Richard Johnson, *Yankees Century: 100 Years of New York Yankee*

Baseball (New York: Houghton Mifflin, 2002), 77.
9. Herbert G. Goldman, *Fanny Brice: The Original Funny Girl* (New York: Oxford University Press, 1992), 88.

Chapter 4

1. Matthew Bruccoli, *F. Scott Fitzgerald: A Life in Letters* (New York: Scribner's, 1994), xix–xx.
2. James R. Gaines, *Wit's End: Days and Nights of the Algonquin Round Table* (New York: Harcourt Brace Jovanovich, 1977), 8–12.
3. Cleveland Amory and Frederic Bradlee, editors. *Vanity Fair: A Cavalcade of the 1920s and 1930s* (New York: Viking, 1960), 13.
4. Gaines, 28.
5. Gaines, 43.
6. Churchill, 238.
7. Gaines.
8. Thomas Kunkel, *Genius in Disguise: Harold Ross of The New Yorker* (New York: Random House, 1995), 67.
9. Eve Brown, *Champagne Cholly* (New York: E.P. Dutton, 1947), 45–46.
10. Brown, *Champagne Cholly*, 278.
11. Brown, *Champagne Cholly*, 45–46.
12. Brown, *Champagne Cholly*, 145–147.
13. Neal Gabler, *Winchell: Gossip, Power and the Culture of Celebrity* (New York: Alfred A. Knopf, 1994), 50–51.
14. Gabler, 104.

Chapter 5

1. Thomas A. DeLong, *Pops: Paul Whiteman, King of Jazz* (Piscataway: New Century, 1983), 27.
2. Arnold Shaw, *The Jazz Age: Popular Music in the 1920s* (New York: Oxford University Press, 1987), 43.
3. Nevin Busch, "The Paid Piper," *The New Yorker*, 27 November 1926, 26.
4. Neal Bascomb, *Higher: A Historic Race to the Sky and the Making of a City* (New York: Doubleday, 2003), 25–26.
5. Bascomb, 150.
6. Bascomb, 188.
7. John Kenneth Galbraith, *The Great Crash 1929* (Boston: Houghton Mifflin, 1954), 15–21.
8. Galbraith, 78.
9. *New York Times*, 20 October 1929, 1.
10. Gordon Thomas and Max Morgan-Witts, *The Day the Bubble Burst: A Social History of the Wall Street Crash of 1929* (Garden City: Doubleday, 1979). 395
11. John Tauranac, *The Empire State Building: The Making of a Landmark* (New York: Scribner, 1995), 269.

Chapter 6

1. "Woman Author-lecturer Who Wrote 'Born in a Crowd'—Really Was," *Lakeland Ledger*, 10 January 1963.
2. Lucius Beebe, *Snoot If You Must* (New York: D. Appleton-Century, 1943), 70.
3. Annette Tapert and Diana Edkins, *The Power of Style* (New York: Crown, 1994), 111.
4. Alexis Gregory, *Families of Fortune: Life in the Gilded Age* (New York: Rizzoli, 1993), 28.
5. Christopher Grey, "The Astor Legacy in Brick and Stone," *New York Times*, 10 September 2006.
6. John Foreman and Robe P. Stimson, *The Vanderbilts and the Gilded Age* (New York: St. Martin's Press, 1991), 105.
7. Foreman and Stimson, 319–323.
8. Philip Van Rensselaer, *Million Dollar Baby: An Intimate Portrait of Barbara Hutton* (New York: Putnam's, 1979), 23–25.
9. Howard Pollack, *George Gershwin: His Life and Work* (Los Angeles: University of California Press, 2006), 194–195.
10. Pollack, 474.
11. Pollack, 510, 513.
12. Pollack, 676.
13. Lucius Beebe, "The Great Depression," *The Lucius Beebe Reader* (New York: Doubleday, 1967), 81–82.

Chapter 7

1. Margaret Case Harriman, "Dolly and Polly, Billy and Cholly–1," Profiles, *The New Yorker*, 16 October 1937, 23–27.
2. Brown, 29.
3. Wolcott Gibbs, "The Diamond Gardenia–1," Profiles, *The New Yorker*, 20 November 1937, 24–39.
4. Wolcott Gibbs, "The Diamond Gardenia–2," Profiles, *The New Yorker*, 27 November 1937, 26–29.
5. Lucius Beebe, "This New York," *New York Herald Tribune*, 22 September 1934.
6. Lucius Beebe, "This New York," *New York Herald Tribune*, 10 November 1934.
7. Gloria Braggiotti Etting, interview with

the author, Palm Beach Gardens, Florida. May 23, 1981.
8. Gabler, 125.

Chapter 8

1. Margaret Case Harriman, "Two Waiters and a Chef–1," *The New Yorker*, 1 June 1935, 22–24.
2. Margaret Case Harriman, "Two Waiters and a Chef–2," *The New Yorker*, 8 June 1935, 23.
3. Iles Brody, *The Colony—Portrait of a Restaurant and Its Famous Recipes* (New York: Greenberg, 1945), 16–17.
4. Eve Brown, *Champagne Cholly*, 288.
5. Brody, 15.
6. Harriman, "Two Waiters and a Chef–1," 20.
7. Eve Brown, *The Plaza: Its Life and Times* (New York: Meredith Press, 1967) 32.
8. Brown, *The Plaza*, 79.
9. Daniel Okrent, *Great Fortune—The Epic of Rockefeller Center* (New York: Viking Penguin, 2003) 83.
10. Gloria Braggiotti Etting, interview with the author, May 23, 1981.

Chapter 9

1. Marilyn Kaytor, *"21": The Life and Times of New York's Favorite Club* (New York: Viking, 1975), 8.
2. Kaytor, 30–31.
3. Lucius Beebe, "The Grand Closing at 42 West Forty-Ninth Street," *The Lucius Beebe Reader* (New York: Doubleday, 1967), 84.
4. Arnold Shaw, *The Street That Never Slept* (New York: Coward, McCann & Geoghegan, 1971), endpapers.
5. H. Peter Kriendler, *"21": Every Day Was New Year's Eve* (Dallas: Taylor, 1999), 116.

Chapter 10

1. Ralph Blumenthal, *Stork Club: America's Most Famous Nightspot and the Lost World of Café Society* (New York: Little, Brown, 2000), 95.
2. Gabler, 188.
3. Blumenthal, 121.
4. Beebe, *Snoot If You Must*, 190.

Chapter 11

1. Kriendler, 16.
2. Beebe, *Snoot If You Must*, 66–67.
3. Brendan Gill, Profile of Jerome Zerbe, "Happy Times," *The New Yorker*, 3 June 1973, 42–43.
4. Interview with Jerome Zerbe, New York City, March 6, 1981.
5. Interview with Gloria Braggiotti Etting, May 23, 1981.
6. Jerome Zerbe, *People on Parade* (New York: David Kemp, 1934), 7.
7. Gill, Profile of Jerome Zerbe, 56.
8. Interview with Gloria Braggiotti Etting, May 23, 1981.
9. Interview with Marion Tiffany Saportas, New York City, March 6, 1981.

Chapter 12

1. Brown, *Champagne Cholly*, 301.
2. Gill, Profile of Jerome Zerbe, 59–62.
3. Richard Goldstein, *Helluva Town: The Story of New York City During World War II* (New York: Free Press, 2010), ix.
4. Lucius Beebe, "This New York," *New York Herald Tribune*, 7 December 1940.
5. Gabler, 303.
6. Ben Yagoda, *About Town: The New Yorker and the World It Made* (New York: Scribner, 2000), 96.

Bibliography

Amory, Cleveland. *Who Killed Society?* New York: Harper and Brothers, 1960.
_____, and Frederic Bradlee, ed. *Vanity Fair: A Cavalcade of the 1920s and 1930s.* New York: Viking, 1960.
Bascomb, Neal. *Higher: A Historic Race to the Sky and the Making of a City.* New York: Doubleday, 2003.
Beebe, Lucius. *The Provocative Pen of Lucius Beebe, Esq.* San Francisco: Chronicle, 1966.
_____. *Snoot If You Must.* New York: D. Appleton-Century, 1943.
Blumenthal, Ralph. *Stork Club: America's Most Famous Nightspot and the Lost World of Café Society.* Boston: Little, Brown, 2000.
Brody, Iles. *The Colony: Portrait of a Restaurant and Its Famous Recipes.* New York: Greenberg, 1945.
Brown, Eve. *Champagne Cholly.* New York: E.P. Dutton, 1947.
_____. *The Plaza: Its Life and Times.* New York: Meredith, 1967.
Bruccoli, Matthew J. *F. Scott Fitzgerald: A Life in Letters.* New York: Scribner's, 1994.
Charyn, Jerome. *Gangsters & Gold Diggers: Old New York, the Jazz Age, and the Birth of Broadway.* New York: Thunder Mountain, 2003.
Churchill, Allen. *The Upper Crust: An Informal History of New York's Highest Society.* New York: Prentice-Hall, 1970.
Clegg, Charles, and Duncan Emrich. *The Lucius Beebe Reader.* Garden City: Doubleday, 1967.
The Complete New Yorker 1925–2005. 8 DVDs. The New Yorker, 2005.
DeLong, Thomas A. *Pops: Paul Whiteman, King of Jazz.* Piscataway, NJ: New Century, 1983.
Dickstein, Morris. *Dancing in the Dark: A Cultural History of the Great Depression.* New York: W.W. Norton, 2009.
Dumenil, Lynn. *The Modern Tempter: American Culture and Society in the 1920s.* New York: Hill and Wang, 1995.
Ewen, David. *American Songwriters.* New York: H.W. Wilson, 1987.
Farrar, Geraldine. *Geraldine Farrar: The Story of an American Singer.* New York: Houghton Mifflin, 1916.
Foreman, John, and Robe P. Stimson. *The Vanderbilts and the Gilded Age.* New York: St. Martin's Press, 1991.
Gabler, Neal, W. *Winchell: Gossip, Power and the Culture of Celebrity.* New York: Knopf, 1994.
Gaines, James R. *Wit's End: Days and Nights of the Algonquin Round Table.* New York: Houghton Mifflin, 1977.
Galbraith, John Kenneth. *The Great Crash 1929.* Boston: Houghton Mifflin, 1954.
Gill, Brendan. *Here at The New Yorker.* New York: Random House, 1975.

Bibliography

———, and Jerome Zerbe. *Happy Times*. New York: Harcourt Brace Jovanovich, 1973.
Goldman, Herbert G. *Fanny Brice: The Original Funny Girl*. New York: Oxford University Press, 1992.
Goldstein, Richard. *Helluva Town: The Story of New York City During World War II*. New York: Free Press, 2010.
Gregory, Alexis. *Families of Fortune: Life in the Gilded Age*. New York: Rizzoli, 1993.
Homberger, Eric. *Mrs. Astor's New York*. New Haven: Yale University Press, 2002.
Kaytor, Marilyn. *"21": The Life and Times of New York's Favorite Club*. New York: Viking, 1975.
Kessner, Thomas. *The Flight of the Century: Charles Lindbergh and the Rise of American Aviation*. New York: Oxford University Press, 2010.
Kingwell, Mark. *Nearest Thing to Heaven: The Empire State Building and American Dreams*. New Haven: Yale University Press, 2006.
Kriendler, H. Peter. *"21": Every Day Was New Year's Eve*. Dallas: Taylor, 1999.
Kunkel, Thomas. *Genius in Disguise: Harold Ross of The New Yorker*. New York: Random House, 1995,
Leinwand, Gerald. *1927: High Tide of the Twenties*. New York: Four Walls Eight Windows, 2001.
Lerner, Michael A. *Dry Manhattan: Prohibition in New York City*. Cambridge: Harvard University Press, 2007.
Lindbergh, Charles A. *We*. New York: Putnam's, 1927.
McAllister, Ward. *Society as I Have Found It*. New York: Cassell, 1890.
McBrien, William. *Cole Porter*. New York: Knopf, 1998.
Montville, Leigh. *The Big Bam: The Life and Times of Babe Ruth*. New York: Doubleday, 2006.
Okrent, Daniel. *Great Fortune: The Epic of Rockefeller Center*. New York: Viking, 2003.
———. *Last Call: The Rise and Fall of Prohibition*. New York: Scribner, 2010.
Parrish, Michael E. *Anxious Decades: America in Prosperity and Depression, 1920–1941*. New York: W.W. Norton, 1992.
Peretti, Burton W. *Nightclub City: Politics and Amusement in Manhattan*. Philadelphia: University of Pennsylvania Press, 2007.
Pollack, Howard. *George Gershwin: His Life and Work*. Berkeley: University of California Press, 2006.
Shaw, Arnold. *The Jazz Age: Popular Music in the 1920s*. New York: Oxford University Press, 1987.
———. *The Street That Never Slept*. New York: Coward, McCann & Geoghegan, 1971.
Shlaes, Amity. *The Forgotten Man: A New History of the Great Depression*. New York: HarperCollins, 2007.
Sloat, Warren. *1929: America Before the Crash*. New York: Macmillan, 1979.
Steeples, Douglas, and David O. Whitten, *Democracy in Desperation: The Depression of 1893*. New York: Praeger, 1998.
Stout, Glenn, and Richard Johnson. *Yankees Century: 100 Years of New York Yankee Baseball*. New York: Houghton Mifflin, 2002.
Stravitz, David. *New York, Empire City 1920–1945*. New York: Harry N. Abrams, 2004.
Tapert, Annette, and Diana Edkins. *The Power of Style*. New York: Crown, 1994.
Tauranac, John. *The Empire State Building: The Making of a Landmark*. New York: Scribner, 1995.
This Fabulous Century: 1930–1940. Alexandria: Time-Life Books, 1969.
Thomas, Gordon, and Max Morgan-Witts. *The Day the Bubble Burst: A Social History of the Wall Street Crash of 1929*. Garden City: Doubleday, 1979.
Turnbull, Andrew. *Scott Fitzgerald*. New York: Scribner's, 1962.
Van Rensselaer, Philip. *Million Dollar Baby: An Intimate Portrait of Barbara Hutton*. New York: Putnam's, 1979.

Waggoner, Susan. *Nightclub Nights: Art, Legend and Style 1920–1960*. New York: Rizzoli, 2001.
Wallace, David. *Capital of the World: A Portrait of New York City in the Roaring Twenties*. Guilford, CT: Lyons Press, 2011.
Walker, Stanley. *City Editor*. Baltimore: Johns Hopkins University Press, 1934.
_____. *The Night Club Era*. Baltimore: Johns Hopkins University Press, 1933.
Ward, Geoffrey C., and Ken Burns. *JAZZ: A History of America's Music*. New York: Knopf, 2000.
Yagoda, Ben. *About Town: The New Yorker and the World It Made*. New York: Scribner, 2000.
Young, William H., and Nancy K. Young. *Music of the Great Depression*. Westport, CT: Greenwood Press, 2005.
Zerbe, Jerome. *El Morocco Family Album*. New York: Federal Printing Service, 1937.
_____. *People on Parade*. New York: David Kemp, 1934.

Index

Numbers in **_bold italics_** indicate pages with photographs.

Adams, Franklin P. (FPA) 61, 66–67, 167, 202
Aeolian Hall 6, 91–92
Algonquin Round Table 65–72, 199
Anthony, Susan B. 25
Anti-Saloon League 27, 30
Arno, Peter 37
Astaire, Fred 36, 116, 156
Astor, Caroline 1, 15–16, 19–22, 193
Astor, John Jacob 13–14, 128, 161
Astor, Vincent 111
Astor, William B. 13, 15, 18

Baskerville, Charles 36–37
Bath Club 186
Beaton, Cecil 63
Beebe, Lucius 1, 3, 5, 8, **_64_**, 88, 108, 111, **_120_**, 125, 127, **_129_**, 132–142, 144, 148, **_152_**, 156, 169, **_171_**, **_179_**, 183, 186, **_189_**, **_191_**, 193–196, 199, 201, 204
Belmont, Alva Vanderbilt 21–22
Benchley, Robert 34, 41, 63, 65–66, 70, 73, 167, 169, 203
Berlin, Irving 6, 58, 118, 119
Billingsley, Sherman 8, 176–184, 203
Biltmore mansion 18
Bloom, Vera 7
Braggiotti, Gloria 1, 108, **_129_**, 141, 161, **_171_**, 192, 195
Breakers mansion 18
Brice, Fanny 58–59
Broadway 5, 57–58
Broun, Heywood 66, 68
Brown, Eve 74, 78, 123–124, 130, 198–199
Bull, Harry **_64_**, 139, 190
Burns, Charlie 163–165, 173–174, 186

Caruso, Enrico 48
Cavallero, Eugene 150–154

Cerrutti, Ernest 149–154
"Cholly Knickerbocker" 2–3, 9, 77–78, 84, 87–88, 111, 119, 145, 198–199, 204
Chromium Mist 3, 10, 203
Chrysler, Walter P. 34, 96–100, 104–105, 140
Chrysler Building 7, 96, 104–105
Clegg, Chuck 10, 142
Colony Restaurant 149–154
Comden, Betty 9
Compton, Betty 47, 171
Condé Nast 62–63, 72
Connelly, Marc 68
Crosby, Bing 95
Crosley Radio Corporation 45
Crowninshield, Frank 62–64, 73, 135, 168

Dahlgren, Elizabeth Drexel 21
debutant ball 13–14
The Delineator 21
Delmonico's 13, 20
DeMille, Cecil B. 49
Dempsey, Jack 44
Distilling Company of America 26
Dorsey, Tommy 9
Duchin, Eddie 157

Eighteenth Amendment 24, 28–29, 41, 43, 172, 182, 185
El Fey Club 34, 87
Elliot, T.S. 63
El Morocco 4, 6, 9–10, 137–138, 142, 145, 159, 185–197, 203
Empire State Building 7, 99, 104
Evening Graphic 5, 86
Evening Journal 5

Farrar, Geraldine 48–50, 59

211

Index

Fifth Avenue 8, 14–16, 18, 20–23
Fish, Mrs. Stuyvesant "Maime" 19–22, 75
Fitzgerald, F. Scott 60, 69–70, 168
Fitzgerald, Zelda 60, 69
Fleischman, Raoul 71–73
Fontanne, Lynn 68

Gershwin, George 6, 69, 91, 93, 115–119, 194
Gibbons, Sarah 12
Gibson, Charles Dana 67–68
Gilded Age 11, 15
Grant, Jane 71–72
Great Depression 2–4, 89, 115, 117, 202, 204
Green, Adolf 9
Guggenheim, Benjamin 23
Guinan, Texas 33–35, 41, 87

Harding, Warren G. 32–33
Harlem 6, 8
Hayes, Helen 68
Hearst, William Randolph 77, 79
Hemingway, Ernest 168, 170
Herald Tribune 83, 122, 125, 132,-134, 140, 146, *201*
Heyward, Edwin DuBose 118
Hollywood 4, 49
Holman, Libby 141–142, *171*, 188
Home Sector 71
Hope, Bob 184
Hunt, Richard Morris 16, 18
Hutton, 113–115
Huxley, Aldous 63

Iridium Room 8, 149
Ismay, J. Bruce 23

Journal-American 122–123, 130

Kaufman, George F. 34, 68, 118, 167, 203
Keeler, Ruby 36
Knickerbocker Hotel 34
Kriendler, Jack 163–171, 186, 203
Kriendler, Peter 168

Lehr, Harry 19–22
Lindbergh, Charles 50–54, 59, 146
Long, Lois 37
Loos, Mary Anita 142, 188, *189*
Lynnewood Hall mansion 23

Marbel House mansion 18
Maughm, William Somerset 63
McAllister, Ward 11–13, 16, 18–20
Merman, Ethel 117
Metropolitan Opera 48–50, 75, 124, 126, 156

Miller, Marilyn 58–59
Morgan, Gloria 82–83
Morgan, J. Pierpont 1, 23

Nast, Condé 108
Nation, Carrie 26
National Liquor League 26
National Prohibition Act 28, 30, 32
New York City (Manhattan) 3–4, 8–9, 11–14, 16–17, 20, 27, 33–34, 37, 40–42, 54, 60–61, 89, 95, 98–99, 112
New York Daily Mirror 5, 88
New York Herald Tribune 1, 3, 5, 18, 66, 111, 131–132, 168, 202
New York Stock Exchange 100
New York Times 1, 22, 33, 47, 61, 65, 71, 137, 147
New York World 16
The New Yorker 36–38, 42, 66, 71–74, 140, 150, 168, 202–203
Newport, Rhode Island 16, 18, 20, 22–23
Niven, David 173

O'Donohue, Joseph J., IV 1, 188
Orteig Prize 50–51

Parker, Dorothy 34, 63, 66–67, 70, 73, 167, 202
Paul, Maury 2–3, 5, 8, 46–47, 74–85, 87–88, 111, 122–131, 140–141, 144, 148, 151, *152*, 153, *171*, 183, 187, 194, 198
People on Parade 138
Perona, John 4, 8, 137, 185, *191*, 203
Persian Room 8, 149, 156–157
Picasso 63
Plaza Hotel 8, 84, 149, 154–157
Porter, Cole 7
Post, Marjorie 114
Prince of Wales 130
Prohibition 4, 24, *30*, 32–33, 40–42, 47, 69, 80, 132, 137, 151, 156, 163–165, 172–173, 182, 184, 186

Radio City Music Hall 158–159
Radio Corporation of America 44
Rainbow Room 4, 7–8, 139, 149, 157–160, 173, 190
Raskob, John Jacob 99–100
"Rhapsody in Blue" 69, 91, 93–94
Rheingold Speakeasy 40
Rockefeller, John David 157–158
Rockefeller Center 7–8, 157
Rogers, Ginger 117–118
Ross, Harold 36–38, 61–62, 71–74, 140, 150, 202
Rothstein, Arnold 47

Index 213

Rum Row 30
Runyon, Damon 34
Ruth, Babe 55–57, 59

St. Regis Roof 149
Saportas, Marion Tiffany 1, 27, 159, 188, 193, *196*
Saturday Evening Post 71
Schermerhorn, William 13–14
Severance, Craig 97–98
Shaw, Artie 9
Sherwood, Robert 63, 66, 68, 167, 199
Society 11, 13–16, 18–19, 135, 159–160
Society As I Have Found It 16
speakeasy 4, 32–34, 36, 40
Starlight Roof 149, 160–162
Stars and Stripes 61, 65
Steichen, Edward 63
Stein, Gertrude 63
Stewart, A.T. 15
Stork Club 6, 8–10, 137, 144–146, 176–184, 203
Stotesbury, Edward T. and Eva 109–110
Surf Club 185
Swanson, Gloria 34, *120*

Texas Guinan 33–34, *35*, 87
"This New York" 2, 6, 9, 111, 145
Titanic 22
Toscanini, Arturo 49
Town & Country 5, 64, 190
Trocadero Club 36
Trumbauer, Horace 110, 155
Twenty-First Amendment 172, 182
"21" Club 9, 163–174, 203
Twombly, Mrs. Hamilton McKown 16, 113, 125

Van Allen, William 96–100, 104

Vanderbilt, Cornelius 15, 18, 113
Vanderbilt, Grace 113, 125, 128, 150
Vanderbilt, Reginald 34, 82
Vanderbilt, William H. 18, 169
Vanderbilt, William K. 18, 112–113
Vanity Fair 5, 37, 42, 56, 62–67, 71, 131
Vogue 5, 42, 62–63
Volstead, Andrew (Volstead Act) 28–30

Walker, Jimmy 34, 43–47, 54, 58, 86, 104, 118, 132–133, 151, 166
Walker, Stanley 5, 88, 131–133, 136–137, 140
Wanamaker, Tom 20–21
White Star Line 23
Whiteman, Paul 6, 10, 56, 89–96, 105, 117, 137
Whitney, Cornelius Vanderbilt 80
Whitney, Harry Payne 34
Widener, George D. 23
Widener, Joseph E. 151
Williams, Mr. & Mrs. Harrison 108–109, 111, 187
Wilson, Edmond 63
Wilson, Pres. Woodrow 23
Winchell, Walter 5, 9, 34, 83–88, 137, 142–148, 180, 183–184, 202
Wolfe, Thomas 63
Women's Christian Temperance Movement 23–26, 32, 42
Woolcott, Alexander 61–62, 65–67, 69, 70, 72, 167, 203
Woolworth, Frank 113
Woolworth Building 7

Zanuck, Darryl 147–148
Zerbe, Jerome 1, 4, 8–9, 138, 141, 160, *189*
Ziegfeld Follies 58